THE NEW FU[illegible]

Who organises charitable giving in contemporary society?

Beth Breeze

First published in Great Britain in 2017 by

Policy Press
University of Bristol
1-9 Old Park Hill
Bristol
BS2 8BB
UK
t: +44 (0)117 954 5940
pp-info@bristol.ac.uk
www.policypress.co.uk

North America office:
Policy Press
c/o The University of Chicago Press
1427 East 60th Street
Chicago, IL 60637, USA
t: +1 773 702 7700
f: +1 773-702-9756
sales@press.uchicago.edu
www.press.uchicago.edu

British Library Cataloguing in Publication Data
A catalogue record for this book is available from the British Library

Library of Congress Cataloging-in-Publication Data
A catalog record for this book has been requested

ISBN 978-1-4473-2502-4 paperback
ISBN 978-1-4473-2500-0 hardcover
ISBN 978-1-4473-2503-1 ePub
ISBN 978-1-4473-2504-8 Mobi
ISBN 978-1-4473-2501-7 ePdf

Cover design by Andrew Corbett
Front cover image: Bigstock
Printed and bound in Great Britain by CMP, Poole
Policy Press uses environmentally responsible print partners

To all fundraisers, whose work enables so many good things to happen, and in particular to those fundraisers who so kindly made time to contribute to the research presented in this book.

[Fundraisers] empower those with financial resources to convert the dross of their money into the gold of a better society … by providing opportunities to give, they empower us to breathe more meaning into our lives.

Arthur C. Brookes, *New York Times*, 29 March 2014

Contents

List of tables and boxes

Tables

Boxes

About the author

Beth Breeze is a Senior Lecturer in Social Policy, and Director of the Centre for Philanthropy at the University of Kent. She previously worked as a fundraiser and charity manager. She has served as a charity trustee and is involved as a volunteer in a number of charitable organisations.

Her previous books are: *Richer Lives: Why Rich People Give* (Directory of Social Change, 2013), co-authored with Theresa Lloyd; *The Logic of Charity* (Palgrave, 2015), co-authored with John Mohan; *The Philanthropy Reader* (Routledge, 2016), co-edited with Michael Moody.

She has also written numerous reports on charitable giving and philanthropy, including the annual Coutts Million Pound Donor Report, which has tracked trends in donations worth £1 million or more since 2008.

Information on all the Kent Centre for Philanthropy publications is available at www.kent.ac.uk/sspssr/philanthropy/publications

Acknowledgements

The research contained in this book was funded by a Leverhulme Trust Early Career Fellowship (ECF-2012-488). The support of the Leverhulme Trust has been crucial not only for this specific study, but also for enabling me to secure a permanent academic position and launch my research career. I am deeply grateful for the original philanthropic act of William Hesketh Lever in establishing the Trust in 1925, and to the ongoing efforts of the Trust's staff, especially the director, Professor Gordon Marshall, and my Grants Administrative Officer, Andreas Heiner.

LEVERHULME
TRUST

I also wish to acknowledge the essential contribution of the UK's Institute of Fundraising, whose support as a research partner enabled me to recruit participants for the research and gave me a direct means of sharing – and refining – the research with members, especially at their annual summer conventions, and also at regional events around the country.

Robert Johnston gave me my first job in fundraising, at the Cardinal Hume Centre in London, which provides homeless young people, families in need, and individuals living in poverty with the support they need to realise their full potential. I am grateful for that opportunity, and proud to be associated with such a worthwhile and well-run charity.

I very much enjoyed sharing some of this research journey with Gloria Jollymore, whose Canadian data and practitioner insights greatly enhanced my thinking, and whose reflections on the art of fundraising were especially invaluable.

My Kent colleagues Dr Rob de Vries and Dr Heejung Chung both provided generous help with the analysis of quantitative data, and Emeritus Professor Hugh Cunningham kindly offered insights and feedback for the historical chapter.

Professor Gareth Morgan is a constant and generous source of insight on charity finances. Amanda Delew and Dr Chris Einolf are both busy, in-demand people who somehow found the time to read and comment on the whole draft. I wish to record my particular thanks to the members of my research advisory committee for their patience, generosity and wisdom: Kate Brown, Donna Day Lafferty, Dr Jane Hudson, Paul Marvell and Associate Professor Wendy Scaife.

I was also fortunate to receive excellent research assistance from Lesley Alborough, Dr Kayleigh Flaxman and Dr Yeosun Yoon.

My sincere gratitude to all those named above does not alter the fact that remaining errors are mine alone.

My husband Michael and our lovely children Beren and Meredith patiently endured my distraction during the writing of this book. I'm very grateful for the constant supply of cups of tea and the even more constant supply of pictures to brighten the wall above my desk.

Preface

Some years ago, a university colleague told me he had once applied for a job as a fundraiser before realising that, in his words: "I didn't want to spend my working life trying to make people do things they don't want to do". I had worked as a fundraiser for a decade before becoming an academic in the emerging field of Philanthropic Studies, and that colleague's depiction of fundraising simply did not ring true: most people *do* want to give, and the role of the fundraiser is not to twist arms, but to help people put their altruistic intention into action. That conversation was one of many moments that prompted me to write this book, which seeks to explain the importance of fundraising and the need for a better understanding of fundraisers.

For me, being a fundraiser was as close to a dream job as a newly graduated, idealistic and penniless 20-something could hope for. From my first day as a fundraiser at a youth homelessness charity I felt I was doing something useful and fulfilling, I met interesting people, had a fair amount of autonomy, and got paid a reasonable salary. What's not to like about a job like that? But even at the time, I knew my view was not widely shared: family worried it "wasn't a proper job", friends asked how I could bear to "beg", and my then-boyfriend, who worked in sales, told his colleagues (admiringly, I think) that "Beth makes a living out of selling *nothing*!"

Many fundraisers report similar reactions, including these amusing words from a book written by a fundraiser:

> When responding to the question "So what do you do?" with "I'm a fundraiser. I ask people for money". There's silence, then confusion, then "I could never do that", or "Do you get paid to do that?" No one says: "That must be interesting", or, "I'll bet you get to meet lots of fascinating people". After a while you begin to imagine that right now there is someone cleaning up zebra droppings at a zoo thinking: "It could be worse. At least I didn't have to ask someone for the money to buy this shovel". (Perdue, 2014, pp 3–4)

This book is a response to those who shudder at the idea of trying to raise funds for shovels, or to put a roof over homeless people's heads, or any of the tens of thousands of other good works that simply cannot happen without voluntary income.

It has been an enormous pleasure to spend three years studying the practices, personalities and perspectives of hundreds of UK fundraisers, in order to offer this explanation of what fundraisers do, what kind of people are good at doing it, and why it matters. While conducting this research, the persistent but mostly low-level concern at the very existence of paid fundraisers, and concern about some of the methods and techniques they use, turned into an avalanche of criticism in the summer of 2015, which has not yet abated. This 'crisis', and the proposed heavy-handed legislative response, has worrying implications for the ability of charities to raise the money they need to fulfil their missions. The task of explaining how fundraising actually works, and what kind of people are good at it, is more urgent and important now than ever.

Beth Breeze
June 2017

Introduction

One typically busy morning in a charity office, an older woman walked in unannounced and asked to see someone about making a donation. The fundraiser, who was about to start a full day of meetings and activities, came to the reception and asked how he could help The visitor explained that her husband had recently died and that she wished to make a gift in his name. Aware that the clock was ticking, the fundraiser could have simply asked: "How much would you like to give?" or "How would you prefer to pay?" But instead, he invited her to take a seat, arranged for some hot drinks, and said these words: "Tell me about your husband". The newly widowed woman was glad – indeed, relieved – to be asked this question, and in the course of talking about her late husband, the fundraiser learnt a lot of useful information that helped him to understand why the couple had a connection to the cause, what level of donation was likely, and what sort of recognition would be most suitable. That first chat was the start of a mutually beneficial, lifelong relationship that ended with a generous bequest for the charity.

How do successful fundraisers know the right way to react in these sorts of situations? This book answers that question by shining a light on the hitherto neglected subject of the social characteristics and daily practices of fundraisers. It documents the history and development of fundraising, explores the knowledge contained in 'how to fundraise' books, and discusses the everyday reality of raising money for good causes for a living. New data from a large study of UK fundraisers helps to show what kind of people are employed to raise money for good causes, how they go about their work, and the qualities that enable them to successfully meet the needs of both donors and charities. It is written to illuminate fundraisers' crucial, but usually overlooked, role in enabling charitable work to happen, and as a corrective to the increasingly widespread, though illogical, view that giving is good yet asking is bad. The book discusses all kinds of paid fundraisers, but with a particular focus on those working face-to-face with wealthy donors.

Why study fundraisers?

The belief that asking for money is demeaning for the asker and annoying for the asked is rejected by Desmond Tutu, the Archbishop Emeritus of Cape Town and Nobel prize winner, who described fundraising as a 'noble profession' undertaken by people who have 'an important calling' (cited in Breeze and Scaife, 2015, p 570). Such language stands in stark contrast to public perceptions of fundraisers as at best, a type of salespeople, and at worst, high-pressure beggars (Payton et al, 1991, p 275). Archbishop Tutu was clearly aware and appreciative of the work undertaken to secure the resources needed to win the fight against apartheid. But many people see no inconsistency in admiring the work that fundraising pays for while simultaneously disparaging, or simply overlooking, those who make sure that the costs of fighting good fights, or doing good deeds, can be met. This results in fundraising being viewed as inherently problematic, a 'necessary but unfortunate task' (Moody and Breeze, 2016, p 316).

Yet despite this, most of us freely give money to charity, and the vast majority of those donation decisions are prompted (Schervish and Havens, 1997; Bryant et al, 2003; Bekkers, 2005; Gunstone and Ellison, 2017, p 4). The annual UK Giving survey finds that around two thirds of people give each year (CAF, 2016), while UK government statistics find even higher levels, with around three quarters of respondents saying they gave to charity in the preceding four weeks (Cabinet Office, 2016). The fact that charitable giving is a common part of daily life is something of a puzzle. We live in an era in which self-interest is accepted as the main driver of action, and in which individualism, wealth accumulation and consumerism are celebrated: none of these values are self-evidently present in collective charitable efforts, which persist nonetheless. Existing studies of the 'paradox of philanthropy' are focused on donors, exploring why most people choose to act in ways that challenge the accepted narrative of personal utility maximisation, rather than accounting for those who ask, and encourage others to overcome self-interested objectives.

This chapter begins by defining fundraising, explaining why charities fundraise, and enumerating the demand for, and supply of, fundraisers. It then sets out the essential yet invisible role of fundraisers, why fundraising matters, and how it relates to the wider philanthropic sector. This provides the context for the original contribution made by this book, which explores the other, hitherto neglected side of the giving equation: those who organise generosity in contemporary society.

What is fundraising?

The Oxford English Dictionary offers this narrow definition of fundraising: 'persuading individuals or organisations to provide financial support for a cause, enterprise, etc' (Brown, 1993, p 1042). A wider definition is offered by the UK's membership body for fundraisers:

'Fundraising is the act of raising resources (especially, but not only money) by asking for it, to fund the work your organisation carries out, including the front-line activity and the overheads' (Institute of Fundraising, 2015, np). Yet both definitions understate the complexity of the task, and the onerous responsibility held by those securing the financing that keeps good causes in business. To conceive of the job of fundraising as simply asking for money is misleading, even 'insultingly narrow' (Worth and Asp, 1994, p 6), because it is a complex process that includes defining the needs to be met, cultivating the interest and involvement of prospective donors, matching their interest and desires with the needs and goals of the institution, soliciting the gift, providing feedback on how the gift was used, and stewarding donors to keep them informed and involved (Worth and Asp, 1994, p 5).

A further complication when trying to define this activity is that many fundraisers do not use the word 'fundraising'; rather they speak of 'development', 'advancement' or 'partnerships'. While those words can be interpreted as mealy-mouthed euphemisms or, at best, a polite way to avoid mentioning money (Walker, 2015, p ix), they are often a more accurate reflection of how the person doing the fundraising spends their time – developing and advancing their institution by building partnerships with potential supporters. One US study found that 'solicitation' (the equivalent North American term for 'fundraising') occupied just 13% of the typical fundraiser's working week, with the bulk of their remaining time being occupied with administration (33%), followed by interacting with 'constituents' (16%) and volunteers (11%) (Duronio and Tempel, 1997, p 38).

Why charities fundraise

Charities cannot run on goodwill alone. They need money to put their charitable missions into practice, whether that is paying the telephone bill to run a helpline, paying for scientific equipment to search for cures for illness, paying qualified staff to tend to the dying, or paying expenses of volunteer lifeboat men and women. However worthy the cause, and however impressive the charity's achievements, it will not attract donations without a concerted and organised effort to raise funds (Payton et al, 1991, p 13).

There is nothing new about charitable work costing money, but rapid growth in the number of charities seeking voluntary income has intensified competition for donations and new donors (Hughes, 1996, p 175; Swindoll, 2015), and financial survival in this new charity landscape relies on ever more innovative and attractive fundraising campaigns (Bennett and Savani, 2011, p 121; Swindoll, 2015). According to figures compiled by the National Council for Voluntary Organisations (NCVO, 2015), drawing on data held by the Charity Commission, the number of registered charities in England and Wales almost doubled from 77,000 in 1970 to 145,000 in 2015. The emergence of other types of fundraising organisations over these decades, including 35,000 charitable companies and 13,000 community interest companies, makes the market for generosity even more intense.[1]

But the wider context for fundraising involves more 'profound change' than simply a more crowded marketplace (More Partnership, 2012, p 2). The new financial pressures also include dramatic cuts in public funding for charities (NCVO, 2014), and the shift towards restrictions being placed on how some income can be used creates a particularly competitive environment for charities (Burlingame and Hodge 1997, p 10; Duronio and Tempel, 1997, p 16; Neilson et al, 2012, p 3). These new pressures are occurring in tandem with increased scrutiny from the media and from politicians with regard to the management of, and spending on, fundraising. This convergence of factors, described as a 'perfect storm' hitting charities (Walker et al, 2012, p 10), means that 'the work of fundraising has never been more demanding, more challenging, or more important' (Duronio and Tempel, 1997, p 16).

The number of fundraisers

Little is known about the workforce charged with this important task: even its size. Data published in the US by the Bureau of Labor Statistics indicates there are at least 153,000 paid fundraisers in that country (Bureau of Labor Statistics, 2016), but there is no equivalent figure available for the number of fundraisers working in the UK. There are no established entry requirements and fundraising practitioners are not required to register with a professional association, so there is no central list of qualified practitioners. At the end of 2016, there were 6,000 members of the UK's Institute of Fundraising,[2] but not all fundraisers choose to pay to join this body, and members may include people (like myself) who are not currently working as fundraisers. A precise headcount is also complicated by the fact that responsibility for fundraising is often part of another job, so there are many people *doing* fundraising who do not necessarily identify *as* fundraisers.

The best estimates of the size of the UK fundraising workforce that do exist vary from 10,000 to 31,000 paid fundraisers. The lower figure is quoted in an Institute of Fundraising report, which reiterates the point that 'many more paid staff have fundraising as part of their broader responsibilities' (Institute of Fundraising, 2009, p 10). And even the higher figure (reported in Breeze et al, 2015, p 293) seems inadequate compared to the number of charitable organisations reliant on fundraised income. Of the 160,000 active charities in the UK, around 100,000 are estimated to be generating income from donations and fundraising activities (NCVO, 2016, p 14), and some 47,000 charities report that these were the income sources of greatest importance to the achievement of their objectives (Mohan and Breeze, 2015, p 72). As the majority of charities are actively seeking support from donors, and a significant percentage is reliant on fundraised income, fundraising is an essential, rather than an optional extra (Hughes, 1996, p 173).

Yet despite the need for employees who are capable of raising voluntary income, demand for experienced fundraisers seriously outstrips their supply, resulting in a 'talent crisis' (Saint, 2011; More Partnership/Richmond Associates, 2014b, p 3; Laskowski, 2016, p 16). This situation is by no means unique to the UK. A survey of 17 national fundraising associations across Europe found 40% believe the shortage of fundraising skills is one of the three biggest barriers to successful fundraising, rating this issue on a par with concerns about the economic climate (also chosen by 40% of respondents) and of greater concern than funding cuts from government and corporate sources (chosen by 33% of respondents) (European Fundraising Association, 2014, p 8). Nor is this solely a European phenomenon. A study in the US conducted in a similar time period identified 'an inadequate and uneven talent pool' of fundraisers, such that over half (53%) of hiring processes attracted an insufficient number of qualified candidates (Bell and Cornelius, 2013, p 8). A similar under-supply of qualified fundraisers for US charities was reported in earlier surveys (Duronio and Tempel, 1997; Looney and Looney, 2005, p 106). In other countries where the supply of fundraisers has been explored, such as Australia, the same picture of scarcity in qualified fundraisers is evident (Scaife and Madden, 2006, p 7).

While the challenge of recruiting fundraising talent is one of the biggest issues facing charities of all sizes (Caldicott, 2013), small charities find it particularly difficult to recruit suitable fundraisers (May and Broomhead 2014, p 10). Salary expectations are the prime reason stated, but a lack of applicants with relevant experience is reported by a quarter (25%) of respondents (May and Broomhead 2014, p 11).

The scarcity of fundraising talent is likely related to a number of issues, including the lack of a clear pathway into the job, ambiguity in defining what the role involves, and lack of affirmation for the task of fundraising, both within charities and in the wider society. Whatever the relative importance of these factors, and however they might be rectified in future, the global shortage of qualified fundraisers brings us back to a point raised earlier in this introductory chapter: that we cannot hope to understand and promote giving without paying attention to asking. The mutual interdependence is clear: 'When fundraising campaigns fail, it's not because there aren't enough potential donors, it's because there aren't enough askers' (Warner, 2001, p 2).

The essential yet invisible role of fundraisers

The task of asking for donations is one of the most intriguing, and yet largely unexplored, parts of the puzzle of charitable giving. In the UK, around a third (38%) of total charity income is raised from voluntary donations, which is primarily fundraising from individuals but also includes support from charitable trusts and foundations, companies, the National Lottery and funding grants from government.[3] The reliance on donated income is even higher among the vast majority of smaller charities that receive no public funding and have no mechanism for earning income (Clifford et al, 2013, p 255). Yet despite its importance, our awareness and understanding of the role that fundraisers play in securing donations is low.

One reason for overlooking fundraisers is a preference to interpret generosity as entirely innate, viewing it as a personal and private decision to respond to needs that exist in society. Instinctive kindness, and gifts that appear to be freely given, are far more highly culturally valued than reacting to a request (Derrida, 1992; Osteen, 2002; Komter, 2005), yet the inconvenient truth is that almost all gifts are prompted and facilitated to some degree (Bekkers, 2005; Bryant et al, 2003; Silber, 2012, p 323; Sokolowski, 1996). This is not necessarily because donors are unwilling to offer spontaneous help, but rather due to lack of awareness of the existence and urgency of some needs, and also lack of clarity about why and how to respond. We do not personally encounter some needs because of geographical proximity, but also because our highly stratified modern lives mean we exist in different social worlds to our neighbours and can easily be unaware of needs a few streets away.

Furthermore, the largely intangible nature of some needs, such as environmental issues, disaster prevention and the search for medical cures, mean that we often only become aware that something important needs funding as a result of someone drawing our attention to it, offering us a viable and trusted means of responding, and making us feel our contribution was worthwhile. That 'someone' is often a professional fundraiser, and in a nutshell that is what fundraisers do: they foster the philanthropic impulse, frame charitable needs, and facilitate donations.

Later chapters explore the questions of what fundraisers do and how they do it, but this introductory chapter is concerned with the question of why fundraising matters. Fundraising secures the resources for anything and everything that charities do: from paying the bills on major, established programmes such as welfare services helping children, veterans and the homeless, to covering the capital costs of new buildings and equipment (from tiny school clubs to major arts venues), to funding innovative solutions to intractable problems. Fundraising also covers a very wide range of activity, from volunteers shaking a tin to well-paid professionals masterminding multi-million-pound campaigns, and every layer of technique, scale and complexity in between. There is no necessary relationship between degree of sophistication and impact, as the following story highlights.

In 1967 a jumble sale was organised by the Mothers Club of Lakeside secondary school in the US city of Seattle. The proceeds were used to buy a basic computer terminal for the school's new computer club and to rent time to connect to a more powerful computer located elsewhere. Two of Lakeside's students, Bill Gates and Paul Allen, used their lunch hour to teach themselves programming and the rest is, quite literally, history.[4] What is especially interesting about that story is that most people don't know it. Bill Gates is a cultural icon and many facts about his life are well known: that he dropped out of Harvard University, became the richest man in the world, married Melinda, and together they are now philanthropically distributing most of their fortune. But the early role of fundraising in this story is usually overlooked.

Philanthropy research: a growing field

There has been a growing interest in explaining the persistence of the charitable impulse in contemporary conditions, with economists, sociologists and psychologists at the forefront of a boom in research on charitable motives and donor behaviour. Many studies that seek to explain why people give focus on revealing supposedly hidden benefits to donors. This was originally due to the greater enthusiasm for studying the topic among economists, whose dominant model assumes that rational individuals will always maximise their own self-interest, and is therefore challenged by evidence of widespread selfless behaviour. Their solution lay in redefining 'self-interest' to include even the most intangible 'warm glow' experienced by donors as a benefit (Andreoni, 1990), thus enabling charitable expenditure to be accommodated within a neoclassical economic world view.

Interest in the topic of charitable giving and philanthropy has spread to other disciplines, and a growing body of research now echoes the economistic 'hidden benefit' premise to demonstrate that, despite donations leading to some depletion in financial resources, generosity enables the accumulation of other, non-financial, rewards. For example, sociologists identify social benefits including enhanced reputation and access to elite networks (Bekkers and Wiepking, 2011); psychologists find that generous people are 'significantly more happy, healthy, and purposive people' (Smith and Davidson, 2014, p 95); and sociobiologists argue that altruistic behaviour has an evolutionary advantage (Okasha, 2013).

However, a number of studies dispute the suggestion that some sort of advantage must necessarily lurk behind all giving. Philosophers in particular have argued that people are willing and able – and ought – to act morally without consideration of personal reward (Singer, 2010, 2015), while others have identified 'extreme altruists', whose lack of self-regard comes at great cost to themselves (Macfarquhar, 2015). The proposition that contemporary capitalism is anathema to genuine 'acts of compassion' has been disputed (Wuthnow, 1991), and there is a growing understanding that material incentives are not the sole drivers of contemporary behaviour, and indeed that 'ethical and other-regarding motives are common' (Bowles, 2016, p 4), making it unnecessary – and socially costly – to assume that moral and ethical behaviour will not occur without tangible rewards. Such studies underline the need to move beyond a narrow economistic interpretation of charitable giving, as the research contained in this book sets out to do.

Donor-centric studies

The substantive and fast-growing body of knowledge on charitable giving, philanthropy and wider pro-social behaviour is not done justice by the reductionist paragraphs above. Yet these very edited highlights of recent research on charitable giving contain an interesting commonality. Despite their differences in explaining *why* people give, these accounts all share a focus on the actor who is assumed to be at the heart of the decision: the donor. The decision to donate (or not) is depicted as being entirely in the hands, head and heart of the one making the gift. And yet even a moment's reflection on our own experiences of making charitable donations reveals this is not an accurate depiction, because giving is intimately connected to being asked. For the most part, *we give because we are asked*. We are constantly encountering requests to make charitable donations, and our philanthropic decisions are understood to be largely reactive, not proactive (Jencks, 1987; Clotfelter, 1992; Schervish and Havens, 1997; Levy, 2009, p xxiii).

At least 20 billion 'asks' are made by UK charities[5] each year, including adverts, direct mail, telephone fundraising, email marketing, and face-to-face requests (Fundraising Standards Board, 2014, p 8). Alongside professionally organised fundraising efforts, we are also constantly being asked to give by people shaking tins and selling poppies, ribbons or stickers; by friends sending emails asking us to sponsor their 10k run or mountain climb; by colleagues encouraging participation in the workplace 'charity of the year'; and by children getting involved in telethons such as Children in Need or Comic Relief, as well as numerous other charitable requests from many quarters. As Greenfield notes: 'Asking for money goes on all the time' (Greenfield, 2002, p 27). While our decision to make a donation in any of these situations involves a mixture of motivations (Silber, 1998, p 144; Frumkin, 2006, pp 11–18), the transition of those mixed motives into action largely occur as a result of someone asking for a donation (Schervish and Havens, 1997; Bryant et al, 2003; Bekkers, 2005; Andreoni, 2006; Barman, 2007, p 1422).

Yet interest in the supply side (those who make donations) almost entirely overshadows interest in the demand side (those who ask for donations). This donor-centric approach also squeezes out other essential parties, including the beneficiaries and the charities, who 'disappear altogether' (Clohesy, 2003, p 134). Useful contributions have sought to rectify these problems, notably Ostrander and Schervish's attack on 'donor ascendancy', which obscures 'the most fundamental sociological fact about philanthropy; namely, that philanthropy is a social relation of giving and getting between donors and recipients' (Ostrander and Schervish, 1990, p 68). However, their useful diagnosis and important call for greater equality in the donor–recipient relationship continues to omit fundraisers from the equation.

Research on the efficacy of fundraising

We know that donors do not really exist in splendid isolation and can easily recall how our own giving is largely reactive to requests. The direct connection between asking and giving is, unsurprisingly, a truism among professional fundraisers (Yörük, 2012, p 220), confirming what

Andreoni calls the 'iron law': that people are more likely to give and also tend to donate more when they are asked (2006). Experimental studies confirm the positive effect of asking in securing donations (Okten and Weisbrod, 2000, p 271; Yörük, 2009; Oppenheimer and Olivola, 2011) and conclude 'that giving is rare without fundraising' (Meer, 2016, p 5). Studies also show that, on average, fundraising is very productive (Andreoni and Payne, 2011).

Capturing figures on the precise extent of fundraising success is not easy because the charity sector is so broad, and methods of fundraising are too various to make global figures particularly meaningful or easy to come by. But a recent study, based on data from 1,200 UK charities,[6] finds that for every £1 they invested in fundraising, £4.20 was raised (Centre for Inter-Firm Comparisons, 2014, cited in Sargeant and Shang, 2016), indicating a return on investment that would delight any venture capitalist. Furthermore, *not* fundraising is the surefire route to *not* raising voluntary income: most people say their reason for not giving is because they were not asked (Piliavin and Charng, 1990, p 35; Duronio and Tempel, 1997, p 173).

However, despite the proven efficacy of fundraising, it is too simplistic to suggest that more asking will lead directly and unproblematically to more giving. Fundraisers are not like a light bulb 'which performs one unambiguous task … at the flick of a switch' (Clark Kerr, quoted in Panas, 1988, p 8): there is huge variability in the quality of 'the ask' (as it is called by fundraisers), which is why the complexity and subtlety of the fundraising role is the subject of this book. The importance of good-quality asking is emphasised in this quote from a wealthy female philanthropist who was reflecting on her good and bad experiences of being approached for donations:

> When fundraising is done by less gifted people, they keep asking for one thing after another and it's really quite eroding, but when it's done well and I really feel that I am helping to do something special that I will look back on with pride, that's a feeling of joy.[7]

Successful fundraisers know that the request for a gift should only come after a lengthy and careful process that begins by developing a strong case for support, conducting research to identify potential supporters, strategic planning of the fundraising campaign, recruiting appropriate volunteers to assist in approaching potential donors, developing mutually beneficial relationships over months and years, then monitoring and evaluating the outcomes (Lindahl and Conley,

2002, pp 101–2). This process requires an investment of time and resources that is far removed from most people's perception of what fundraising involves, and this understanding gap has at least three main causes.

First, fundraisers are intentionally low-key and 'backstage' in their efforts (Duronio and Tempel, 1997, p 29). Donors prefer to feel they give spontaneously and from their own free will, so fundraisers know they must not assume control over the giving process (Radley and Kennedy, 1995, p 688; Hibbert and Horne, 1997, p 269). Second, the preparatory, organisational and follow-up tasks are extensive but not immediately obvious, even to close colleagues. The nature of this background work, and how it combines with the more visible public image of fundraisers, is discussed in greater detail in Chapter 3.

Third, people underestimate the complexity of professional fundraising because they have often raised some money in their private lives and assume it is essentially the same. Raising money is the most common form of volunteering (Cabinet Office, 2016), but asking friends and family for one-off support for a cause with which you (and perhaps the person you are asking) have a direct connection is a qualitatively different task to approaching strangers for ongoing funds for a charitable organisation. The difference between asking for money from friends and family and asking for support from strangers might usefully be compared with the difference between busking and fundraising. In the former case, people respond to the person making the request and are motivated by their assessment of the effort and talent of the asker (or busker, to keep the analogy going). In the latter case, the worthiness of the cause plays a much bigger role at the outset, but in order to sustain and grow support, a relationship must develop. The distinctive features of contemporary professional fundraising, including building and stewarding relationships with donors, is explored in much greater detail in Chapters 3, 4 and 5.

The need to shift research attention to askers

One way of encapsulating the essential role of fundraisers is to note that the process of making a donation is not friction-free: it is mediated even when the intermediaries are not visible (Mohan and Breeze, 2015, p 120). So-called 'friction-free' giving, usually exemplified by online giving or text giving, still requires someone to design and update a website or to set up the text-giving number, to manage the bank account that receives gifts, and (ideally) to let the donor know that their contribution has been safely received and how it has been used.

The conclusion that the existence and infrastructure of asking leads to more positive responses has been reached in many contexts beyond financial donations to charitable organisations. The importance of asking to prompt a response has been identified in relation to volunteering (Musick and Wilson, 2007, pp 288–91), giving blood (Drake et al, 1982; Healy, 2000), and donating kidneys (Simmons et al, 1977). Even those who rescued Jews during the Second World War were more likely to have been directly asked for help than those who did not (Oliner and Oliner, 1988; Yaish and Vaese, 2001). These diverse studies all show that in many different contexts, a situational factor (that is, receiving a direct appeal for help) triggers the underlying motivations that lead to altruistic action (Yaish and Vaese, 2001).

This is why it is argued that more studies need to focus on the macro-level context within which people make decisions to donate, rather than the micro-level context of individual donor characteristics such as income, age or religion (Barman, 2007). The organisational context includes factors such as a conducive fiscal framework (for example, tax reliefs for donations) and high levels of confidence in charities as a result of robust regulation. But the contextual factor of prime concern in this book is potential donors' encounter with frequent, plausible and attractive requests for support.

A shift in focus from givers to askers is not only necessary to redress the existing imbalance in research, but also because fundraisers' responsibility for triggering giving decisions makes them a more fertile locus of analytic attention. Indeed, research solely focused on donors is arguably guilty of what social psychologists call a "fundamental misattribution error", which occurs when behaviour is explained with reference to the actor's personal characteristics rather than the situation in which they find themselves. Difficulties in correctly identifying the site of giving decisions is further complicated by the fact that:

> There are no 'social laws' that explain who is generous and why. There is no simple list of variables that 'produce' or 'predict' generosity … [P]ossessing the natural general power for some given practice like generosity does not guarantee that it will be activated and exercised in any given case. Not all human capacities are triggered, cultivated, and expressed. Some, perhaps especially virtues like generosity, need to be actively prompted and tutored in order to become regular practices. That shifts our analytic attention from deep human neurology to more proximate triggering and routinizing factors promoting generosity. (Smith, 2014, np)

Most charitable acts are the result of both an 'asker' and a 'giver', but the donor's role is clearly visible, understood to be essential, and largely appreciated (excepting major donors whose gifts can sometimes generate suspicion rather than admiration), while the asker's role is usually either invisible or problematised. The substantially greater interest in philanthropy over fundraising is normative. Donors – especially wealthy donors – are of general public interest and attention, both historically and contemporaneously, whereas those asking for donations have never yet breached the public consciousness. The names of leading philanthropists, such as Andrew Carnegie, John D. Rockefeller, Bill Gates, and Warren Buffett, are well known, but no fundraiser shares a similar high profile. There are no plaques recording or honouring the contribution of fundraisers, despite giving and asking being two sides of the same coin – or, to use a more evocative metaphor that also highlights their differences:

> Donors and fundraisers occupy the same landscape yet they carry utterly different maps. Fundraisers maps are full of routes to donors and potential donors. In contrast, donors, would-be donors and their advisers use maps in which fundraisers are non-existent. (McLoughlin, 2014, p 6)

The recent flourishing of research on philanthropy is also driven by a practical goal: to identify the factors that encourage people to give, in order to encourage more people to become givers, and to encourage those who are already donors to give more. While understandable, given the increasing expectations of philanthropically funded goods and services, this creates an expectation that there is a 'donor type' or a set of sociodemographic characteristics and personal motivations that are allegedly typical of those most likely to give. Chasing this elusive donor profile has absorbed much intellectual and practical energy (see, for example, Prince and File, 1994; Rooney and Frederick, 2007; de Las Casas et al, 2013). However, given the global variation in levels of giving, and the fact that people can move from being non-donors to donors while retaining all other personal characteristics, it would seem that efforts to identify enduring and essential qualities of givers and non-givers would be better spent on gaining a better understanding of askers.

Fundraisers have not only been neglected by academic researchers (Duronio and Tempel, 1997; Andreoni, 1998; Kelly, 1998, p 106) – they have also been overlooked by policy makers, whose attempts to promote charitable giving and philanthropy are firmly focused on encouraging people to give, with apparent indifference to the needs and concerns of those charged with *asking* them to give (Saxton and Madden, 2010). Recent UK governments (Labour (1997–2010), the Coalition (2010–2015) and Conservative (2015 to date)) have all endorsed the role of philanthropy and philanthropists in numerous papers (see, for example, Home Office, 2005; Cabinet Office, 2011; Breeze, 2012a) but have been curiously silent on the role of fundraisers. Indeed, a House of Lords Select Committee on Charity that explicitly strove to encourage and support charitable activity, nonetheless states: 'we consciously chose not to focus on fundraising in our inquiry' (House of Lords, 2017, p 58). Since the passing of the Charities Act 2006, the Charity Commission for England and Wales (henceforth 'the Charity Commission') has had a duty to promote philanthropy by 'act[ing] in a way that is compatible with encouraging charitable giving' (Charities Act, 2006), yet this appears to have been interpreted only in terms of encouraging donors. Where the Charity Commission has considered fundraising, it has focused on the role of trustees rather than paid fundraisers, and on guarding against potential negative impacts of fundraising on organisational reputation, public trust and confidence (Charity Commission, 2016).

A 2011 summit on growing philanthropy in the UK concluded there was a need to promote better public understanding of fundraising (Sargeant and Shang, 2011, p 8), yet in the same year, an independent initiative called 'The Philanthropy Review' focused almost exclusively on donors. The final report of this review argued that the 'road to a new philanthropy' lay primarily in new tax reliefs and new products (such as 'lifetime legacies' and charity bank accounts), with scant attention paid to the people who would be using these tools to engage and encourage donors to either start or increase their giving (Philanthropy Review, 2011, p 14). The only policy proposal to focus squarely on fundraisers is the 'Better Asking campaign' proposed by NCVO in its *Funding the Future* report, which was intended:

> to increase the quantity, and improve the quality of, asking for donations … the campaign should aim to increase the confidence and competence of all those involved in asking for funds for charities, including trustees, chief executives, paid fundraisers, volunteer fundraisers and communications staff. (NCVO, 2010, p x)

Yet in the few years since that report was published, the reputation of fundraising has deteriorated further.

The aim of this book

This book is not the first to note that fundraising is neglected as a topic of study. Philanthropy has long been conceived of as a world exclusively populated by donors (Ostrander and Schervish, 1990), and when asking receives any consideration, it is viewed as a generic activity undertaken by charitable organisations, rather than specific actions of practitioners (Kelly, 1997, 1998, p 106). The lack of extensive empirical research was noted by Payton et al (1991, p 276), and the unequal treatment of donors and askers was highlighted almost 20 years ago:

> Economic research on altruism, public goods, and charitable giving has flourished over the past decade. The analysis to date has focused almost exclusively on donors – the supply side of charity – and has left unexplored the role played by fund-raisers – the demand side. Yet fund-raising is a vibrant, innovative, and highly professional industry. (Andreoni, 1998, p 1186)

In the intervening two decades, there has continued to be a slew of books published on the identity, motivation and experiences of philanthropists, with no equivalent attention paid to fundraisers, aside from a handful of biographical and quasi-autobiographical accounts written by and about fundraisers (Gurin, 1985; Knott, 1992; Johnson, 2011b; Walker, 2015). Studies of fundraising have recently grown more numerous, including some testing of techniques in field experiments (Oppenheimer and Olivola, 2011; Jasper and Samek, 2014), but are typified by what Kelly disparagingly – though accurately – describes as 'the search for magic buttons' (Kelly, 1998, p 109) – meaning an attempt to identify characteristics, behaviours and attitudes that are causally correlated with inclination to give. The result is that fundraising must 'skate on thinner intellectual ice than is prudent' (Payton et al, 1991, p 277).

The studies of fundraising that do exist are biased towards certain topics and settings. For example, there are more studies of fundraising in higher education institutions and hospitals than other cause areas (Lindahl and Conley, 2002, p 91), and there are more studies of mass solicitation (Bekkers and Wiepking, 2011) that make use of transactional marketing techniques than there are studies of major donor fundraising, which is based on relationships (Burnett, 2002; Burk, 2003). The bias towards studying mass fundraising is likely to be due to this being more amenable to both field and laboratory experiments, as well as to issues regarding access to samples.

But in practice – as explored in later chapters – relationship-based fundraising, rather than transactional marketing, is the recommended approach, especially in relation to higher-value donors. This is because the biggest donations are understood to occur as a result of longstanding, trusting relationships between donors and charitable organisations, rather than as a result of a one-off, transactional, 'ask'. Therefore the academic studies that do exist often betray a lack of insight into the actual practice of fundraising and donating. Laboratory experiments are among the worst offenders, consisting of artificial scenarios in which the decision making of participants (typically undergraduate university students) is deemed relevant to real-life philanthropic scenarios. In reality, giving happens within social and organisational contexts that directly influence action, such that 'altruism is structured, promoted, and made logistically possible by organizations and institutions' (Healy, 2004, p 387).

The need to understand and acknowledge the 'social-organisational approach to altruism' has a long pedigree in social science. It dates back at least to the early 1970s with Richard Titmuss's influential study of blood donating in the UK and the US, which argued that different rates and quality of donations are achieved, depending on the structural context (Titmuss, 1970). Yet studies seeking to understand fundraising continue to take place in scenarios that are denuded of any meaningful context, and frequently fail to understand what the task of fundraising actually involves. For example, a study of 'excessive fundraising' is founded on the belief that fundraisers do nothing other than mail out brochures to prospective donors (Rose-Ackerman, 1982). It is unsurprising that practitioners often find academic studies frustratingly detached from the reality of their everyday practices.

The structure of this book

Chapter 1 reviews the historical roots and development of fundraising in the UK, highlighting important milestones and key issues that have emerged over time and that remain contentious today.

Chapter 2 presents findings of a major survey of over 1,200 UK fundraisers to paint a picture of the type of people currently working as fundraisers in the UK. Data on personality traits and emotional intelligence, as well as trust levels, social lives, hobbies and many other factors, are presented and compared with data on the general public in order to identify the extent to which, and in what ways, people who raise money for a living either share characteristics or appear to be distinctive.

Chapter 3 explores 'the science of fundraising' through an analysis of 60 books, widely read within the profession, that explain 'how to' fundraise. The content of these guides, and the language used in them, suggests that fundraising is often presented as a set of skills that can be learnt and mastered by anyone who puts in the time and effort. Yet advice on how to implement the suggested steps – such as building personal relationships and stewarding donors – is usually ambiguous or absent. I therefore argue that the 'scientific' approach is more relevant for impersonal types of fundraising such as direct mail, and less applicable to fundraising that relies on strong interpersonal relationships, notably working with major donors.

The fourth chapter focuses on 'the art of fundraising', exploring how the social and personal skills of fundraisers enable them to succeed. By focusing on the metaphors that fundraisers use to describe their work, the data highlights the importance of skills such as reading body language, 'hearing the unsaid', exercising good judgements about how, and how fast, to progress relationships with donors and potential donors, as well as understanding the distinct motivations of each supporter and what type of acknowledgement they want. The importance of seemingly trivial decisions, such as the precise wording of an email or whether or not to send a birthday card, illustrates the difficulty of codifying this knowledge.

The fifth chapter focuses on what fundraisers do. Despite the apparently self-explanatory job title, most fundraisers do not see 'raising funds' as their central task. Rather, their daily work involves building strong, mutually beneficial relationships with people who share a conviction about the importance of the charity's work. I suggest this work can be understood as involving three sets of tasks, as follows.

- Fostering the philanthropic culture within the charity and among potential supporters and donors.
- Framing, which involves raising awareness of the nature and extent of need and the charity's ability to solve or mitigate them.
- Facilitating the involvement and ongoing engagement of potential supporters.

The successful implementation of this triad relies on fundraisers utilising and regulating their personalities and emotions in the course of their work, which can therefore be described as 'emotional labour'

(Hochschild, 1983), within which I suggest the concept of 'gratitude work' is particularly important.

Chapter 6 draws together the findings of the previous chapters to explore the status of fundraising work: is it a profession, a job, a calling or a vocation? The continuing lack of a verifiable, agreed body of knowledge, the absence of widespread formal qualifications, the emphasis on experiential learning, the frequent involvement of volunteers and the lack of public recognition of fundraisers' expertise, are all shown to undermine claims regarding the professionalisation of fundraising. As contemporary fundraising involves a combination of creative innovation and managerial skills, I argue that fundraising is both an art and a science, and that fundraisers are best understood as a type of creative professional.

The concluding chapter suggests that we are witnessing the emergence of 'The New Fundraisers' who exist in a necessarily complementary relationship with 'The New Philanthropists', said to typify the most recent generation of major givers. Contemporary askers and givers possess many similar traits and attitudes, including shared connections to the cause and convictions about its importance; a desire for impact; and a joy in asking and giving. These similarities enable them to build mutually beneficial relationships, despite a general lack of public affirmation in the UK for both givers and askers.

The current context: fundraising in 'crisis'

This book is not only written as a corrective to the lack of meaningful academic interest in this subject. It is also a response to the growing hostility to fundraising in both the public and political spheres. The research presented here started in 2013, two years before the current 'crisis' in fundraising began, and these subsequent events have heightened the relevance of its message.

The persistent, but mostly low-level, concern about the methods and techniques used by fundraisers turned into an avalanche of criticism after the death in May 2015 of an older charity supporter, 'the UK's longest serving poppy seller',[8] Olive Cooke, after a friend attributed her suicide to "exhaustion" and "pressure" from charitable appeals.[9] Despite disagreement with this analysis from close family,[10] and despite the coroner's report failing to concur that an excess of charitable requests played any part in Mrs Cooke's tragic death, the culpability of fundraising became firmly established in both the public and political consciousness. A succession of prominent national newspaper headlines lambasted the work of charities in general, and of paid fundraisers in particular; these included 'Killed by Her Kindness (*The Sun*, 15 May 2015); 'Hounded to death by Cold Callers' (*Daily Mail*, 15 May 2015); and 'Charities Must be Less Brutal' (*The Observer*, 17 May 2015). Politicians queued up to profess themselves outraged at the practices used by charities to raise money, including the then-Prime Minster David Cameron, who referred to the "frankly unacceptable"[11] actions of some fundraisers. William Shawcross, the current chair of the Charity Commission for England and Wales, felt that events constituted a "crisis", and stated:

> The sad case of Olive Cooke is the most recent example of how strongly charities' actions – good and bad – resonate among the public .... regardless the specifics of the Olive Cooke case, the issues it highlighted have clearly caused great anxiety among the public ... I believe this is a crisis for the charity sector.[12]

The fundraising environment was already tough before the media storm of 2015 (Aldrich, 2016). Support for charities remains high, but large sections of the public feel no contradiction in simultaneously feeling sympathy for charitable causes and antipathy towards those who raise the funds for those causes. Political and media critiques of fundraising techniques have found their echo in more substantive and academic texts including critiques of corporate fundraising (Einstein, 2012) and charity awareness campaigns (King, 2006; Moore, 2010), creating a 'volatile and complex' environment in which charities exist and fundraise (Neilson et al, 2012, p 3). Furthermore, negative media stories tend to take a homogenous approach, rarely differentiating between the different types of organisations that are trying to raise funds or the many different approaches that can be taken to asking for support, each of which has its own costs, dynamics and complexities. This results in 'an overall negative and very confusing picture' of fundraising (Duronio and Tempel, 1997, p 12).

Of course, there is nothing new about widespread discomfort with the act of raising funds for good causes. The historical overview in the next chapter explains that asking is as old as giving, and that those doing the asking have long attracted criticism. As an item in *The Times* (London) newspaper in 1880 wearily notes,

> When a name has once been printed on a subscription list, its owner becomes a marked man. He has joined, by his own act, the unhappy class to which an appeal can be

> made with some chance that it will be met. From that day forward his persecution will never cease. (Cited in Davies, 2015, p 143)

It may also be of some comfort for UK fundraisers to learn that their transatlantic counterparts, who are often assumed to be working in a more fundraising-friendly context in the US, have in fact long been facing 'severe public criticism' (Duronio and Tempel, 1997, p 171) and that 'the public image of fundraisers in the United States is in some disarray' (Pribbenow, 1999, p 29) and has worsened as a result of a series of scandals (White, 2007).

While much hostility to fundraising is expressed with reference to methods and techniques, such as the extent, timing and tenor of specific types of communications, the source of antipathy likely runs much deeper and relates to the essential nature of the act rather than any particular quarrel with its execution. Money and morals are viewed as a private matter, which means that any sort of request for donations can offend deeply held values regarding privacy (Harrah-Conforth and Borsos, 1991, pp 28–9). Levy claims most people 'would rather walk slowly over hot coals' than ask others for money because 'it's widely viewed as a bold and presumptuous act, one filled with the potential for awkwardness, embarrassment, disappointment, and rejection' (Levy, 2009, p 1). Fundraisers can also be perceived as exhibiting moral superiority, and hence exposed to the 'do-gooder derogation' experienced by those whose existence threatens the self-worth of those who feel 'judged and found wanting' by moral minorities (Minson and Monin, 2011, p 205).

Antagonism to fundraisers can come from within charities: some board members describe the work of raising funds as 'demeaning' (Dorsey, 1991, p xiii) and a fundraiser explains that 'Our CEO [chief executive officer] hates fundraising [even though] we rely on donors' (Jerberg, cited in Pudelek, 2014b). While it might be tempting to counsel acceptance of this lack of affirmation, the ability for fundraisers to do their job is influenced by how they are perceived (Hughes, 1996, p 177). The interaction of fundraisers with their colleagues is explored further in later chapters.

Disparity in esteem for fundraisers and their charities

The longstanding stream of concern and criticism about fundraising, which occasionally – as in the summer of 2015 – turns into a torrent, occurs despite a general appreciation of the work that fundraising pays for. In general, the British public likes and admires the work of charities, with a firm majority (68%) viewing their contribution to society as 'highly important' (Glennie and Whillans-Welldrake, 2014, p 4). Attitudinal surveys conducted in 1991 and repeated in 2015 find greater agreement over time that charities should play a role in responding to issues such as homelessness, food aid to poor countries, and conservation, along with a growing recognition of the importance of, and need for, charitable activity (Mohan and Breeze, 2015, pp 10–11). Yet despite this increasing reliance on charities, the public perception of fundraising is suspicious and often hostile.

One of the earliest uses of the word 'fundraiser' in print appeared in a seminal mid-20th-century book titled *The Hidden Persuaders*, which exposed the ways that advertisers manipulate customers. Setting the tone for future writing on the topic, the word was defined pejoratively, with those raising funds for good causes undifferentiated from the 'merchants of discontent' selling anxiety-inducing and unnecessary products (Packard, 1957). Half a century later, fundraising is still often viewed as a form of high-pressure salesmanship or even begging (Breeze and Scaife, 2015, p 571), 'rather squalid' (Allford, 1993, p 105) and 'an odious activity' (Bloland and Tempel, 2004, p 16), while fundraisers are viewed as 'hucksters' (Kelly, 1998, p 105), 'pushy and somewhat sleazy' (Joyaux, 2011, pp 94–5) or even 'the white collar equivalent of cleaning toilets' (Pink, 2012, p 2). These negative sentiments have sometimes been appropriated by fundraisers themselves, for example a book about fundraising techniques has the words '[This] book is *the* manual for the honest pickpocket' (Warner, 2001) emblazoned on its front cover.

Fundraising as the servant of philanthropy

Despite recent claims that philanthropy has been 'revived and reinvented' (Bishop and Green 2008, p 3), fundraising continues to be viewed with suspicion and disdain (Daly, 2013, p 29) and there is considerable anxiety about how fundraising is presented to – and perceived by – the world (Bloland and Bornstein, 1991, p 120). This is perplexing to fundraisers because their work does not occur as an end in itself: money is only raised in order to make something good happen. The primacy of need over funding is crystallised in arguably the field's most famous aphorism: 'fundraising is the servant of philanthropy' (Rosso and Associates, 2015, p 6), penned by Hank Rosso, who was the originator of university-level education programmes for fundraisers.

Rosso's phrase echoes the sentiment of Basil O'Connor, a 'singleminded and ingenious fundraiser' (Whitman, 1972) who emphasised fundraising as the means rather than the end. O'Connor noted that charitable organisations 'do not exist to raise money. We *do* have to have money to exist. That is the whole difference' (O'Connor, 1959, p 16). O'Connor led one of the world's most successful fundraising organisations: the US-based National Foundation for Infant Paralysis, which raised the equivalent of over £520 million in the late 1930s to early 1950s to pay for the development of the Salk vaccine that ended the scourge of polio in much of the world. The organisation became known as the March of Dimes Foundation after its annual fundraising event, which asked every household in the US to donate dimes (Lindahl, 2010, p 81). This collective effort raised 7 billion dimes to fund the successful scientific research and educational effort, prompting O'Connor to tell a gathering of fundraisers, then a newly emerging profession, that: 'you are part of something that is real … of great consequence, and of great meaning to the American people.' (O'Connor, 1959, pp 15–16).

The successful conclusion to O'Connor's fundraising is rare because charities typically tackle complex and enduring problems. Some of the most popular issues addressed by contemporary UK charities are curing cancer, promoting child welfare, responding to natural and man-made disasters, providing hospices that care for the dying, and protecting historic buildings, landscapes and coastlines. These are self-evidently all important issues, and none of them has any obvious end in sight, so the need to continue – and ideally increase – raising funds is an enduring task. There is therefore a pressing need to reconcile the disparity between the widespread negative public image of fundraising, with the vital importance of voluntary income generation to charities, and to the welfare of wider society (Burlingame and Hulse, 1991, p xxii–xxiii; Gurin, 1991, p 149).

The role of fundraised income in the mixed economy of charities

The simple fact is that charities cannot do their good work unless they have enough income to cover their costs and pay their bills. As Wagner explains: 'Most work in the nonprofit sector, whether it is advocacy, healing, educating, entertaining, preserving, or some other activity, will not happen unless someone brings in money' (Wagner, 2004, p 170). There is a great lack of understanding about where the money comes from to pay for charitable activity. Some charities can charge some fees (usually below market price) or get some money from government or a founding endowment, but the rest must be raised through fundraising (White, 2007, p xvii). Of course, charity leaders are aware of the vital role that fundraising plays because they can see the evidence on their balance sheet, and because recruiting good fundraisers is one of their main managerial headaches. But there remains a disconnect between understanding the importance of the role and valuing the people filling that role. There is a widespread sense that fundraisers are tolerated because of the pressing need for the funds they can bring in, rather than a genuine appreciation of their skills and wider contribution (Bloland and Bornstein, 1991, p 104). In somewhat of an understatement it is suggested that, 'the role seems to have a mystique or be underrated … the role and its complexities perhaps much misunderstood' (Scaife et al, 2011, p 64).

This book responds to the problems set out above by explaining the practices of fundraising, and illuminating the characteristics of those who work as fundraisers. My goal is to create a better understanding of this important aspect of social life, and to challenge the illogical position whereby charities are admired, but the people who keep them in business are not.

Notes

1. This data is available here: https://data.ncvo.org.uk/a/almanac15/big-picture/#Charity_registration_over_time (last accessed 1 July 2016).
2. The figure of 6,000 members of the Institute of Fundraising is reported here: www.linkedin.com/groups/3064668/3064668-6217725125731577859 (last accessed 22 December 2016).
3. This data is available here: https://data.ncvo.org.uk/wp-content/uploads/2016/04/voluntary-sector-income-sources-types.png (last accessed 7 June 2017).
4. This story is related in Flanagan, 2002, p 1; Gladwell, 2009, p 51; Lowe, 2001, pp 7–8; Schuman, 2007, pp 23–4.
5. The charities referred to are the 1,203 members of the UK Fundraising Standards Board (FRSB), which supplied figures in the cited report.
6. The 1,200 UK charities report their figures as a result of being members of the Fundraising Standards Board.
7. This statement was made at an event on women and philanthropy held at Murray Edwards College, Cambridge on 25 September 2015.
8. Mrs Cooke received a Points of Light award from the then-Prime Minister in 2014 for being for being the UK's longest-serving poppy seller: http://www.bbc.co.uk/news/uk-england-bristol-32748923
9. For example, http://www.bbc.co.uk/news/uk-england-bristol-32748923
10. In the days after Olive Cooke's death in May 2015, her granddaughter told the BBC that charities had been "intrusive" but were not responsible for her suicide (http://www.bbc.co.uk/news/uk-england-bristol-32788128). The Cooke family made a statement to the FRSB report published in January 2016, which stated: "We want

Olive to be remembered for her incredibly kind, generous and charitable nature. Far from being a victim she was a strong believer in the importance of charities in UK society and local communities".

[11] David Cameron's words appear in this government-issued press release: www.gov.uk/government/news/new-law-to-protect-vulnerable-from-rogue-fundraisers

[12] William Shawcross's words appear in this speech: www.gov.uk/government/speeches/rathbones-charity-conversations-series-2015-william-shawcross-speech.

ONE

A history of fundraising in the UK

Asking is as old as giving – but fundraising has been overlooked and problematised throughout history, receiving minimal academic attention while frequently attracting public hostility. This chapter explores why invisibility and infamy have been dominant motifs in the history of fundraising, and suggests that a focus on what the raising of funds has achieved over the centuries, rather than simply documenting the changing techniques and technologies used by fundraisers, offers an alternative account of the emergence of the profession. This chapter is also concerned with the broader context that makes fundraising possible, looking beyond the rare documented instances of historic solicitation to focus instead on the social conditions that are necessary for fundraising to exist and to be effective.

Fundraisers have much lower profiles than philanthropists

Askers leave far fewer traces than philanthropists. The actions of donors are recorded in the history books as well as on buildings, benches, plaques and pillars. Yet no one recalls who asked Andrew Carnegie or Bill Gates to make their first donation, or who funded the speaking tours and campaigning that led to the abolition of slavery or more recent equalities legislation, or who organised the fundraising for voluntary schools and hospitals in the pre-welfare state era, or for museums and science laboratories today.

This collective amnesia is even-handed, as it also overlooks fundraising's more problematic contributions, most notably the infamous sale of indulgences that motivated Martin Luther to start the Reformation in 1517. One of the reasons that fundraising's role in the schism that split the Christian church is easily overlooked is due to changes in terminology. The men licensed to sell papal pardons and indulgences to raise funds for religious foundations were called 'Pardoners' rather than 'Fundraisers'. Notable examples include Johan Tetzel, whom Luther encountered when he was professor of scripture in Wittenberg and whose name was later attached to the annual Tetzel Award, organised by the American *Philanthropy Monthly* magazine, for 'the most discreditable fundraising performance' each year (Mullin, 2007, p 14), and the fictional Pardoner who is one of the 24 storytellers in Geoffrey Chaucer's *The Canterbury Tales*, written in the late 14th century. The word 'fundraiser' did not become the common term for people undertaking this activity until many centuries later, possibly as late as mid-20th century (Turner, 1991, p 38). But changes in terminology should not obscure the continuity in goals, methods, approaches and criticisms that are charted in this chapter.

It is also noteworthy that, despite fundraising having played a part in many important social, cultural and political developments in the UK, a substantive historiography has not been written. The intangible nature of much fundraising practice, including conversations and other informal face-to-face interactions, makes it less amenable to historic study, which tends to rely on documentation (Cunningham and Innes, 1998, p 11). There is an admittedly slim and mostly quite dated bookshelf of volumes on UK philanthropy (Gray, 1905; Jordan, 1959; Owen, 1965; Prochaska, 1990a; Cunningham, 2015; Davies, 2015), and biographies have been written of some notable British, or British-born, philanthropists including Andrew Carnegie (Krass 2002; Nasaw 2006), Titus Salt (Balgarnie, 2003), William Hasketh Lever (Macqueen, 2004) and Henry Wellcome (Flannery and Smith, 2011). But there are no book-length accounts of the emergence and development of fundraising in the UK that compare with Cutlip's study of fundraising in the US, which was first published in 1965. There are a handful of useful but brief overviews, notable examples being the chapter on 'The history and development of fundraising practices' in Sargeant and Jay (2014), and Mullin's lively summary entitled 'Two Thousand Years of Disreputable History' (2007) – yet both are relatively brief chapters containing interesting vignettes rather than a coherent or comprehensive story. Meanwhile, substantive academic articles such as Lloyd's (2002) study of charity dinners in 18th-century London, offer fascinating material and analysis of specific fundraising practices, yet lack contextualisation in the broader story of fundraising.

In the absence of such a guide, this chapter reviews what is known about the roots of contemporary fundraising, and offers an alternative to the accepted wisdom that modern fundraising 'began' in the US in the late 19th/early 20th century (as suggested by, for example, Bremner, 1988; Cutlip, 1990; Worth and Asp, 1994; Duronio and Tempel, 1997; Wagner, 2004). This alternative account highlights much continuity in practice over the centuries, despite radical changes in the technology available to fundraisers to communicate with potential donors.

Fundraising's origin myth

The standard explanation for the 'invention of fundraising' cites the 1890 appointment of Charles Sumner Ward (1858–1929) as General Secretary of the Young Men's Christian Association (YMCA) in Grand Rapids, US. Ward succeeded in raising funds through short-term, intensive fundraising drives, with the brevity being a response to donors' alleged desire 'to get the agony over with quickly' (cited in Cutlip, 1990, p 41). In 1905 Ward was invited to repeat his 'whirlwind' campaign on the national stage by assisting a colleague, Lyman Pierce (1868–1940), in raising $90,000 for a new YMCA in Washington, DC. As summarised by Sargeant et al (2010, p 31), the three main ingredients of the Ward–Pierce approach were as follows.

1. A highly organised 'backroom' operation undertaken by paid, including the recruitment of local, well-connected volunteers to 'front' the campaign and securing pledges of 'pace-setting' gifts in advance equal to the value of up to a third of the intended goal.
2. Cutting-edge public relations techniques to launch the public phase of the campaign, with maximum publicity in local media to emphasise the urgency of reaching the goal.
3. A concentrated time-span of around a fortnight to secure the support of busy local business leaders and keep the campaign in the headlines.

The success of this approach was evident in subsequent campaigns, including Ward's 'triumphant tour of Britain' (Wooster, 2000) in 1912 when he ran drives for the YMCA in London and Edinburgh (Cutlip, 1990, p 84), and the deployment of the same techniques to respond to needs created during the First World War, such as supporting soldiers on the front line and those returning with injuries, the families of those killed in action, and civilians affected by bomb damage (Grant, 2014). Those leading the wartime fundraising in the US were largely the same people who had worked on YMCA campaigns, as Ward and Pierce were 'on loan' during wartime to the Red Cross (Wagner, 2004, p 167); the implementation of those same successful techniques enabled them to raise unprecedentedly large sums for the Red Cross, including $114 million (equivalent to over £2 billion in 2016) in just eight days in 1917 (Cutlip, 1990, p 116). When the First World War ended in 1918, the 'mass campaign' had become an established fundraising method (Aldrich, 2016, p 504), and for those skilled at organising such campaigns, fundraising had become established as a paid job (Sargeant et al, 2010, p 32). It was also emerging as a profession able to make claims for having a 'scientific basis' rather than simply relying on the personal appeal of fundraisers asking their existing contacts (Worth and Asp, 1994, p 8; Aldrich, 2016, p 504). Soon after the war ended, a number of profitable fundraising businesses were created in the US, primarily led by key figures from the 'YMCA School' of fundraisers (Cutlip, 1990, p 43) – notably the firm of Ward, Hill, Pierce and Wells, established in 1919 (Mullin, 2007, p 16).

A younger man, Jonathan Price Jones (1877–1964), joined the ranks of 'fundraising's first superstars' (Wooster, 2000) as a result of the phenomenal success of the consultancy he established in the same post-war period: the John Price Jones Corp (Cutlip, 1990, p 43; Lindahl, 2010, p 79). Jones originally worked in journalism and his distinctive contribution was to transfer techniques from the newly emerging field of public relations into fundraising (Cutlip, 1990, p 171) and finding innovative ways to highlight campaigns, such as putting fundraising messages onto milk bottles, utility bills and bank statements. The results were so successful that his obituary was headlined: 'Fund-Raiser who Collected a Billion, Dead' (*New York Times*, 24 December 1964). During this period, the techniques and practices of fundraising were established and passed on to junior colleagues through a process of personal tutoring (Harrah-Conforth and Borsos, 1991, p 24; Wagner, 2004, p 168). Decades later the names of pioneers were still attached to 'The Ward Plan' and to 'The Pierce Plan' (Cutlip, 1990, p 39), and their ideas were codified in the first 'manual' on fundraising, written by Harold 'Sy' Seymour in 1966.

The influence of Ward, Pierce and Jones was not confined to introducing new techniques and accomplishing ever-higher campaign goals. It also included their emphasis on fundraising as a values-based enterprise, rather than purely a commercial venture, summed up most pithily in Ward's assertion: 'I would leave this work immediately if I thought I were merely raising money. It is raising men that appeals to me' (cited in Cutlip, 1990, p 43). However, as others have noted, positioning for-profit fundraising consultancy as an overtly ethical enterprise could be interpreted as an astute marketing move when trying to win business from charitable organisations (Wagner, 2004, p 168).

The contribution of Ward, Pierce and Jones is undoubtedly impressive, and it is reasonable to describe them as the creators of the for-profit fundraising consultancy industry. However, it is inaccurate to claim that they founded fundraising per se, or that systematically asking strangers for donations began in the US in the first years of the 20th century. We know that funds were raised for a wide range of causes over many preceding centuries, from building cathedrals to providing accommodation and food for the poor. Specific examples will be discussed further below, but first we consider how fundraising's 'origin myth', which relies on a 'Great Man' interpretation of history, has been replicated in the UK.

'Great Men' and the origin myth of fundraising

The 'Great Man theory' is a 19th-century idea most famously articulated by the Scottish philosopher Thomas Carlyle, who asserted that history is essentially driven by the acts and personalities of rare and heroic 'great men' (Carlyle, 1841). The view that the agency of a few individuals can shape the destiny of the many was soon questioned by those asserting the greater influence of social conditions, notably Herbert Spencer, who insisted that so-called 'great men' are also products of their time and shaped by the same social conditions as the rest of the population (Spencer, 1896). Modern social science continues to debate the extent to which 'agency' (autonomous individual action) and 'structure' (prevailing social conditions) influence outcomes, but a 'great man' view of history persists in the popular imagination, and is clearly evident in the accepted account of the emergence of fundraising, described above.

The historiography of fundraising, such as it exists, has tended to focus on a handful of key personalities who shaped the profession, and there is symmetry in the number of 'great men' cited on either side of the Atlantic. As discussed above, in the US credit is given to Charles Sumner Ward, Lyman Pierce and Jonathan Price Jones (see Marts, 1961, p 35), while the UK triumvirate, active a few decades later than their US counterparts, is Leslie Kirkley (1911–89), Harold Sumption (1916–98), and Guy Stringer (1920–2009), described as 'three quite remarkable men' and 'an intriguing trio whose collective achievements created the business in which we now all work ... They were "good" men, fuelled by a quiet zeal to make the world a slightly better place' (Smith, 2009).

Kirkley led a small group formed during in 1942 called the Oxford Committee for Famine Relief, which aimed to help civilians by getting vital supplies to those living in occupied Europe. Kirkley's social vision, rooted in Quaker values combined with his fundraising acumen, enabled him to grow the organisation until it became one of the UK's biggest and best-known charities – Oxfam – which remains one of the most successful global fundraising organisations. While Kirkley was employed first as the 'General Secretary' and then as 'Director', he understood the role and importance of professional fundraisers, and the importance of support for the fundraising function by the charity leadership (Smith, 2009).

Harold Sumption, like Kirkley, was a Quaker. He had a background in sales, but after experiencing life-threatening ill health in his twenties, he decided that a career in fundraising offered the best way to use his professional skills in a manner compatible with his faith and desire to do good (Sumption, 1995, pp 57–9). He worked at a number of major UK charities including Oxfam, ActionAid and Help the Aged, where he established the viability of what are now mainstream fundraising techniques such as direct mail, off-the-page press advertising, trading catalogues and cinema commercials (Smith, 2009). His obituary claimed that 'little in today's fund-raising repertoire was not tried first by Sumption' (*The Guardian*, 27 March 1998) and he is described as the man who 'practically invented' modern fundraising (Sherrington, 2015). But Sumption's successes involved re-invention as much as invention, seeing the untapped potential in old-fashioned practices such as the humble collecting box: 'he had volunteers deliver 6 million collection boxes – an exercise that added 400,000 new donors to Oxfam's first computerised database' (Smith, 2009).

Guy Stringer is the youngest of the UK 'Great Men of fundraising'. He served in the army during the Second World War and in Korea, then returned to the UK to become a successful businessman, before becoming commercial director of Oxfam in 1969. As a self-described 'commercial man with a conscience' (Black, 1992, p 163) he introduced the selling of crafts made by people in the developing world in Oxfam shops – what is now called fair trade (Smith, 2009). He became director of Oxfam in 1982, but still spent Friday afternoons on the phone personally thanking all donors who gave £500 or more. By the time he retired in 1986, the charity's income had increased from £2.5m in 1969 to £51m (Smith, 2009). His obituaries described him as a 'pioneering practitioner' of fundraising (*New Internationalist*, 1 September 2009) and a 'fundraising genius' (Black, 2009, np).

All six of the 'Great Men' of US and UK fundraising described above clearly deserve credit for their innovative and successful efforts, in the consultancy business for the US triad and within major charities for the three UK men. But to describe them as the 'inventors' of fundraising in their respective countries raises some awkward and unanswerable questions. How can this account be squared with the existence of systematic, organised fundraising campaigns before their times? And how did fundraising develop in any country other than the US and the

UK? Is there a male triumvirate waiting to be named in every region that now has a thriving fundraising industry?

There is a further complicating factor in understanding the emergence of fundraising, which relates to accepted versions of the historical timelines for philanthropy and fundraising. Philanthropy is alleged to have enjoyed 'golden ages' in the 18th and 19th centuries, yet it is also suggested that fundraising only really began in the early 20th century. Given the known symbiotic relationship between asking and giving, as discussed in the previous chapter, this unlikely sequence is undermined still further by evidence from the 19th century that the collective contributions of the poor, who were prompted to give 'pounds, shillings and pence' by door-to-door collectors and via the church collection plate, came to 'many millions each year' (Prochaska, 1988, p 60). As there is no reason to assume that poorer donors need prompting while richer donors give proactively without prompting, we appear to be overlooking the existence of fundraising during the 'golden ages' of philanthropy, and indeed in earlier periods.

An alternative approach: the history of fundraising impact

To date, the history of fundraising has been concerned with process rather than purpose, with the focus firmly on the methods used (such as personal requests, newspaper adverts, direct mail and so on) rather than on the outcomes they achieved. This is understandable, as the development of fundraising has been tightly linked to the development of communication techniques and the possibilities they present for reaching potential donors, from the pulpit, which was an effective site for fundraising for centuries (Mullin, 2007, p 14), to the vastly increased opportunities for mass communication enabled by the invention of the printing press, the postal service and, most recently, social media. Yet as emphasised in the introductory chapter, fundraising is a means to an end, not an end in itself. Unlike private wealth accumulation, there is no praise for, or purpose in, accumulating fundraised income for its own sake: as one of the UK 'great men' said: 'Fundraising is not about money, it's about work that needs doing' (Sumption, quoted in Lee, 1998). Therefore the only meaningful measure of fundraising success is what is achieved with the accumulated funds: what is improved, ameliorated, or preserved in society as a result of 'raising money by asking for it'.

Therefore the approach taken in this chapter is to describe and discuss the *impact* of fundraising over the centuries. It includes an eclectic mix of examples, from within and beyond the UK, chosen primarily because of the availability of evidence but also to illustrate the breadth and variety of ways in which fundraisers – those willing to ask others to make voluntary contributions – have shaped our society.

Ten examples of the impact of fundraising through history

1. Care for the poor and other good works in antiquity

The oldest documented evidence of charitable giving to help the poor comes in the Egyptian *Book of the Dead*, dating back to the 4th century bce, which praises those who gave bread to the hungry and water to the thirsty (Emerson Andrews, 1950, p 30; Gurin and Van Til, 1990, p 4). While there is no explicit reference to asking, the scribes who wrote it helped establish norms around benevolence and offered the ultimate donor benefit of admittance to the afterlife. Other peoples of the Ancient Mediterranean world helped shape the definition and practice of philanthropy.[1] The Greek origins of the word philanthropy ('philos' meaning loving and 'anthropos' meaning mankind), and its first use in the 5th century bce Greek myth *Prometheus Bound*, in which the title character steals fire from the gods as a gift for humankind in need of light and warmth, underlines the centrality of the concept in Ancient Greece, where subjects even addressed the emperors of Byzantium as 'Your Philanthropy'.

Emulating the peoples they had conquered, philanthropy was also a central part of life in Ancient Rome, where rich citizens paid for civic institutions including libraries, theatres, stadia, and schools for poor children. Donations for the school endowments encouraged by Pliny were 'carefully sourced' (Lee and Mullin, 2006, p 51) and a 'rich man of Gytheion', who funded oils for the public baths in ad 161–9, was given prominent recognition of his gift on marble pillars. In keeping with the standard practice over the centuries, we know the name of the donors, but nothing about the person who negotiated the terms of the gift and the inscription.

The organised transfer of resources from private individuals to the public good was therefore clearly evident long before it became codified as essential within the Judaeo-Christian tradition, and later in Islam. Every major religion encourages its followers to be charitable (Ilchman et al, 1998), and these three faiths provide specific directions for followers: notably, the practice of tithing by Jews and Christians, which was first described in the Old Testament book of Genesis,[2] and *zakat*, one of the five pillars of Islam, which specifies what percentage of savings should be set aside for alms giving. These rules and traditions were well established and well known, but nonetheless it is clear from passages in various religious texts that it remained necessary to encourage the charitable impulse and to designate individuals to oversee charitable giving. People within the Jewish and Christian communities were appointed to organise the collection and distribution of charity, and it is possible that some of them were paid to undertake this task (Mullin, 2007, p 11).

A further mention of fundraising in the Bible's Old Testament appears in Exodus 30: 11–16, when the Israelites are told to make a contribution to pay for the tent where religious services take place (Jeavons, 1991, p 58). As this was essentially paying for a facility that the donors themselves would use, the first mention of fundraising for the benefit of others appears in the New Testament, in Acts 6: 1–6 (Jeavons, 1991, p 54) when the disciples appoint seven men 'of good reputation filled with spirit and with wisdom' to gather and distribute food for needy widows; the wording in this passage highlights the enduring importance of the personal characteristics of those tasked with organising generosity.

Some of the techniques used by these earliest fundraisers would be familiar today. Mullin describes St Paul's letters to the Corinthians as 'a remarkable precedent for [modern] fundraising letters' and offers this illuminating paraphrased version of one such letter, in which Paul urges the Corinthians to donate money to help those suffering from famine in Palestine:

> There is famine in Palestine; give your support. I am sending Titus to receive the money you promised and have told people how generous you will be. Every week before he arrives, set aside a considered sum, calculated according to your means ... If you are not as generous as promised to be, I and you will be shamed. There were previous complaints about the handling of funds, so please appoint trustees to account for the money. (Mullin, 2007, pp 9–10)

These words make clear that fundraising was an accepted and understood practice, as no explanation was necessary to clarify or justify the making of this request. Furthermore, it is clear that fundraising was organised, both at the individual level of calculating a reasonable size of donation, and at the community level with the appointment of trusted individuals to collect and account for the funds raised.

Despite suggestions that the systematised delivery of assistance to needy strangers is a quintessential feature of modern philanthropy (Zunz, 2011), examples of such practices are found in the first centuries of the Christian church. There was fundraising in Carthage to assist 'devastated Numidia', care for refugees in Rome and the paying of ransoms for prisoners in the Balkans, as well as 'federated' efforts in the local community, organised by guilds which coordinated the collection and distribution of money for the benefit of members and non-members (Mullin, 2007, pp 11 and 13), including 'a large flow of legacies to the Christian church and its causes' (Mullin, 2007, pp 10–11).

There is also documented evidence of ancient fundraising practices and organisations in other countries, including 6th-century Japan, where Buddhist temples coordinated *kanjin* to raise money for social welfare needs, including orphaned children and the elderly. Likewise, the Pania funds collected in Hindu temples and phuongs in Vietnam enabled the organisation of generosity (Lindahl, 2010, p 71).

While the terms 'fundraiser' and 'fundraising' were not used in the Ancient world, it is clear that their meaning: 'the act of raising resources for a charity, cause or other enterprise', was indeed a familiar feature in Antiquity.

2. Cathedrals

Leaping forward to the Medieval period, the fruits of fundraising efforts are most obviously seen in the enormous – and enormously expensive – cathedrals built across northern Europe during the Middle Ages, which required capital appeals for their construction as well as ongoing income for running costs: '[The] detailed fundraising strategies that ushered in the completion of the cathedrals of northern Europe required concerted investment in sophisticated prospect research techniques' (Lee and Mullin, 2006, p 51). In what has been described as 'a high period for fundraising' (Mullin, 2007, p 11), monies were raised by and for the church using a variety of methods, from the simplest – such as the installation of collection boxes and practice of passing a plate round the congregation during services – to the most discreditable chapter in fundraising's history, the selling of indulgences. Whether simple or complex, ethical or disreputable, somebody had to take the initiative to establish and run these schemes. For example, somebody must have commissioned each collecting box, composed the wording of the sign, chosen a propitious location to install it, encouraged people to use it, and ensured the contents were emptied, counted and put to good use. That person is doing many recognisable fundraising tasks.

Mullin offers another helpfully paraphrased letter to demonstrate the longstanding existence of fundraising appeals, this time from Bishop

Stephen after the destruction in 1174 of the monastery of St Evertius near Orleans in France: 'Standing in the smoking ashes of our church among the scorched timbers of its walls, soon to rise again, we are forced to approach the general public and shamelessly to ask for support from outside gifts' (Mullin, 2007, pp 11–12).

Two centuries later, a wide range of fundraising activity is evident in the efforts to pay for the building of Milan Cathedral, including jumble sales, street and house-to-house collections, major donors and legacy fundraising. The Milan campaign was typical of fundraising around Europe in the Middle Ages, which utilised a wide range of methods including collection boxes, matched funding between bishops and chapters, 'high society fundraising', major patrons, and even events such as a sponsored bell-ringing at Rouen (all examples cited in Mullin, 2007, pp 11–12). We must assume that some individuals were organising these efforts, because the only tangible evidence of asking that can be found is in fundraising letters: indeed, a set of model fundraising letters produced by 14th-century Cistercian monks in Austria exists, which advise writers of such missives to include 'a honeyed salutation, a tactful exordium … a narration … a petition … and a graceful peroration' (Sargeant and Jay, 2014, p 8).

The fundraising instincts of many members of religious orders, and of their advisers, is often evident. To give three further examples: in 1157 the adviser to the Archbishop of Canterbury, John of Salisbury, wrote to his friend Peter of Celle in France, recommending that the relics of saints and letters authenticating them be used to stimulate support for a fundraising appeal to rebuild a church that had recently been destroyed by fire (John of Salisbury, 1955, pp 53–4). In the 16th century, the founder of the Jesuits, Ignatius Loyola, set out in the Constitutions of the Society of Jesus how donors should be acknowledged and thanked in annual rituals such as the blessing and lighting of the 'founder's candle' (Hufton, 1998, pp 127–8; Hufton, 2008). And in 1655 the first fundraising dinner organised by the Sons of the Clergy was held in London, an annual event that continues today.

3. Universities

The UK's oldest universities, such as Oxford, Cambridge and St Andrews, all relied on philanthropic benefactors for their original establishment and have continued to seek private support throughout the many centuries of their existence (Cannadine, 2013; Squire, 2014). Fundraising has also been a part of American higher education from the beginning (Worth and Asp, 1994, p 13): '[T]he creation of the great endowments and subsequent grand fundraising designs at Oxford, Cambridge, Harvard, etc., all found their grounding in the persistent application of individual prospect research undertaken and managed through informal, peer-to-peer networking programs' (Lee and Mullin, 2006, p 51).

In 1641 three clergymen – Hugh Peter, Thomas Weld and William Hibbens – sailed from Boston in the US to London to raise funds for the fledgling Harvard College, which had been founded five years earlier, as well as to raise general funds needed for the colony of New England and for 'the conversion of Indians' (Morison, 1998, pp 256–7). The clergymen wrote back from London requesting a document to support their fundraising efforts, what in modern terminology would be called 'a case for support' to use in their campaign. The result was the pamphlet *New England's First Fruits*,[3] published in England in 1643, which was 47 pages of densely argued text setting out the need for funding and culminating in the 'ask': 'Lend us, we beseech you … your prayers, and helpe in heaven and earth for the furtherance of this great and glorious worke' (New England's first fruits, 1643, p 21).

The pamphlet ends with 'model answers' to be used when responding to common objections of donors who might need convincing that New England is a suitable place to send support. Potential objections include: 'Your ground is barren', 'Your winters are cold' and 'Many speake evil of the place' (New England's first fruits, 1643, pp 42–5). This attention to detail in anticipating problems and preparing responses is a clear illustration that pre-20th-century philanthropy was not, as some (for example, Sargeant et al, 2010, p 27) suggest, entirely spontaneous and lacking in organisation.

4. Hospitals and health care

Voluntary hospitals were the prime providers of free health care for the UK population until the tax-funded National Health Service (NHS) was established in 1948. Hospitals were attached to monasteries and convents until their dissolution in 1540, after which secular support for medical institutions emerged. In rare cases, a single donor established a new hospital with enough money to pay for its ongoing running costs, as was the case with the three London 'endowed hospitals': St Bartholomew's, St Thomas' and Guy's (Waddington, 2003, p 365). But in the vast majority of cases, a major effort was required to raise the original sums needed to buy the land, then build and equip a new hospital, followed by continuous fundraising efforts to pay for medical staff salaries and annual running costs, as well as for capital repairs and modernisation. This meant that '[h]ospital administrators were constantly worried about fundraising' (Waddington, 2000, p 3). It is therefore unsurprising that hospital fundraising was a significant element of charitable activity in the UK, especially during the 19th century (Prochaska, 1992).

The extent of demand for voluntary income for hospitals meant that every available method was used, including charity dinners, gala events, street collections and public collections. Innovations included the Hospital Sunday Fund, begun in 1873, to receive the proceeds of one church collection per year, and the Hospital Saturday Fund, launched the following year, when workers (who were paid on Saturdays) pledged a donation from their wage (Waddington, 2000, p 68). Royal endorsements played a key role in hospital fundraising. Both Edward VII and his wife Alexandra prioritised this cause by encouraging donations to the Prince of Wales fund (as he was called prior to coronation in 1902), established in 1897 and which continues today as the influential health charity, the King's Fund (Prochaska, 1992); and the Queen Consort launched the Alexandra Rose Days in 1912, which raised the equivalent of £2 million (£32,000) for London hospitals on its first day.[4]

It was even possible to receive naming rights for hospital beds: at London's Evelina Hospital, founded in 1869, the going rate was 30 guineas;[5] by 1917, donors giving £105 to the Brompton Hospital for Consumption and Diseases of the Chest 'may name a Bed and also become Governors of the Hospital'[6] (Fry, 1917). One of the best-known approaches that helped to raise the crucial regular income needed for institutions with ongoing high running costs was private subscriptions. These regular gifts typically gave donors a say in electing the hospital management committee and the opportunity to nominate beneficiaries; in around 5% of cases, donors were given a vote to determine which patients were admitted (Kanazawa, 2016). The influence of donors on medical decisions was a controversial issue, and despite defenders describing it as an 'earnt right' and beneficial for creating links between rich benefactors and those in need, the practice was gradually phased out, although it persisted in 50 London hospitals until as late as 1924 (Kanazawa, 2016).

During the inter-war period, the insufficiency of voluntary funding to meet the health needs of a nation in an era of increasingly complex and costly medical interventions became clear. Private fees became a significant source of income until a new financial settlement was established with the post-war nationalisation of hospitals and health care (Mohan and Gorsky, 2001, p 91). Yet the creation of the NHS did not mark the end of fundraising for hospitals, three of which (The Christie, Great Ormond Street Hospital, and Guy's Hospital) continue to raise more than 10% of their total income from donations (Mohan and Gorsky, 2001, p 99), and which continues to be one of the most popular cause areas supported by donors and major philanthropists in the UK (Breeze, 2015; CAF, 2016, p 8).

Hospitals are a prime example of the invisibility of fundraising success. It is widely assumed that a welfare state with a well-funded NHS will no longer have need of voluntary donations, but that view misunderstands the common drivers behind donations, which include a desire to show support for valued institutions, a wish to 'pay back' for help received and an expectation that philanthropy can pay for 'the icing on the top' of state-funded services (Breeze and Lloyd, 2013, p 96).

5. Schools

As with other provision that is now a central part of the welfare state, it is easy to forget that for much of history, education in the UK was funded by donors and fee-paying customers rather than through taxation (Prochaska, 1990a). During the 18th and 19th centuries, in an era when philanthropic activity expanded from a focus on the problem of poverty to broader social improvements, money was raised to fund a wide range of scholastic provision for those who could not afford to pay fees, including Ragged schools, Sunday Schools, and Industry schools (Owen, 1965).

Those raising funds to build such schools used similar methods and techniques as their contemporaries who were fundraising for other causes. The invention of the printing press became increasingly important as a tool to reach and reward supporters: charities placed adverts requesting contributions and listed the names of donors in newspapers. An early version of a direct marketing appeal was issued by the Quaker John Bellers, listing the price of specific items needed and the annual running costs for a new 'College of Industry', which later became the Saffron Waldon Boarding School (Mullin, 2007, p 15). Those seeking to raise the funds for annual running costs, which (then as now) is considered more difficult than capital fundraising, used methods often assumed to reflect more recent concerns. For example, evidence of the impact of donated funds to encourage donor confidence is illustrated in a 1715 painting. The View of the Charity Children in the Strand by George Vertue. This historic 'proof of impact' depicts an annual event, first held in 1704, at which the trustees of London Charity schools demonstrated the charitable need served by their organisations, and the positive impact achieved, by marshalling thousands of clean, clothed children in the streets of London, to sing psalms giving grateful praise for the Queen and assembled dignitaries (Payne, 2006; Jones, 2013).

6. Saving lives at sea

As an island nation with a significant fishing industry for many centuries, the task of keeping seafarers safe has been a longstanding philanthropic goal in the UK. As with all other areas of fundraising, the little we know about how this work was funded comes from historical documents such as legacies containing charitable bequests, which are a particularly prominent form of philanthropic documentation as testamentary giving was extensive at least as far back as the 17th century (Jordan, 1959). One such legacy, left in 1721 by Nathaniel Crewe, Lord Bishop of Durham of Bamburgh Castle, records that he left a charitable endowment which supported many causes, including the costs associated with rescuing lives at sea off the coast of the north east of England, where he had once lived (Cunningham, 2007, p 12). Specifically it paid for: rewards for fishermen who participated in rescues; the equipment needed to raise stranded ships; store rooms to hold cargo that might otherwise be looted; accommodation for up to 30 shipwrecked sailors; and even free coffins and funerals for those who died. Although we cannot know what 'ask' was made in advance of his death, Crewe's understanding of the wide variety of tasks involved in responding to shipwrecks suggests familiarity with the need that could well have come from interactions with those seeking his support.

In 1824, the National Institution for the Preservation of Life from Shipwreck was founded to coordinate national life-saving efforts at sea, and is still in existence today, having been renamed in 1854 the Royal National Lifeboat Institution (RNLI). Almost 100 years after Crewe's death, Grace Darling was born in that same town of Bamburgh and, in 1838, at the age of just 22, she participated in a daring rescue of the shipwrecked paddle steamer Forfarshire. As an embodiment of the bravery required to undertake rescues at sea, Grace Darling's name and image was swiftly and successfully appropriated by the nascent RNLI, and there continue to be lifeboats named after the Victorian heroine, as well as an RNLI Grace Darling museum in Bamburgh. The charity has also had longstanding success in securing royal patronage, from being granted a Royal Charter in 1860 by Queen Victoria, to enjoying the patronage of the present queen, Elizabeth II, since her accession in

1952. Today the charity is funded almost entirely by donations and legacies and accepts no government funding.

Reliance on voluntary support has long necessitated finding innovative ways to keep the cause in the public eye. In 1891 a local businessman, Sir Charles Macara, inspired by a recent tragedy off the coast of nearby Merseyside in which 27 lifeboat crew lost their lives and left numerous widows and children, organised a 'grand cavalcade' of lifeboats pulled by horses through the streets of Manchester to draw attention to their courageous work and encourage donations to help the bereaved families. This successful event was repeated and became known as the Lifeboat Saturday Movement, with similar goals to the Hospital Saturday Fund, 'to enlist the sympathies of all classes of the community' (RNLI, n.d, p 5) and to replace 'spasmodic help' with reliable income (Dibdin, 2010, p 23); public collections for the RNLI have been part of British life ever since (Pudelek, 2014a). As with so many other philanthropically funded activities, mass fundraising is necessary to pay for running costs which have always proved difficult to cover, as this quote from 1894 shows:

> The [Royal National Lifeboat] Institution has generally had a plethora of money for supplying lifeboats, whereas the funds at its disposal for their maintenance, and for suitably rewarding and otherwise providing for the brave men who man them, have been lamentably deficient. (Dibdin, 2010, p 5)

The lifeboats example also illustrates how funding can shift from one person – such as Nathaniel Crewe – taking responsibility for funding a charitable good, to a wider movement of people providing collective support. For other causes this idea, known as 'associational philanthropy', was entrenched from the start – and therefore required proactive fundraising effort from the outset.

7. *Preserving the nation's natural and built heritage*

The Victorian social reformer Octavia Hill (1838–1912) was involved with a range of philanthropic efforts, from providing decent housing for the poor to advocating a more 'scientific' approach to organising charity. Her belief in the value of fresh air and the joy of plants and flowers prompted her involvement in creating a number of London's public parks before co-founding the National Trust in 1895. One of her founding principles was to value donations from working-class supporters more than the support of 'big moneyed people' (Waterson, 2011, p 137), stating that 'The pennies of one are as of much importance as the pounds of another'. This principle was tested in the Trust's first public appeal in 1902, which aimed to put Brandelhow, 100 acres of woods and parkland on the shores of Derwentwater in the Lake District, under the protection of National Trust ownership. The successful response included a donation of 2s. 6d. from a Sheffield factory worker along with a note which said: "All my life I have longed to see the Lakes. I shall never see them now, but I should like to help keep them for others" (Waterson, 2011, p 14).

The work of the National Trust, which now cares for over a quarter of a million hectares of countryside, 700 miles of coastline, and hundreds of significant buildings, has depended over time on a combination of gifts of properties and land from rich owners, and on the smaller donations of over 3 million members whose subscriptions support the ongoing work (Breeze, 2006, p 4). The Trust's more cautious approach to accepting major acquisitions that require costly upkeep and repairs (Breeze, 2006, p 13), and an expansion in the membership of the Trust, has led to a shift in reliance on smaller donations, including membership fees, returning the fundraising focus to the founders' original intentions of drawing support from a broad base.

8. Campaigning to change laws

Despite widespread assumptions that the primary role of charitable organisations is to *do* good and useful things, such as provide direct help for those in need, many charities are not primarily service deliverers, but rather are focused on campaigning to change the way things are run, so that problems are averted rather than tackled after the fact. Seeking systemic change, often via new legislation, has long been a feature of charitable activity: a poll of UK charity experts to identify the greatest philanthropic achievements named the campaign to abolish the slave trade and more recent campaigns to introduce equalities legislation such as gay marriage (Breeze, 2006). Campaigning is not free and fundraisers have developed innovative ways of funding such activities over the centuries.

The politician William Wilberforce has rightly achieved enduring acclaim for introducing and pushing anti-slavery motions in parliament, but he was fronting a campaign that was run, organised, and paid for by supporters of The Society for the Abolition of the Slave Trade, founded in 1787 by Granville Sharp and Thomas Clarkson. Funds were needed to pay for the printing of pamphlets setting out the anti-slavery argument and personal testimonies of former slaves; for organising signatures to be collected in every English county so that 500 mass petitions could be presented to the House of Commons; and to pay for speaking tours, such as when the former slave Olaudah Equiano travelled across Britain from 1789 to 1794 (Kaye, 2005, pp 8–9). A noted fundraising method for this campaign involved selling ceramic 'slave medallions' designed and produced by the famous potter Josiah Wedgwood, which 'became something of a rage' (Owen, 1965, p 13). It is estimated that around 15,000 of these medallions, depicting a black man in chains with the words 'Am I not a man and a brother?', were sold for a likely price of 3 guineas each (Guyatt, 2000, pp 96–7). The medallions were worn by fashionable men and women who also incorporated them into snuff box lids, hat pins, and brooches, just as modern fundraising often features the widespread sale and prominent wearing of iconic designs, colours and symbols – such as the annual Royal British Legion poppy appeal and Marie Curie's daffodil appeal, as well as pink items to denote support for breast cancer charities and wristbands bearing logos and slogans for a wide variety of causes.

Jumble sales are a mainstay of modern community fundraising, relying on an attractive combination of recreation, bargain-hunting and duty, that proved effective in funding another major historical campaign. The Anti-Corn Law League was founded in 1839 to protest against Corn Laws that imposed high taxes on imported grain and thus artificially raised domestic food prices to protect landowners' interests. Supporters of the League organised numerous bazaars, including one in 1845 which raised £25,000 (about £2.5m in today's money), making it 'probably the most profitable and long-lived fancy fair of the century' (Prochaska, 1990b, p 54). Most Anti-Corn Law League bazaars raised much smaller sums, but their popularity created a buzz which 'set up' the situation for fundraising from big donors (Shapely, 2000), just as capital appeals today continue to rely on a mutually dependent relationship between major and small donations.

9. Child welfare

Many of the UK's longest-established and best-known charities are concerned with the protection of children. The National Society for the Prevention of Cruelty to Children (NSPCC) was founded in 1889 in an amalgamation of a number of city societies in which the dominant figure was a Congregationalist minister, Benjamin Waugh. Beginning as a London society, it took on a national role and was granted a Royal Charter in 1895 when Queen Victoria became its patron. Fundraising involving members of the royal family is longstanding and is arguably now the main role of our 'welfare monarchy' (Prochaska, 1995), but it dates back at least as far as the 15th century, when Henry VII encouraged preachers to 'Exhort, move, stir and provoke people to be liberal and bountifully to extend their alms and contributions toward the comfort and relief of poor, impotent, decrepit, indigent and needy people' (Mullin, 2007, p 15). Mullin also notes that many monarchs, including Queen Anne, George I, George II, George III, George IV, William IV, and Queen Victoria all wrote fundraising letters on behalf of organisations such as the Society for the Propagation of the Gospel (Mullin, 2007, p 15).

Alongside 'celebrity patrons', the early fundraising efforts of the NSPCC relied on 'the loyalty of its local militia: the lady collectors' (Behlmer, 1982, p 144). Extensive door-to-door collections were modelled on the district visiting principles fashionable among Victorian upper-class women. By the end of the 19th century, the NSPCC had 6,000 women 'in the field' collecting donations house by house and street by street (Prochaska, 1990a, p 384). Child welfare remained a priority concern for donors, and voluntary income for this purpose was achieved as a result of 'astutely organised and well publicised' appeals (Owen, 1965, p 539). Technological developments, including cheap printing and postage, and the domestic ubiquity of telephones, televisions and personal computers in various formats, have made it possible for fundraisers to reach larger numbers of potential donors through impersonal communications such as letters, television adverts and websites.

The end of the 20th century saw a return to the personal approach in NSPCC's 'Full Stop' fundraising campaign, launched in 1999, which raised the as-yet highest UK single campaign total of £250 million. Although direct mail, posters and TV adverts were all used, the campaign recruited 100,000 people to help with raising funds in person, including from a large number of networks of wealthy donors. The singular success of this appeal is attributed to the devolution of power to 'an extraordinary network of volunteer fundraisers' (Burnett, 2010).

10. International development and disaster relief

Disaster relief and international development charities are now among the most popular causes supported by UK donors (Micklewright and Schnepf, 2009, p 320). Public enthusiasm for this type of philanthropic action has been attributed to the relatively recent media coverage, fronted by the BBC reporter Michael Buerk, of the 1984 famine in

Ethiopia (Franks, 2013); and indeed, the fundraising inspired by Buerk's reportage – including charity singles in the UK and the US,[7] and the global concert Live Aid – raised over £50 million (Davis, 2010). This is the equivalent of over £150 million in 2017, exceeding the contemporary annual totals raised by either Comic Relief or Children in Need.[8]

Impressive as the sums and the scale of the 1984 fundraising were, this was by no means the first time the UK public had responded to great need overseas. On 1 November 1755, a devastating earthquake hit the Portuguese city of Lisbon, killing over 30,000 people on impact and in the fires that raged for days after (Schwittay, 2015, p 28). As news of the disaster spread across Europe, financial assistance was sent to help the victims, often – but not solely – organised by churches, and money was also raised by the sale of pamphlets containing lurid eye-witness accounts (Schwittay, 2015, p 29). Donations were particularly concentrated in cities connected to Lisbon via Atlantic shipping routes, notably Bristol, which was the leading British outport in the 18th century (Morgan, 1993, p 27), because the direct connection between their citizens galvanised the philanthropic response.

Empathy, particularly with those sharing similar identity characteristics, is a well-established driver of charitable behaviour that lies behind the founding and enduring support for numerous other overseas aid charities, including the British Red Cross founded in 1870, whose first appeal during the Franco-Prussian war (1870–71) raised £250,000 (over £11 million in today's money) comprised donations from 'the royal family, the staff of 100 companies, 257 schools, 5,824 congregations and parishes, 139 concerts and events, and 11,832 individuals' (Red Cross, n.d.). The list of contributors to that first Red Cross appeal in 1870–71, from rich and poor, children and churches, individual and corporate donors, and community fundraising, is easily recognisable as the spread of support still sought, and achieved, by many contemporary charities.

International development charities have continued to harness the empathy and compassion of a wide range of donors, by developing new opportunities to give. Examples include the invention of 'child sponsorship' in 1937, in response to children affected by the Spanish Civil War[9] to the recent harnessing of internet-enabled communications technologies that enable donors to connect and respond to need almost anywhere in the world (Bernholz et al, 2010), from 'crisis mapping' of natural disasters, such as the Haitian earthquake in 2010 (Bernholz et al, 2010, p 25) to developmental initiatives such as 'toilet twinning', where donors receive the GPS coordinates of the sponsored facility.[10]

The ten examples of the impact of fundraising through history challenge the 'origin myth' described above, which suggests that fundraising was invented by a handful of 'big men' around the time of the First World War. It is clear that effective asking has occurred for centuries, with the results of some of that funding still evident in the form of cathedrals and other buildings, and less tangibly – but no less importantly – in the social changes that needed philanthropic funding to be achieved. While the form that fundraising takes has changed significantly over the centuries, the act of asking others for help to achieve a common goal is by no means new.

What social conditions facilitate fundraising?

As searching for the origins of asking is as unlikely to yield a sensible answer as searching for the origins of giving, we will turn our attention to a more fruitful question that can help to trace the historical development of fundraising. This question focuses on understanding the conditions that best facilitate the act, rather than trying to get to the root of the act itself. The question is: what broader social conditions enabled the development of the systematic organisation of generosity? Three potential answers all point to the 18th century as having a particularly conducive context for fundraising.

1. The new ideas and ways of thinking about improving society that became known as the Age of Enlightenment.
2. The emergence of the public sphere which created spaces for collective social action to occur.
3. The rapid spread of wealth across society which enabled a larger part of the population to participate in associational philanthropy.

The Age of Enlightenment is the period in Western thought and culture when revolutions in all parts of society – including science, culture, philosophy and politics – replaced the medieval world view and transformed Western civilisation (Bristow, 2011). A key feature of this period, which peaked in the 18th century, was a renewed respect for the power of reason in all areas of life, contra to the largely unquestioned authority of the Church in the Middle Ages.

Applying reason to thinking about the often difficult conditions in which fellow human beings lived led to a change in sensibilities such that people became less tolerant of suffering and more willing to try to help relieve that suffering (Pinker, 2011, p 160). Extending offers of help beyond family, friends and neighbours involves an enlarged sense of empathy to encompasses unknown others whose lives are nonetheless valued (Singer, 2011), and it also involves confidence in the right to intervene in other people's lives. Philanthropic action became one vehicle for such interventionism as a result of 'an Enlightenment confidence that, given the appropriate environment, people's lives could be reshaped' (Cunningham and Innes, 1998, p 4). The surge of philanthropic activity in this period has been noted by numerous social historians (for example Owen, 1965; Prochaska, 1990a; Cunningham, 2015). Given the symbiotic relationship between giving and asking noted above, it is reasonable to state that fundraising also flourished as a result of Enlightenment conditions.

The public sphere

The idea of the public sphere draws on the work of Jürgen Habermas (1989), whose sociological account of historical conditions in the 18th century points to the emergence of a new public space in which people could act, rather than existing primarily in private domesticity. The public sphere involves both physical spaces (such as coffee houses and salons) as well as conceptual spaces (such as newspapers) where people are able to exchange ideas and collaborate as private citizens outside of (and sometimes in opposition to) the state.

The civic society that flourished in these conditions led to the establishment of many self-governing charitable organisations for the purpose of organising and delivering desired changes. As the public sphere included many people of moderate and minimal wealth, they could not fund these organisations without seeking others to share the costs involved. This led to the birth of 'collective' or 'associational' philanthropy, whereby like-minded people collaborate to fund a shared goal, such as building a new hospital, or to collectively pursue an abstract goal, such as a vision of a better society in which slavery is abolished, manners are improved, or people abstain from alcohol. The ability to pursue shared goals relies, at least in part, on securing sufficient financial resources to cover the costs incurred, be it paying for building materials or the paraphernalia of campaigning activities. The possibility of mass communication, resulting from the invention of the printing press, was also key in enabling like-minded altruistic people to find each other. Fundraising therefore became a necessary element of the emergence of the public sphere, reliant on the new possibilities for charitable communications and resulting in a vast new array of charitable organisations funded by collective contributions. As Davies (2015) explains:

> Here lie the origins of the model that forms the bedrock of modern charitable giving: that of addressing a social issue by supporting dedicated, cause-driven organisations via donations. Philanthropists were no longer required to solve society's problems themselves, but instead could support a range of organisations already working to address those problems. (Davies, 2015, p 45)

The spread of wealth and fundraising

The emergence of a booming civic society that enabled people to collaborate in order to question and attempt to change the existing order, occurred in the same century as the start of the first Industrial Revolution. This involved a transition from a country in which most people survived by working on their own land or in their own homes, to one in which they survived by working for other people in factories, farms, and mines, utilising new technologies and processes that enabled large-scale production. Many diverse positive and negative consequences flowed from this transition, including the emergence of the 'middling orders' (Barry and Brooks, 1994), an increasing proportion of the UK population who had some disposable income, access to printed matter in which they became aware of needs in and beyond their community, and opportunities to act on the new ideals of sentiment and sensibility. As more and more people were willing, and in a position, to make voluntary financial donations, a larger and more organised body of fundraisers was needed to liaise with this ever-widening constituency of potential donors.

Some therefore suggest that increased fundraising and charitable giving are a 'natural' consequence of the spread of wealth across society. However, this teleological interpretation makes assumptions about causation, when the growth in wealth and fundraising may be more accurately described as correlated. There is a potential logical fallacy in suggesting that more 'askers' emerged to encourage giving, as a result of the wider population beginning to use their surplus wealth for charitable purposes. It is perfectly possible that the causation ran in the other direction, as it seems plausible that the masses started to give *after* fundraising emerged to encourage and organise their voluntary efforts. But whatever the exact nature of the relationship between more wealth, more giving and more asking, they are clearly inter-linked and therefore are an important part of the story of the development of fundraising.

The Enlightenment and associated change in sensibilities, the emergence of the public sphere and the rapid spread of wealth meant that the 18th century enjoyed particularly fertile conditions for the practice of fundraising – but what proof is there that it took root and flourished? In the absence of much tangible evidence of asking, the founding of numerous institutions and associations that required philanthropic support is one viable proxy, but the need for financial input could be met by one sole funder rather than via a network of associated donors organised by a fundraiser. Indeed, some of the most prominent charitable projects were founded and funded by the same person. For example, Thomas Guy (1644–1724) used his own fortune to establish Guy's Hospital in London, which remains a landmark institution today.

So one further change occurred around the middle of the 18th century as a consequence of people having ideas for new charitable initiatives, yet – to use Bourdieu's concepts of different forms of capital (1984, 1986) – lacking the economic capital to fund the realisation of those ideas. The absence of economic capital, coupled with enough social and cultural capital to present the idea to others possessing the financial wherewithal to contribute, creates a situation requiring fundraising skills and effort, as the story of Thomas Coram and the Foundling Hospital illustrates.

Thomas Coram (1668–1751): the first UK fundraiser?

Thomas Coram was born in Lyme Regis in Dorset in 1668. His mother died when he was four years old, and at the age of 11 was sent to earn his own living at sea on a merchant ship. After five years he became an apprentice shipwright in Liverpool, where he excelled and became a freeman before being employed to sail to Boston to set up a ship-building business. He returned home aged 21 with an American wife, Eunice, and 'deeply in debt' (Wagner, 2004, p 1) – a financial position from which he barely escaped as decades later, at the height of his success, he still had 'little or no money of his own' (Wagner, 2004, p 41).

After returning to the UK, Coram settled in Rotherhithe and regularly travelled into central London to pursue his business and political interests. On this journey he frequently passed babies who had been abandoned to die on the roadside; horrified by this sight he decided to dedicate his efforts to rescuing them. From around 1720, Coram began gathering support for his idea of a new institution to care for abandoned infants: a foundling hospital. He began by knocking on doors in the wealthier streets of London, one by one, asking the rich and well-connected residents to pledge their support for a Royal Charter, which at the time had to be secured before setting up a new charitable venture. This effort was costly in both time and money, and Coram's personal qualities were crucial to success: 'No one else would have had the tenacity and dogged determination to raise the money needed to pay the fees demanded by the lawyers to prepare the charter, and to collect the large number of signatures that were still needed to ensure royal assent' (Wagner, 2004, p 3).

After 12 years, in 1732, Coram received the first large pledge of financial support – £500 from a Josiah Wordworth – but obtained no more signatories or donors until 1733. His tenacity and patience extended until 1739 when he finally succeeded in obtaining the necessary Royal Charter, at which point – having no financial resources of his own – he had to revisit all those who had pledged support to ask them to make good on their promise.

Coram was an organised campaigner and used his 'subscription books' to pursue donors and also ask for contributions from charitable legacies. His success in persuading people to maintain and extend their support for his idea is evident in the fact that the first foundlings were admitted just two years later, in 1741, and that the following year he raised £10,000 through fundraising activities including events and subscriptions; while it is not possible to calculate the exact equivalent value today, this is many millions of pounds. As Wagner (2004) notes: 'It was entirely due to his perseverance that a powerful and privileged group of men, hereditary aristocrats, landowners and wealthy merchants, members of the small circle of London's social elite, were reluctantly persuaded to join with him' (Wagner, 2004, p 1). Coram also secured donations from some of the biggest names of the day, such as the artist William Hogarth and the composer George Frideric Handel (Owen, 1965, p 57), whose masterpiece *Messiah* was regularly performed to raise funds for the hospital in what has been described as 'an 18th-century precedent for Live Aid'.[11] His prescient use of modern techniques extended to a sophisticated relationship with the media. Anticipating modern PR techniques, which are now so integral to fundraising campaigns, newspaper adverts were placed to advertise that new babies were to be received at the Foundling Hospital, not because their unfortunate mothers would be reading the newspaper but to remind the well-heeled readership of the charity's work (Lloyd, 2002). Coram's importance as a fundraiser was clarified further in 1743 when he was ousted from the General Committee after disagreements with the other governors, and the fundraised income dropped to under £2,000 because the Foundling Hospital had lost is chief fundraiser and best advocate (Wagner, 2004, p 165).

The word 'fundraiser' was not in use during Thomas Coram's lifetime, but his passion for the cause, his application of personal qualities such as tenacity and relationship building, and his skill at harnessing new elements of public culture to raise significant sums of money, all suggest he is a worthy candidate to be considered the UK's first identifiable fundraiser. This example also underlines the suggestion that the historical development of fundraising can be explained as a result of charitable entrepreneurs, operating in a conducive context, who possess significant social and cultural capital, yet lack the economic capital to fund their own charitable ideas.

Continuity and change in fundraising over time

Since the start of recorded history, people have asked other people to help strangers, which means that 'the history of fundraising is much longer than many people believe' (Sargeant and Jay, 2014, p 15). For centuries, as today, this task has primarily been conducted by volunteers, but paying people to organise generosity was 'common enough, though not universal' (Owen, 1965, p 480). Other factors that have remained constant over time include the role of well-known people (such as members of the royal family and celebrities) in fronting fundraising appeals; the greater difficulty in raising funds for ongoing costs as compared to one-off costs such as paying for a new building; the integration of generosity with enjoyable social activities; and the importance of quantifying the good that is achieved by donations (Davies, 2015, pp 142–4).

Yet despite the abundant examples sketched above of all types of fundraising being used to raise money for a wide variety of good causes across the centuries, it is not the case that the task of raising money has remained entirely unchanged over time. Table 1 summarises the key differences in historical and contemporary fundraising, which are discussed in more detail below.

Table 1: Changes in fundraising over time

Typical for most of fundraising history	Typical for contemporary fundraising
Fundraising mostly done to benefit religious institutions and causes	Fundraising mostly done for secular institutions and causes
Only a small number of fundraising organisations in existence	Intense competition among an ever-growing number of fundraising organisations
Fundraisers approach only a small number of people in the financial and social elite	Fundraisers approach the mass of the population who have any disposable income
Mostly personal solicitation	Mostly impersonal solicitation
Main communication tools: face-to-face, word of mouth and, after 15th century, printed literature	Growth of new communication technologies, including telephone, television, online, social media
Fundraising profession dominated by white men	Dominance of females (though less pronounced in more senior posts) and slowly growing diversity in relation to ethnicity
Fundraising knowledge passed on by word of mouth and by example	Fundraising knowledge codified in books and taught via formal training and educational courses
Fundraisers operate independently or via informal collaborations	Fundraisers supported and represented by national membership bodies
Sporadic fundraising for one-off or occasional appeals	Sustained fundraising efforts for ongoing running costs

The secularisation of charity and fundraising began in the 17th century (Jordan, 1959) and reflects wider changes in society. When people's primary concern shifts from saving their soul in the next life to fulfilling their potential in this life, religious leaders became less relevant in encouraging philanthropic acts. The expansion in the number of organisations seeking charitable support, and the growth of the 'mass affluent' resulting from changes in the nature and distribution of wealth, meant the number of private citizens being asked to make a contribution grew rapidly and was no longer confined to the very rich (Harrah-Conforth and Borsos, 1991, p 21). Those doing the asking shifted from predominantly male to predominantly female, with ethnic diversity slowly increasing (Institute of Fundraising, 2013).

Since the middle of the 20th century, this workforce has had access to a codified body of knowledge in 'how to fundraise' books (as discussed further in Chapter 4), as well as access to training and formal programmes. The Fundraising School was founded in the US in 1974, and from 1935 American fundraisers were represented and supported by a professional national membership body, the American Association of Fundraising Counsel (AAFRC). Nearly 50 years later, the Institute of Fundraising was established to fulfil the same role in the UK; there are now more than 20 national professional fundraising organisations established around the world (Breeze and Scaife, 2015, p 582).

A further shift is from intermittent to ongoing fundraising efforts. In the early 20th century fundraising campaigns were still sporadic, with even the largest charitable organisations only launching a campaign once or twice a decade. These campaigns lasted for around three years, leaving 'fallow' periods when charities were not focused on fundraising. But by mid-20th century, fundraising had become a continuous effort within many charities (Worth and Asp, 1994, p 9), requiring more in-house fundraisers as there was work to occupy them year-round (Duronio and Tempel, 1997, p xvi). As Worth and Asp note, 'The transition from occasional campaigns conducted by temporary consultants to ongoing programs managed by full-time staff professionals was gradual' (Worth and Asp, 1994, p 9); but nonetheless meant that the period dominated by fundraising consultants was just a few decades near the start of the 20th century. Despite their short-lived nature, the charismatic individuals who founded and led the most famous US fundraising agencies, such as Charles Sumner Ward and Jonathan Price Jones, have succeeded in securing the status as the originators of 'fundraising'.

Fundraising as a social problem

The final, and arguably most significant change, is the framing of fundraising as a social problem. As we have seen above, fundraising has been prevalent throughout history but it was not significantly problematised until the late 19th century. As noted in the introductory chapter, those doing the asking have long attracted critical comments in the media, and there is no reason to assume that the general public welcomed being approached for donations in the past any more than they do today. Social investigators in the 1940s found that the public was swift to express concerns about the methods and tactics of charity fundraisers (cited in Mohan and Breeze, 2016). But in recent decades charitable fundraising has been re-framed from, at worst, a general irritation, to being commonly understood as an aggressive act.

The confusion between experiencing moral discomfort and actual physical assault continues today, most obviously in the word 'chugger' which is widely used to describe street fundraisers. 'Chugger' is a compound word, created by joining together the words 'charity' and 'mugger'. The neologism is not based in fact: no fundraisers have been convicted for physically attacking or mugging those from whom they seek support for a charitable cause. Rather, the ready acceptance of this language indicates that simply asking people to consider making a donation is now perceived as an aggressive act that invites a belligerent response. To take just one example of many media stories that frame street fundraising as a social problem (rather than as a means to raise the funds to fix social problems), a recent article in the UK broadsheet newspaper the *Daily Telegraph* was headlined 'Hate Chuggers? This is how you can get rid of them'.[12] The author writes that 'chuggers annoy many people' and suggests readers 'sweep them from the streets' by making alternative, tax-effective giving plans. The readers who left comments 'below the line' prefer a more robust response: 'This is how you can get rid of them: Punch them in the face',[13] and another notes: 'the way I deal with chuggers is to tell them straight – if they don't get out of my naffing face I'll deck them!'[14]

Conclusions

This chapter began by noting that, despite the historically parallel practices of asking and giving, philanthropists and beneficiaries have consistently taken centre stage in accounts of charitable transactions. Explanations for this donor-centric bias include the lack of documentation of solicitation, longstanding under-estimation of the importance of prompting giving, and widespread dislike of the experience of being asked to give. Also, until relatively recently, charitable projects could be founded and funded by the same person. I therefore argued, using the example of Thomas Coram, that it was not until the conducive conditions of the 18th century that large-scale organised fundraising became more commonplace, as people with ideas for new charitable initiatives were able to expend their social and cultural capital by reaching out to others with the economic capital to fund the realisation of those ideas.

Fundraising – like all social phenomena – is a product of its time. It develops to reflect changing social norms, technological opportunities, and economic and political realities. Despite asking being as old as giving, we know little about fundraising historically because there are very minimal records of organised efforts to raise funds for good causes. This lack of tangible evidence of the activities of pre-20th-century fundraisers has fuelled an origin myth, which typically states that: 'fundraising as an organised and organisational function only dates back to the early 1900s' (Wagner, 2004, p 167). But it is hard to square that view with the many significant outcomes of fundraising recounted above.

This chapter has challenged the accepted 'origin myth' by showing that the outcomes of fundraising are evident in many preceding centuries, even in the absence of detailed evidence of the inputs of fundraisers. I have also suggested that the broad principles of solicitation have remained relatively unchanged over the centuries, despite extensive changes in the way these principles have been implemented in practice, primarily as a result of new communication technologies, from the invention of the printing press in the 15th century to the rise of social media in the 21st century.

The claim that fundraising 'began' in the early 1900s is predicated on a number of assumptions that have been shown above to lack evidence. The ten examples of the outcomes of fundraising activity demonstrate the existence of a wide variety of fundraising techniques and strategies over many centuries. This challenges the suggestion that pre-20th-century donations were proactive and 'not triggered' (Sargeant et al, 2010, p 27) and that fundraisers lacked a systematic and organised approach (Broce, 1986). St Paul, born in 10ad, has been described as 'the prototype of the certified fund raising executive', because he worked hard and systematically to raise funds to support the early church (Jeavons, 1991, p 63). The Foundling Hospital's donors were 'triggered' and Coram was systematic in his approach, insofar as the technology of the time allowed him to be. The nature and degree of organisation by pre-20th-century fundraisers is unknowable, yet the end result of their efforts is evident for all to see: enormous cathedrals, significant secular buildings, and impactful charitable organisations do not spring up spontaneously.

The proposition that fundraising emerged somehow organically as the number of people with any disposable wealth spread has also been challenged as a potential causal fallacy, because fundraisers also prompt potential donors to make alternative spending decisions. Finally, the suggestion that pre-20th-century fundraising was entirely conducted by volunteers, and that the emergence of fundraising as a job marks the defining 'birth' of the profession, sits uncomfortably with evidence that paid fundraisers have existed for centuries. This last point is also undermined by the ongoing essential role of volunteers in contemporary fundraising; the crucial task of recruiting and managing that voluntary input in order to connect with potential donors who are often peers of wealthy volunteers, will be discussed in Chapters 3, 4 and 5. But before that, the next chapter paints a portrait of the fundraisers of today, by drawing on existing and new data collected for this book.

Notes

[1] This paragraph draws on the entry on 'Philanthropy – Ancient Mediterranean Examples' on the JRank Science and Philosophy website: http://science.jrank.org/pages/10645/Philanthropy-Ancient-Mediterranean-Examples.html (last accessed 14 August 2016).

[2] Tithing involves giving away a tenth of one's possessions, and is first mentioned in Genesis 28:22, when Jacob pledges a tenth of all he has to God.

[3] The pamphlet has been digitised and is available online at: https://archive.org/details/NewEnglandsFirstFruitsInRespectFirstOfTheCounversionOfSome (last accessed 8 August 2016).

[4] These figures are from the website of the modern equivalent of the organisation, the Alexandra Rose Charity: www.alexandrarosecharities.org.uk/ourhistory.html (last accessed 13 August 2016.

[5] This information is from an online history of the Evelina Hospital www.hharp.org/library/evelina/general/history.html (last accessed 29 May 2017).

[6] This information and the reference to Fry's Guide 1917 is from a website maintained by Lee Jackson: www.victorianlondon.org/charities/charities.htm (last accessed 30 May 2017).

[7] These charity singles were, respectively, 'Do They Know it's Christmas' (UK) and 'We Are the World' (USA)

[8] In 2015 the Comic Relief appeal raised £99m and Children in Need raised £37m: www.comicrelief.com/red-nose-day and www.bbc.co.uk/mediacentre/latestnews/2015/cin-2015-total (both accessed 12 November 2016).

[9] Further details on the invention of child sponsorship as a fundraising strategy is available on the SOFII (Showcase of Fundraising Innovation and Inspiration) website: http://sofii.org/case-study/the-plan-the-launch-of-child-sponsorship-spain-1937 (last accessed 12 November 2016).

[10] Toilet Twinning is organised by the UK charity Tearfund: www.toilettwinning.org (last accessed 12 November 2016).

[11] This quote appears in the *Daily Telegraph*, 16 April 2014, citing the historian Amanda Vickery www.telegraph.co.uk/culture/music/classicalmusic/10767955/The-Messiah-Handels-gift-to-the-poor-of-London.html (last accessed 6/11 2016).

[12] This article was published on 6 March 2015: www.telegraph.co.uk/finance/personalfinance/11452129/Hate-chuggers-This-is-how-you-can-get-rid-of-them.html (last accessed 5 November 2016).

[13] This comment was posted by 'YongyBongy'.

[14] This comment was posted by 'Castilian'.

TWO

Who are the fundraisers?

Having clarified the role and importance of fundraising and reviewed the history of fundraising, we turn now to look closely at the people who currently work as fundraisers in the UK: their backgrounds and paths into the career; insights into their attitudes, social lives and hobbies; and data on their personality traits and emotional intelligence levels.

Fundraisers as stakeholders in a cause

The March of Dimes Foundation, which successfully fundraised to support the development of the Salk vaccine, was discussed in earlier chapters. That charity was founded in 1938 by President Franklin D. Roosevelt, whose personal experience of having polio exemplifies the 'stakeholder theory' of the non-profit sector: that is, that one reason charities come into existence is because individuals with a stake in an unmet need decide to organise to meet that need (Young, 1986; James, 1990). So too, a personal connection to a cause, be it a personal passion for opera or a loved one experiencing cancer, is known to be a key driver of donor decisions (Schervish, 2007; Breeze, 2013a; Breeze and Lloyd, 2013). What has not so far been noted, probably as a result of the general neglect of this aspect of charitable activity, is the possibility that fundraisers also have a personal investment in the cause for which they are raising funds.

To take an example, the fundraiser (who is also the Chief Executive Officer (CEO)) for a charity that supports hostages and their families during and after a kidnap, offers this explanation of how she came to be doing this work, and her thoughts on what makes a good fundraiser. Her answer usefully reflects many of the themes covered in this chapter:

> My uncle was held hostage when I was younger, so I know that the families of hostages need the kind of support that we offer. I do think that my personal experience of the cause is relevant to my job – undoubtedly it's why I chose to spend my career working in this field, but I also think it helps make me a better fundraiser. Because it is personal, because I know this work needs doing, I can keep going

> even when I get a lot of 'no's'. My personal background does give me insight and an authority to speak about this issue – I'm able to make a connection really quickly with those who've gone through the same thing, and I'm able to answer questions from those who haven't. There's a certain power in the fact that I can personify 'the ask'. But I don't think it's essential for fundraises to have first hand experience of their cause. Most fundraisers are passionate and mission-driven people, good at telling stories about the kind of people their charity helps, what's happened to them and how the work has made a difference. Stories help to generate empathy, they help potential donors to imagine what it would be like to be in the shoes of the people we help; they can picture it being their uncle or their daughter.[1]

This fundraiser's possession of a personal connection to the cause for which she is raising funds, her tenacity in the face of frequent rejection, and her ability to convey passion for the charity's work, are themes that recur consistently in the data presented in this book. But first, a warning about the risks of painting too idealised a picture of the 'perfect fundraiser'.

The 'perfect fundraiser'

Despite the common negative perception of fundraisers as 'beggars', 'manipulators' and 'sleazy salesman', discussed in previous chapters, there also exists a view that fundraisers must possess an extraordinary mix of positive qualities in order to succeed. This view is held most strongly within the charity sector, where there is greater awareness of the importance of fundraising expertise to the organisation and concern about the scarcity of fundraising talent, particularly in the specialism of working with major donors. A tongue-in-cheek, but nonetheless revealing, summary of the qualities needed by fundraisers suggests they should be 'well-rounded, intelligent, personable, capable, and gifted in communication. In short, he or she should be all things to all people' (Worth and Asp, 1994, p 39). A longer list of attributes sought in fundraising employees include:

> self-confidence, self-esteem, self-motivation, aptitude for personal growth, controlled ego, sense of humor, strong worth ethic, caring nature, commitment to something bigger than oneself, sense of community, civic responsibility,

> adventurous spirit, gentle tenacity, flexibility, positive attitude, tolerance for ambiguity, analytical reflection, inquisitive mind, creative talents, and other similar traits. (Woods, 1997, p 9)

That is quite some person specification, and this idealisation of 'the fundraising type' is longstanding. Over 50 years ago the desired – but clearly implausible – combination of characteristics required by fundraisers was gently mocked by the fundraising pioneer Carlton Ketchum, who described the 'perfect fundraiser' as:

> bold but modest, aggressive but tactful, confident but prudent, alert without presenting the appearance of over-eagerness. He [sic] must be resourceful, far-seeing, discriminating and wise. He must make a fine personal appearance and convey the impression of being both a wonderful fellow to know and be with, and a man of dignity, poise and judgment. A true conservative who is, at the same time, full of originality and invention. He must carry instant appeal to old and young, man and woman, great and small. (Cited in Cutlip 1990, p xxvi)

Ketchum's contemporary, Harold 'Sy' Seymour, who wrote one of the first handbooks explaining how to fundraise (discussed further in Chapter 3), echoes the received wisdom that fundraisers must possess a clutch of positive personal qualities, noting that among the most successful:

> there is a kind of liveliness that generates and communicates enthusiasm, knows and likes people by instinct and preference, exhibits a genuine kind of pleasure and gratitude for good advice and wise talk, and bears proudly the mantle of the job. (Seymour, 1966, p 128)

The latter point – being not just *prepared* to ask, but *proud* to ask – suggests that successful fundraisers require a particular mindset as much as a specific skillset, a point that is developed further in Chapter 4.

The difficulty in ascertaining fundraising proficiency

The emphasis on personal qualities described above reflects the fact that formal training and certification are relatively new phenomena in the fundraising profession. For most of the period since fundraising became a common paid job in the early 20th century, recruitment processes have necessarily relied on embodied qualities, rather than documented qualifications. A track record of success in raising funds was, and remains, an important factor but the extended time periods involved in donor–charity interactions, and the necessary role of colleagues and volunteers, makes it difficult to accurately attribute fundraising success. Simply being in post when a large donation occurs is unlikely to mean that credit is entirely due to the incumbent in the fundraising office, as the donor's relationship with the charity may pre-date their appointment, and the successful ask will likely also follow interactions with others such as non-fundraising colleagues and peers on the board.

Of course, CVs are rarely taken entirely at face value: charities can use a range of tests to assess aptitude, intelligence, attainment and personality (Sargeant and Jay, 2014, pp 348–9), and recruitment consultancies and larger charities have developed more sophisticated methods for assessing and evaluating candidates for positions requiring fundraising competencies (as set out in More Partnership/Richmond Associates (2014b), for example). But the typical charity, being small and financially insecure, is unlikely to have the resources to run an in-house human resources function or to hire a professional recruitment agency, and may struggle to ascertain proficiency in a traditional interview setting because 'people can talk really well about fundraising without being able to do it at all ... unlike a lot of other professions' (Betsy Mennell, quoted in Nagaraj, 2014).

Prior research on the skills and traits required by fundraisers

Given the profound importance of voluntary income to many charities, and hence the crucial need to identify competent people possessing the right attributes to fulfil the fundraising function, it is not surprising that at least six previous studies have explored the question of what traits and skills fundraisers require. Table 2 summarises these studies, highlighting that most research has been focused on US fundraisers and on fundraisers working in Higher Education institutions (HEIs).

Table 2: Summary of previous studies on fundraising traits

Date	Author(s)	Country in which study conducted	Focus of study	Key traits and skills of good fundraisers
1988	Panas	US	Major donor fundraisers	Impeccable integrity Good listener Ability to motivate Hard worker Concern for people
1994	Worth and Asp	US	Fundraisers working in Higher Education	Interpersonal skills Personal charisma Willingness to stay 'behind the scenes' Fit with institutional culture
1997	Duronio and Tempel	US	General	Passion for fundraising Communication skills Authenticity Passion for organisation Knowledge of field Warmth Personal ambition
2011	Scaife et al	Australia	General	Passion for the cause Integrity Communication skills Marketing skills Management skills
2014b	More Partnership/ Richmond Associates	UK	Fundraisers working in Higher Education	Intelligence and intellectual curiosity Good judgement/intuition Influence and persuasiveness Oral communications Empathy/listening
2014	Nagaraj	US	Fundraisers working in Higher Education	Linguistic and behavioural dexterity Intellectual and social curiosity Information distillation – skills for synthesising information Strategic solicitation – assertiveness in soliciting prospects
2016	Garcia	Mexico	Development professionals (HEI)	Effective communicator Broad-view thinker Connector and mentor Passion

Panas's book is based on his own successful career as a fundraiser, plus input from a survey completed by 'thousands' of professionals working in the field of fundraising and interviews with 'over 50' fundraisers who he considers to be exemplary (Panas, 1988, pp 9–10). Despite scant information on methodology, Panas offers a comprehensive discussion of the topic, narrowing down an initial list of 88 criteria to his final top five, and providing an extended discussion of whether fundraising requires innate qualities or learnt skills. He concludes that, while very few people are 'born to raise' good fundraisers do seem to share the five traits listed in Table 2, of which he claims the most important is 'impeccable integrity'.

Reflecting the recent emergence of academic studies of fundraising, Worth and Asp's (1994) report also draws on their experience as senior fundraising practitioners in Higher Education Institutions (HEIs), as well as an extensive review of the practitioner literature. Having identified the personality traits they believe are required for success as a development professional, they suggest there are four overarching 'schools of thought' about the function of fundraiser: as Salesperson, Leader, Catalyst and Manager, with each type requiring a greater emphasis and quantity of certain skills and traits. For example, 'Leaders' must possess large amounts of charisma, while 'Catalysts' must be comfortable with staying behind the scenes and have an ego 'in good shape' to cope with the lack of recognition and credit. However, these types are not discrete, and fundraisers may need to be able to switch between them, especially if – as is often the case – they are the sole fundraiser in a charity. The authors therefore note approvingly the suggestion that 'people in our business have got to be in the "Renaissance Man" mold' (McCord, quoted in Worth and Asp, 1994, p 39), meaning that they need to possess proficiency in many different regards.

The first substantial academic study of the fundraising profession was conducted in the 1990s and focused on the 'careers, stories, concerns and accomplishments' of fundraisers working in the US (Duronio and Tempel, 1997). A survey sent to members of the major organisations representing fundraisers[2] achieved 1,748 responses, and interviews were conducted with a subset of 82 fundraisers who completed the survey. This data enabled the authors to draw conclusions about the sociodemographic profile of the profession, for example, noting female dominance, as well as identifying the personal characteristics, skills and professional knowledge deemed most important for success in this field. This is the only study of those summarised in Table 2 to determine fundraising knowledge (for example, understanding of relevant tax and legal issues) as the top priority, above any particular skill, attitude or trait; but the authors conclude that the data still reveals 'high expectations of fund-raising colleagues [including] … strong characters and warm personalities [and] … a strong value-driven orientation' (Duronio and Tempel, 1997, p 159).

The only one of these studies to be conducted outside the US and UK looks at Australian fundraisers and reaches a similar conclusion, that 'an array of skills and qualities are needed for the role', listing 25 separate areas of personal proficiency ranging across customer service, budgeting, people management and interpersonal communication. However the 'key factors' are said to be passion for the cause and integrity, while the main areas of required competence are in communications, marketing and management. (Scaife et al, 2011, p 27)

Two recent studies conducted on either side of the Atlantic have a focus on understanding the qualities required by fundraisers working in HEIs. Indeed, one was commissioned by the Higher Education Funding Council for England (HEFCE) as part of wider efforts to better understand and encourage an effective 'philanthropy workforce' in universities (More Partnership/Richmond Associates, 2014a). Drawing on evidence from 750 fundraisers (largely via a survey achieving 658 respondents, plus 64 interviews as well as participants in six focus groups), this study was also able to draw conclusions about the composition of the workforce, finding it to be 'young, predominantly female and ethnically un-diverse' (p 11), as well as identifying the qualities of a 'good fundraiser' in a Higher Education setting. An allied 'toolkit' for identifying, recruiting and retaining 'the best people for an emerging profession' concludes that intelligence, intuition and communication skills are the most crucial, but notes that the most important skills and traits will depend on the specialism within fundraising, such that people working with major donors will differ from those working on annual appeals or corporate giving (More Partnership/Richmond Associates 2014b, pp 5–6).

The final prior study listed in Table 2 is based on insights from over 160 research interviews and data from a survey of 1,200 major gift officers at 89 HEIs (mostly in North America and also some in the UK), which aimed to uncover the key profile attributes of high-performing frontline fundraisers (EAB, 2014). The authors conclude that the highest performers possess four key skill sets: behavioural and linguistic flexibility; intellectual and social curiosity; the skill to distill information; and the ability to approach the solicitation process in a strategic manner. Only 4% of the sample was found to possess all four skill sets. This small subgroup, named 'Curious Chameleons', had 78%

higher odds of exceeding their fundraising goals than their peers, and are characterised as follows:

> they are the people who can spend two hours in an 80-degree condominium drinking a warm Tab with an 85-year-old grandmother and then quickly switch gears for a 30-minute pitch to a high-powered lawyer. They are also the people who are equally comfortable sorting through the results of data analytics generated by the development office's prospect-research team and taking in the esoteric work of a university's star scientist. (Blumenstyk, 2014)

All four skill sets are described as learnable, though 'intellectual curiosity' is said to be the hardest to teach. The implication of this last study is that we must either accept there is a tiny talent pool, or find ways to develop the missing skills in order to meet the demand for successful fundraisers.

The extant research goes some way to sketching out the kind of people who are employed, and who excel, at raising money for good causes for a living. The data indicates that fundraisers need a number of different skillsets and, crucially, they also require certain personality traits, outlooks and mindset, not least because 'it is difficult, if not impossible, to separate attitude and skills when determining what is required for doing effective major gift fundraising. As critical as they are, skills are not enough … attitude is of paramount importance' (Woods, 1997, p 11).

However, prior research is focused almost exclusively on identifying skills and traits and, excepting Duronio and Tempel (1997), tells us very little about the sociodemographic characteristics of people who work as fundraisers, or anything about their wider social and personal characteristics beyond the workplace. The data gathered for this book takes that broader perspective, and is presented below after pausing to clarify that there is no intention of claiming that there is – or should be – any 'ideal' type of fundraiser.

Fundraisers are not a homogenous group

While the study presented in this book seeks to identify those characteristics most often associated with fundraising success, there is no intention of suggesting that there is – or should be – a blueprint for hiring fundraisers. As all previous studies of the fundraising profession have also insisted, fundraisers are not a homogenous group and are in fact 'highly diverse in many aspects' (Duronio and Tempel, 1997, p 26). As Panas explains, with typical panache:

> One thing is certain, fundraisers are a totally dissimilar group. They look different. Act differently. Work differently. They are diverse – hard charging and hard driving, quietly effective. They include used-car salesman types, ministers and priests, scholars and backslappers. Computer freaks and computer frightened. Great writers and virtually illiterate. They do not have the same characteristics or personalities. (Panas, 1988, p 8)

There is therefore no such thing as a 'typical' or 'perfect' fundraiser, any more than there is an 'ideal' type of teacher, doctor or lawyer. Expected qualities can be held in various combinations and people who fall outside the anticipated character mould can still succeed, and even excel, so long as they possess the requisite skills which 'work equally well for the introverted or extroverted, quiet or exuberant fundraiser' (Woods, 1997, p 13).

New data on UK fundraisers including 'Million Pound Askers'

The findings presented below are based on an extensive online survey of people working as paid fundraisers in the UK, which was conducted in the summer of 2014. The survey was disseminated with the help of the UK's Institute of Fundraising, the professional membership body, which at the time of survey distribution had around 5,000 individual members. Only respondents confirming that they were currently employed as a paid fundraiser, either in-house, freelance or as a consultant, or on a planned career break such as maternity leave, were able to complete the survey, which resulted in 43 potential respondents being filtered out. The survey was live for three months and achieved the relatively high response rate of 25%, with 1,243 completed surveys.

Within the 1,243 completed surveys, 174 respondents self-reported that they had succeeded in securing a donation of £1 million or more. To take account of the teamwork involved in making asks for large amounts, the wording of this question was as follows: 'What is the single biggest gift you have ever secured? Please note that colleagues and volunteers may have been involved in the process, for example by helping with cultivation and asking.' This subset of 'million pound askers', which constitutes 14% of respondents, is highlighted in the data presented below, to explore whether and how they vary from 'all paid fundraisers'. While there are clearly many different measures of 'fundraising success' that need to be contextualised in relation to factors such as the maturity and turnover of the organisation, public trust and confidence in the charity and the degree of investment in fundraising functions, it was not possible to ascertain these variables from an online survey that promised anonymity to respondents. While recognising that 'success' also depends on the type of fundraising being conducted – with direct marketing clearly generating smaller average amounts than major donor fundraising – there is sufficient interest in gaining an understanding of those fundraisers able to raise £1 million or more, just as 'million pound donors' attract particular public and academic attention (see, for example, Breeze, 2015), to warrant using that factor as the definition of 'success' in this element of the study.

Survey respondents

The achieved sample is broadly in line with what is known of the social profile of UK fundraisers. Data collected by the UK's membership body for fundraisers indicates that contemporary fundraising is a predominantly young and female profession, in which the most common role is to be a generalist fundraiser. The Institute of Fundraising finds that 50% of fundraisers are aged under 40, 74% are female, and 46% work in general fundraising rather than a specialist role (Institute of Fundraising, 2013). In my sample, 54% are under the age of 40, 77% are female, and 27% indicate they are generalist fundraisers. The over-representation of specialists in my sample should not unduly affect the results, as the focus here is on the social and personal characteristics of all paid fundraisers, and in any distinctive qualities of those who succeed in asking for £1 million or more.

Reflecting normative professional patterns, senior fundraising positions have a higher proportion of men than junior positions, but the common correlation between age and seniority is less marked in fundraising: 41% of 35–44-year-olds report holding director/senior management roles, and 59% of 25–34-year-olds report being at manager or senior officer level (Institute of Fundraising, 2013). The impact of gender, age and years of professional experience on fundraising success is explored in further detail below.

Survey questions

The survey was substantial and took on average (median) 15 minutes to complete, with the shortest recorded time being 9 minutes and the longest 46 minutes. The 17 questions (which can be found in full in Appendix A were divided into four sections as follows.

1. Experience as a paid fundraiser (5 questions).
2. Background, training and professional qualifications (5 questions).
3. Attitudes and hobbies (5 questions).
4. Standardised tests of Big 5 Personality traits and Emotional intelligence scale (2 questions, with respectively 44 and 10 parts).

In addition, four sociodemographic variables (gender, age, geographical location and educational level) were elicited.

To enable comparisons, a further online survey of a representative sample of the UK population was conducted in June 2015, using the same questions insofar as they were relevant to a non-fundraiser sample. Here, 1,059 completed surveys were achieved. This newly commissioned data is used in conjunction with existing data from reputable sources, such as UK government data and OECD data, in order to identify any distinctive characteristics of paid fundraisers. To avoid drawing unwarranted conclusions and overlooking alternative explanations, such as findings being related to the typical age or gender profile of fundraisers, rather than the status of being a fundraiser, the data was weighted where feasible and as appropriate. For all relevant questions where education might have proved a confounding variable (levels of trust, hobbies, personality traits and emotional intelligence) the data was re-analysed to include only responses from participants in the general population survey that have at least a first degree. This ensures that any differences identified between fundraisers and the general population cannot be attributed to the generally higher education levels of fundraisers. This data is presented in the final row of each relevant table.

In the survey of fundraisers, participants could skip questions if they so chose, hence the number of responses varies between tables. In the general population survey, responses were compulsory and attention filters[3] were used to ensure that respondents were paying attention. In all tables, numbers have been rounded to 1 decimal point, so rows may add up to 99% or 101%.

Socio-demographic traits of the UK fundraising profession

Gender

Fundraising is a female-dominated profession in the UK, with just over three quarters (77%) being female, as shown in Table 3.

Table 3: Gender of UK fundraisers

	Male	**Female**
All paid fundraisers (N=1,129)	23% (259)	77% (870)
Million pound askers (N=159)	36% (57)	64% (102)

Most studies of women as philanthropic actors focuses on their roles as donors or as recipients, but it is clear that gender is also relevant in relation to asking. The global 'feminisation of fundraising' dates back almost three decades to 1989 when the membership of the US National Society of Fund Raising Executives first reported a majority female membership (52%) and reported that women were entering the field at twice the rate of men (Conry, 1991, p 144). However, the reason for the female dominance of fundraising remains debated. The answer may lie in practical matters such as low barriers to entry (for example, lack of compulsory qualifications) and greater flexibility in daily work regimes than comparable careers. But some take an essentialist approach, suggesting that women are naturally better equipped for fundraising success than men: for example, Greenfield describes 'a woman's natural ability to engage people in social settings, to cope with diverse personalities, and to nurture relationships' (Greenfield, 2002, p 522). Others suggest the feminisation of fundraising is in line with normative gender expectations (for example, Dale, 2014), such that women are more willing than men to undertake work that lacks recognition and culturally ascribed value.

Whatever the explanation, the reliance of charities on women's fundraising work is clear. However, fundraising success (as defined here) is slightly gendered, with a disproportionate number (one third, or 36%) of those who have raised £1 million donations being male, which most likely reflects the normative spread of gender, favouring males in more senior positions.

Age

Fundraising is a youthful profession in the UK, as shown in Table 4, with the majority (54%) of paid fundraisers aged under 40, and over a fifth (21%) in their twenties.

Table 4: Age range of UK fundraisers

	Under 30	30–39	40–49	50–59	60+
Million pound askers (N=161)	4% (6)	28% (45)	36% (58)	20% (32)	12% (20)
All paid fundraisers (N=1,136)	21% (237)	33% (380)	22% (253)	18% (204)	5% (62)

Million pound askers are on average older, with two thirds (68%) aged over 40, and very few (4%) in their twenties.

Education

Table 5 shows that fundraisers are substantially better educated than the general UK population, with the vast majority (84%) holding at least a first degree, compared to 38% in the newly commissioned survey of the general population; this latter figure is in line with existing data, which states that 38% of the UK working-age population have a degree or higher qualification (ONS, 2013).

Those who have raised £1 million or more are slightly more likely to have a postgraduate degree, but otherwise their educational attainment level is similar to that of all other paid fundraisers.

Table 5: Highest level of educational attainment

	None	GCSEs/'O' levels or equivalent	'A' levels/ Highers/Bac or equivalent	First degree	Masters degree	PhD
Million pound askers (N=161)	1% (1)	0 % (0)	8% (13)	60% (96)	29% (46)	3% (5)
All paid fundraisers (N=1,139)	2 (0%)	3% (36)	13% (144)	59% (672)	23% (263)	2% (22)
General Population (N=1,059)	4% (43)	27% (288)	31% (325)	29% (310)	7% (74)	2% (19)

Professional profile of UK fundraisers

Route into fundraising

Very few respondents, just 5%, had a long-term plan to work as a fundraiser and the vast majority came into it 'gradually' or 'by accident', as shown in Table 6, with most (52%) of the 'million pound askers' describing themselves as having 'fallen into' this line of work.

Table 6: Route into fundraising

	Million pound askers (N=174)	**All other paid fundraisers (N=1,198)**
I always wanted to work as a fundraiser	5% (8)	5% (64)
I came into this work gradually through related professional and volunteering roles	36% (62)	42% (502)
I fell into fundraising by accident	52% (90)	44% (524)
Other	8% (14)	9% 108)

This is not a new phenomenon, nor is it confined to the UK. Fundraisers in the 1930s and 1940s 'had no preparation other than on-the-job training [and] drifted into fund raising from a variety of other occupations' (Gurin, 1985, p xi). Cutlip describes then-contemporary professionals, even at the end of the 20th century, as having 'risen to their positions by serving an apprenticeship under others who came up the same way' (Cutlip, 1998, p xi). Most of the US fundraisers studied by Bloland and Bornstein 'came into the field accidentally, after having done a number of other things' (Bloland and Bornstein, 1991, p 107), while a 'surprising number' of US fundraisers working in Higher Education Institutions attribute their career to chance, though some had been appointed after volunteering, doing some fundraising at university or knowing others who worked as fundraisers (Carbone, 1987, p 9). A gendered angle to routes into the career was found in a US study, with women being twice as likely to become fundraisers after volunteering experiences (Duronio and Tempel, 1997, p 135); but the data on UK fundraisers presented here shows no difference between genders in terms of routes into professional fundraising roles.

There is some evidence from the US that the 'accidental' nature of fundraising careers is beginning to change 'as younger professionally minded people see the opportunity, need, and potential for a career in the not-for-profit world that is rewarding, adventuresome, challenging, and meaningful' (Woods, 1997, p 10; Josyln, 2016). A lack of longitudinal data on the characteristics of UK fundraisers prevents similar claims being made on this side of the Atlantic, but the situation is likely to be evolving along similar lines, particularly among new graduates, who may have been aware of, or even participated in, fundraising campaigns while at university, particularly since 2008 when the UK government launched a major matched funding scheme to encourage philanthropic giving to universities (HEFCE, 2012).

Many fundraisers had different sorts of jobs before taking on their present role, most commonly (around 10%) having previously worked in marketing, sales and advertising. The transferability of skills was highlighted by many of these respondents, who typically sought an opportunity to apply their existing expertise in a more 'worthwhile' domain. For example, one respondent said: "I started in marketing but decided I'd rather 'sell' a cause than a product", while another explained: "I'm from a marketing background. I became disillusioned with the sector I was in and wanted to use my skills for a good cause". The other most common prior careers are retail, event management, personal assistant/secretary, and office management.

However, the total number of people moving from these five careers is outnumbered by the much larger number of contemporary fundraisers who have moved from a wide range of disparate prior careers including commercial pilot, teacher, journalist, banker, photographer, bookseller, air cabin crew, engineer and asbestos surveyor. Some responded to the question of their route into fundraising by describing personal triggers such as having a child with special needs or losing a loved one to cancer, which prompted their desire to find a job working for a charitable organisation working in that field. The lack of an obvious career path into fundraising, and the frequency with which events from personal lives, rather than formative career experiences, are cited as factors behind moving into fundraising, highlights the difficulty in identifying the tributaries into the talent pool for fundraising.

Acquiring fundraising skills and knowledge

Once in post, and as has been the case since fundraising emerged as a paid occupation, 'learning on the job' is by far the most common method for acquiring fundraising skills and knowledge (Gurin, 1985, p xi; Kelly, 1998, p 2; Lindahl, 2010, p 1). Table 7 shows that over half of contemporary UK fundraisers describe their expertise as some variation of "caught not taught".[4] While this may often happen by default, it is not necessarily an unsatisfactory way to learn, as Wagner notes: 'On-the-job training is a time honored way of learning ... some people learn best by experience, observation, and experimentation', though this approach may also be the result of scant budgets and lack of awareness that other types of learning are available (Wagner, 2002, pp 117–18).

Table 7: Main method for acquiring fundraising skills and knowledge

	Million pound askers (N=165)	All paid fundraisers (N=1,158)
Learning on the job	53% (88)	53% (608)
Learning by working alongside a more experienced fundraiser	27% (45)	28% (328)
Attending courses	7% (12)	11% (126)
Being mentored	5% (8)	2% (26)
Informal discussions with other fundraisers	3% (4)	2% (24)
Attending events	2% (3)	1% (11)
Reading books about fundraising	2% (3)	1% (15)
Finding information online	1% (2)	1% (13)

The same situation exists in the US, where data collected in the mid-1990s indicated that 74% learnt to be a fundraiser 'on the job', compared to less than 10% who acquired fundraising expertise through formal education (Duronio and Tempel, 1997, p 134). The greater availability of training, education and certification in fundraising over the past decade, in both the US and the UK, may eventually affect these proportions, but for now informality remains the dominant motif of both career entry and career progression.

Learning by working alongside a more experienced colleague is the prime route to acquiring skills and knowledge for over a quarter of fundraisers. The more formalised concept of 'mentoring' is indicated by a much smaller proportion, though twice as frequently among 'million pound askers'; it is not possible to ascertain whether they were allocated a mentor as part of formal processes that exist in their organisation, or organised a mentor for themselves. In the latter scenario, being a person who takes the initiative might be the more important driver of success than simply having a mentor.

Possession of qualifications

Learning by attending courses is half as common among those who have raised £1 million or more, and – as shown in Table 8 – they are slightly less likely to hold a professional qualification, though they constitute the larger part of the small numbers studying for the new Advanced Diploma, which was launched in 2013.

Table 8: Percentage of fundraisers holding a professional qualification

	Hold any qualification	Of those stating they hold a qualification, what type:*			
		Introductory Certificate in Fundraising	Certificate in Fundraising	Diploma in Fundraising	Advanced Diploma in Fundraising
Million pound askers (N=174)	21% (37)	14% (5)	41% (15)	24% (9)	11% (4)
All paid fundraisers (N=1,189)	28% (329)	19% (61)	59% (195)	27% (88)	1% (5)

* As fundraisers may hold more than one qualification, totals do not add up to 100%.

Table 8 also shows that only just over a quarter (28%) of UK fundraisers hold any sort of qualification, including the Introductory Certificate in Fundraising, which is aimed at people who are new to fundraising and involves an exceedingly minimal outlay of time and money, costing less than £100 and requiring typically one day of study, to gain 'a basic knowledge and understanding of fundraising and the sector itself, the surrounding legal framework and ... some fundamental fundraising tools and techniques'.[5] The low take-up of formal training may be due to the low availability of such courses, although new providers are emerging, but is more likely due to the minimal budgets available for staff development in the small charities that typify the UK sector (May and Broomhead, 2014, p 2). A further factor potentially impeding the take-up of formal training and educational opportunities is the absence of a clear connection between gaining qualifications and career progression: 'Career lines in fundraising are problematic so that it is difficult to trace a smooth upward career path ... it is not clear what experience, talents, training, and expertise they must have to be successful' (Bloland and Bornstein, 1991, p 108).

Areas of work within the fundraising function

While specialism is a sign of progression in many careers, Table 9 shows that UK fundraisers typically work in generalist roles, and interact with all types of donors.

Table 9: Main area of focus in paid fundraising role

	Million pound askers (N=174)	**All paid fundraisers** (N=1,213)
Major donors	36% (62)	14% (166)
Generalist (including major donors)	34% (60)	22% (271)
Trusts and Foundations	11% (19)	19% (227)
Other	10% (18)	9% (108)
Legacies	5% (8)	6% (71)
Corporate	2% (4)	4% (51)
Community/Individuals	1% (2)	13% (154)
Generalist (not including major donors)	1% (1)	5% (64)
Direct marketing	0% (0)	8% (93)
Digital	0% (0)	0% (6)
Trading	0% (0)	0% (2)

Unsurprisingly, those raising donations worth £1 million or more are most likely to be in a major donor fundraising role (36%), or in a generalist role that includes working with major donors (34%); trusts and foundation fundraisers are the next most likely to generate million pound donations, and legacy fundraisers also occasionally deal with gifts of that size. The fact that no fundraisers working in direct marketing, digital, or trading have secured a donation worth £1m or more (therefore are not 'million pound askers') underlines the problematic nature of defining 'fundraising success' as there are obviously many successful fundraisers working in those specialisms; future research could usefully explore how to identify them and explore their distinctive social and personal characteristics.

Existence and impact of an organisational 'culture of philanthropy'

Prior research highlights the correlation between fundraising success and working in a 'fundraising-friendly' environment, which is one that understands, supports, and invests in, the fundraising function (Bell and Cornelius, 2013; More Partnership/Richmond Associates, 2014a). As Table 10 shows, only a fifth of UK fundraisers claim to be working in a charity that has a consistent 'culture of philanthropy', which is defined as:

> Most people in the organisation (across positions) act as ambassadors and engage in relationship-building. Everyone promotes philanthropy and can articulate a case for giving. Fundraising is viewed and valued as a mission-aligned programme of the organisation. Organisational systems are established to support donors. The chief executive/director is committed and personally involved in fundraising. (Bell and Cornelius, 2013, p 3)

Table 10: Fundraisers stating they work in an organisation with a 'culture of philanthropy'

	Yes	**Most of the time**	**Probably not**	**Definitely not**
Million pound askers (N=166)	22% (36)	39% (65)	26% (43)	13% (22)
All paid fundraisers (N=1,155)	19% (225)	38% (435)	28% (327)	15% (168)

Over four in ten (43%) of respondents say they 'probably' or 'definitely' do not work in a charity with a culture of philanthropy, and of these, almost all (95%) say it affects their ability to fundraise to some extent, as shown in Table 11. 'Million pound askers' are only slightly more likely to feel they are operating in a conducive setting, and when a culture of philanthropy is probably or definitely not present, they are only slightly more likely to feel that hampers their efforts.

Table 11: Belief that absence of a 'culture of philanthropy' adversely affects ability to fundraise

	Yes	Sometimes	No
Million pound askers (N=64)	50% (32)	48% (31)	2% (1)
All paid fundraisers (N=494)	51% (250)	44% (218)	5% (26)

Differences in professional profile between million pound askers and all other paid fundraisers

The most obvious explanation for career success is greater experience, and this is clearly a key factor for UK fundraisers, as shown in Table 12. In this table, the subset of 'million pound askers' is compared with 'all other paid fundraisers', which shows that those who have successfully secured a gift worth £1 million or more have, on average, worked as a fundraiser for almost twice as long as those who have not.

Table 12: Average number of years employed as a fundraiser

	Average number of years employed as a fundraiser
Million pound askers (N=174)	15.8 years
All other paid fundraisers (N=1,041)	8.8 years

But success (as defined in this element of the study) is not only a function of longevity in post. Statistical analysis of the data shows that million pound askers are significantly more likely to be: male, in their forties, to claim to have fallen into fundraising by accident, to have been mentored, and to work in major donor fundraising. And all these differences remain significant even after accounting for years of experience.

As this study seeks to understand the characteristics of fundraisers beyond their professional profile, the next sections explore factors relating to social and personal factors such as attitudes, hobbies, personality traits and emotional intelligence.

Personal profile of UK fundraisers

Trust

The extent to which members of a society are generally trusting of their fellow citizens is known as 'generalised trust' and is understood to be an important contributing factor to healthy democracies and to economic growth (Putnam, 1993; Fukuyama, 1995). Governments are therefore interested in tracking trends in generalised trusts levels among the general population, and the following question was included in the British Household Panel Survey (BHPS) which ran from 1991 to 2009:[6] 'Generally speaking, would you say that most people can be trusted, or that you can't be too careful in dealing with people?'.

Table 13: Generalised trust levels among fundraisers and the general population

	Most people can be trusted	You can't be too careful	It depends
Million pound askers (N=166)	51% (85)	5% (8)	44% (73)
All other paid fundraisers (N=1,016)	51% (520)	6% (59)	43% (437)
General population (N=1,059)	22% (234)	32% (335)	46% (486)
General population with at least a first degree (N=403)	26% (105)	24% (96)	50% (202)

Table 13 shows that fundraisers have significantly higher levels of generalised trust than the general population. A majority (51%) of both paid fundraisers and 'million pound askers' believe that 'most people can be trusted', but that view is held by only just over a fifth (22%) of the general population, rising only slightly to a quarter (26%) when only those with at least a first degree are compared with fundraisers (to ensure that like populations are being compared with like). Very few fundraisers (5% or 6%) hold the view that 'you can't be too careful' when it comes to trusting unknown others, whereas a half (50%) of the general public hold that view.

Experience of, and attitudes towards, exchange and gift-giving

It has been suggested that fundraisers have distinctive expertise in gift giving, for example Konrath describes fundraisers as 'the high priests of giving' (Konrath, 2016, p 12). In order to test this suggestion, a set of questions was designed to ask respondents about their early experiences of helping others and asking for help, as well as their current attitudes to borrowing from neighbours, gift-giving, and sending thank-you cards, and whether or not they are a blood donor. The results, shown in Table 14, indicate that a number of significant differences are apparent between fundraisers and the general population.

Table 14: Self-reported attitudes to gift economy in personal life

	I grew up in a family where it was normal to help others and to ask for help	I borrow things from, and exchange favours with, my neighbours	I enjoy gift giving and choosing presents for loved ones, friends and relatives	I always send a thank-you message when I receive a gift from loved ones	I am a blood donor
Million pound askers (N=168–171)	74% (127)	62% (105)	82% (140)	82% (140)	31% (52)
All paid fundraisers (N=1,163–1,189)	74% (880)	46% (547)	87% (1,025)	79% (940)	34% (395)
General population (N=1,059)	62% (659)	34% (355)	79% (833)	67% (712)	24% (249)
General population with at least a first degree (N=403)	64% (257)	36% (145)	80% (322)	68% (276)	29% (118)

Note: Responses were on a 5-point Likert scale, Y = 'definitely agree' and 'tend to agree' merged; N figures are given as a range, as not all respondents answered all questions.

All types of fundraiser indicate greater familiarity and ease with gift-giving scenarios than the general population, including growing up in a family where it was normal to ask for help and enjoying choosing presents. 'Million pound askers' were much more likely than all other paid fundraisers to borrow things from, and exchange favours with, neighbours (62% versus 46%), and were slightly more likely to claim to always write thank-you notes (82% versus 79%), but in all scenarios the gap was greater between fundraisers and the general population, and this finding holds when controlling for the effects of education, as the last row in Table 14 shows. To help illustrate this point, and other quantitative findings presented below, some data from interviews with 50 successful fundraisers is included in this chapter (please see Chapter 4 for an explanation of the methodology and identifiers in parentheses).

In relation to early experiences of asking for, and giving help, an interviewee explains:

> When I was younger, I was never afraid to ask people for a favour. It sounds silly but quite a lot of people are afraid to ask someone for a favour. It's not exactly the same as being bold enough to ask people for money, but I think it's linked to making things happen. (Male, A, B)

Another interviewee concurs:

> The best fundraisers are people who want to give back in some sort of way because they have themselves been on the receiving end of gifts and understand reciprocity. They are people who get something out of giving back. They have usually done it before – you can track back to scouts, guides, shaking a tin with their mum, maybe being involved at church. There's something in their past so that asking for money is normal and they have that way of looking outside themselves. Without that experience and way of seeing the world, they'd be a salesperson rather than a fundraiser. (Female, A)

While the link to early experiences was obvious for many interviewees, some noted that fundraising is a widespread part of childhood, and suggested that a more crucial factor is maintaining the view that asking is an appropriate reaction to meeting need, as this interviewee reflects: "As a child I was horrified by seal clubbing and wanted to do something about it, so did a sponsored jog in my garden. Fundraising is an innate part of childhood and yet at some point it becomes inappropriate when adults ask. Why is that?" (Female, A).

Blood donation has long been considered an archetypical example of gift exchange (Titmuss, 1970). All fundraisers are more likely than the general population to self-report that they are blood donors, but it is likely that all four figures in the final column of Table 14 are over-statements, as the UK National Blood Authority reports that only 4% of eligible British adults donate.[7] However, assuming the tendency to over-state is uniform across fundraisers and non-fundraisers, the former are around 17% more likely to be a blood donor.

Sociability

The widespread assumption that fundraisers are naturally very sociable people (see Chapter 5) was explored by questioning both fundraisers and the general population on how often they meet up with friends or relatives who are not living with them, and who tends to organise such gatherings.

As Table 15 shows, fundraisers do socialise more frequently than the general population, with the latter – whether they hold a degree or not – being nearly three times as likely to socialise less often than once a month.

Table 15: Frequency of socialising with friends and relatives

	On most days	Once or twice a week	Once or twice a month	Less often than once a month
Million pound askers (N=166)	9% (15)	51% (85)	31% (51)	9% (15)
All paid fundraisers (N=1,163)	11% (127)	52% (610)	30% (347)	7% (79)
General population (N=1,059)	9% (96)	41% (434)	28% (292)	22% (237)
General population with at least a first degree (N=403)	9% (35)	42% (172)	29% (119)	19% (77)

But the starker contrast in sociability lies in who organises these gatherings, as shown in Table 16. Fundraisers are far more likely to claim that they 'usually' organise social gatherings, and few fundraisers admit to 'rarely' organising such occasions, whereas this is the case for around a fifth of the general population – with or without a degree. This finding supports a theme discussed in Chapter 5, that a key characteristic of the 'art' of fundraising involves being a 'scene setter' and 'choreographer' of social situations.

Table 16: Frequency of taking responsibility for organising social gatherings

	I usually organise the gathering	I sometimes organise the gathering	I rarely organise the gathering
Million pound askers (N=166)	25% (41)	70% (116)	5% (9)
All paid fundraisers (N=1,162)	29% (336)	67% (773)	5% (53)
General population (N=1,059)	13% (138)	65% (686)	22% (235)
General population with at least a first degree (N=403)	17% (67)	66% (267)	17% (69)

Hobbies and reading habits of UK fundraisers

Hobbies

In order to understand what people who work as paid fundraisers do outside of the workplace, and whether this differs from the general population, the survey included a number of questions about hobbies. A list of 15 common hobbies was offered as a prompt, and, as Table 17 shows, there is much consistency in the pattern of hobbies declared by all fundraisers and the general population, but also some interesting differences emerge.

Table 17: The hobbies of UK fundraisers

	Million pound askers (N=174)	All paid fundraisers (N=1,110)	General population (N=1,059)	General population with at least a first degree (N=405)
Reading	81%	79%	72%	79%
Outdoor pursuits that do not generally involve danger (e.g. walking, cycling)	70%	69%	54%	57%
Going to the cinema	66%	61%	49%	54%
Going to the theatre	61%	53%	29%	36%
Non-competitive sport or exercise	54%	57%	32%	39%
Visiting art galleries	52%	38%	23%	30%
Watching sport	33%	26%	42%	46%
Competitive sport	23%	14%	12%	11%
Yoga, meditation or other forms of relaxation	23%	25%	13%	16%
Attending night classes or part-time study of any kind	17%	19%	9%	12%
Making music other than singing in a choir	16%	15%	10%	13%
Visual art (e.g. painting)	14%	12%	15%	17%
Outdoor pursuits that involve some degree of danger (e.g. rock climbing)	13%	11%	5%	6%
Singing in a choir	11%	11%	2%	2%
Performing art (e.g. amateur dramatics)	7%	7%	4%	5%
I have no hobbies	0%	1%	2%	1%

Most notably, singing in a choir was substantially more likely to be a hobby for fundraisers (11%) compared to the general population (2%). Qualitative research is needed to explain this differential, but considering the other hobbies that show significant differences, such as artistic pursuits, non-competitive sport, and yoga/meditation/relaxation, it is possible that fundraisers seek out communal-oriented, non-competitive activities. The next biggest differential is for 'attending night classes or part-time study of any kind', which is over 50% more common among fundraisers, even when controlling for education. In the interviews, some successful major donor fundraisers describe taking night classes as a way to expand their general knowledge, for the pure pleasure of learning, and also to enhance conversation with donors who pursue the interest taught in the class, suggesting that some hobby differentials may be the result of conscious strategies as well as personal preferences. As one interviewee explains: "You need something else to be able to talk to people about before you start talking about your job, your role, what you're asking for money for. And it needs to be real, it can't be artificial" (Female, A).

The only hobby that is more popular among the general population is watching sport. A tiny fraction (2%) of the general population report having no hobbies, whereas no 'million pound askers' make this claim, and only 1% of all other paid fundraisers do so, although this difference is eliminated when comparing all paid fundraisers with the subset of the general population that has a degree. It appears that – on the whole – fundraisers are likely to be more active and engaged in a range of activities in their free time.

There are also some differences in the hobbies pursued by those fundraisers who have secured donations of £1 million or more and all other paid fundraisers. A majority of 'million pound askers' claim to visit art galleries (52%) compared to just over a third of all fundraisers (38%), and the former are substantially more likely to attend the theatre (61% versus 53%). Such findings could indicate greater appreciation of 'higher culture' among fundraisers who are able to raise the largest sums, or there could be a simpler explanation, such as arts organisations being more frequent recipients of seven-figure donations and hiring people who are passionate about the arts. However, the finding that million pound askers are almost twice as likely as all paid fundraisers to participate in competitive sport (23% versus 14%) is less easy to explain away as a proxy for other variables, and indicates there may be some significant difference in the types of people who succeed in asking for bigger gifts.

Reading habits

Reading is the most popular hobby among fundraisers and the general population, so a further pair of questions probed this activity further, asking how much they read and what kind of books are preferred. Table 18 shows that most fundraisers are slightly keener readers than the general population, though the gap shrinks when controlling for education levels, and 'Million pound askers' are the most avid readers.

Table 18: UK fundraisers' reading habits

	I am an avid reader and always have at least one book on the go	**I like to read and get through three or more books each year**	**I like to read but only get through one or two books a year**	**I don't like to read books**
Million pound askers (N=166)	61% (101)	28% (46)	10% (17)	1% (2)
All paid fundraisers (N=1,018)	56% (652)	26% (303)	16% (184)	2% (23)
General population (N=1,059)	46% (488)	27% (288)	19% (203)	8% (80)
General population with at least a first degree (N=403)	53% (215)	29% (118)	14% (57)	3% (13)

Unlike the propensity to read, reading preferences differ more sharply, as shown in Table 19, with fundraisers being more likely to claim that they read literary fiction and popular social science, and a third (34%) claiming to read in connection with their job. There is little difference between 'million pound askers' and all other paid fundraisers, though the former are less likely to read lightweight (non-literary) fiction, and slightly more likely to read popular science books, compared to all paid fundraisers. Psychology books aimed at a non-academic readership, such as those on the topics of decision making, influencing and happiness, written by the likes of Malcolm Gladwell, Daniel Kahneman, Dan Ariely and Steven Pinker were mentioned in the qualitative phase of this study. As one female interviewee noted: "There's a lot more psychology involved [in fundraising] than people realise. People who have studied psychology or read popular psychology books, have an advantage" (Female B).

Table 19: Type of books read by UK fundraisers

	Fiction (serious/ literary)	Fiction (lightweight/ non-literary)	Non-fiction	Popular social science	Books related to your job
Million pound askers (N=166)	73% (121)	60% (99)	64% (106)	28% (46)	34% (56)
All paid fundraisers (N=1,110)	70% (800)	70% (793)	63% (717)	23% (258)	34% (389)
General Population (N=1,059)	54% (530)	68% (669)	64% (627)	9% (85)	6% (59)
General population with at least a first degree (N=391)	64% (251)	72% (280)	69% (270)	10% (40)	14% (53)

Personality traits and emotional intelligence

The final sections of the surveys completed by both fundraisers and the general population sample consisted of a 44-question personality test (John and Srivastava, 1999, p 70), followed by a 10-factor emotional intelligence scale (Davies et al, 2010, p 204). Despite some contestation regarding the construction and measurement of these traits (for example, as discussed by Conte, 2005; Davies et al, 2010, p 198) their widespread usage in both academic and popular literature, coupled with assumptions about the personality profile of the 'ideal' fundraiser, as noted above, makes them a topic of interest for this study. A number of researchers have explored the relationship between personality traits and job performance (for a meta-analysis, see Barrick and Mount, 1991; Barrick et al, 2001), including some that focus on fundraisers (Croteau and Smith, 2012; Nagaraj, 2014). The relevance of this line of enquiry to human resource functions and recruitment consultancies has resulted in a number of organisations and training agencies making use of personality testing of fundraisers for instrumental reasons, whereas this study is focused on gaining insight into the social and personal characteristics of fundraisers, rather than generating new tools for the purposes of recruitment.

The first columns in Tables 20 and 21 indicate how these questions are used to create global scores for, respectively, the 'Big 5' personality traits: extraversion; openness; conscientiousness; agreeableness; and neuroticism; and for five measures of emotional intelligence: appraisal of own emotions; appraisal of others' emotions; regulation of own emotions; regulation of others' emotions; and utilisation of emotions.

In both tests, the respondent is asked to indicate the extent to which they agree with a series of statements. In the personality test, the question asks about: 'the extent to which you agree or disagree that you see yourself as someone who …' (for example, 'Is talkative', 'Does a thorough job' etc.). For the emotional intelligence scale, respondents are asked to 'indicate the extent to which you agree with the following statements' (for example, 'I know why my emotions change' etc.).

There are five response options as follows: 'Disagree strongly' = 1 point; 'Disagree a little' = 2 points; 'Neither agree nor disagree' = 3 points; 'Agree a little' = 4 points; and 'Agree strongly' = 5 points. The average (mean) for each of the Big 5 traits is calculated by adding up the points allocated to all the statements that measure a particular trait, then dividing by the number of statements used to measure that trait. For example, if a trait is measured by six statements, and a respondent 'agreed strongly' with three of those statements, and 'disagreed a little' with the other three, their mean score for that trait would be calculated as follows:

(3 x 5) plus (3 x 2) divided by 6 = 3.5

Statements marked (R) measure the 'reverse' of the relevant trait, for example, within 'Extraversion' the statement 'Is reserved (R)'. In such cases, the scoring is reversed, such that 'Agree strongly' = 1 point, and so on.

The data on the general population's personality traits comes from two sources: (1) the British Household Panel Survey 2009, wave 18; and (2) the 'comparison' survey undertaken for this book. The former is a well-regarded data source with a large sample size, and the latter enables a comparison that controls for education levels.

Personality traits of uk fundraisers

Fundraisers score more highly (positive perspective) on every personality trait than the general UK population; this finding persists when removing the effects of education. The largest differential between 'all paid fundraisers' and 'general population with at least a degree' is for Extraversion, and the smallest difference between these two groups relates to Neuroticism. Furthermore, the standard deviation of responses from fundraisers has a much smaller range of distribution than that of the general population, indicating less range in

Table 20: Personality traits of UK fundraisers

	Personality trait	N	Mean	SD
Extraversion • Is talkative • Is reserved (R) • Is full of energy • Tends to be quiet (R) • Has an assertive personality • Is sometimes shy (R) • Is outgoing, sociable	Million pound askers	153	3.996	0.864
	All paid fundraisers	544	3.892	0.858
	General population (BHPS)	8,697	2.565	3.147
	General population with at least a first degree	403	2.97	-
Openness • Is original, comes up with new ideas • Is curious about many different things • Is ingenious, a deep thinker • Has an active imagination • Values artistic, aesthetic experiences • Prefers work that is routine (R) • Likes to reflect, play with ideas • Has few artistic interests (R) • Is sophisticated in art, music or literature	Million pound askers	150	4.26	0.631
	All paid fundraisers	541	4.097	0.649
	General population (BHPS)	8,697	2.600	3.157
	General population with at least a first degree	403	3.53	-
Conscientiousness • Does a thorough job • Can be somewhat careless (R) • Is a reliable worker • Tends to be disorganised (R) • Tends to be lazy (R) • Perseveres until the task is finished • Does things efficiently • Makes plans and follows through • Is easily distracted (R)	Million pound askers	152	4.349	0.576
	All other paid fundraisers	1,129	4.320	0.636
	General population (BHPS)	8,697	3.238	3.292
	General population with at least a first degree	403	3.74	-
Agreeableness • Tends to find fault with others (R) • Is helpful and unselfish • Starts quarrels (R) • Has a forgiving nature • Is generally trusting • Can be cold and aloof (R) • Is considerate and kind to almost everyone • Is sometimes rude to others (R) • Likes to cooperate with others	Million pound askers	150	4.082	0.739
	All other paid fundraisers	544	4.069	0.694
	General population (BHPS)	8,697	3.241	3.293
	General population with at least a first degree	403	3.72	-
Neuroticism • Is depressed, blue • Is relaxed, handles stress well (R) • Can be tense • Worries a lot • Is emotionally stable, not easily upset (R) • Can be moody • Remains calm in tense situations (R) • Gets nervous easily	Million pound askers	151	2.525	0.915
	All other paid fundraisers	544	2.766	0.930
	General population (BHPS)	8,697	1.814	2.963
	General population with at least a first degree	403	2.92	-

Note: N is Number, SD is Standard deviation.

the responses given by fundraisers. The personalities of 'million pound askers' differ from that of all other paid fundraisers in two out of the five traits: those who have secured seven-figure donations are more open and less neurotic than all other paid fundraisers, but do not differ in a statistically significant way in terms of extraversion, conscientious and agreeableness.

Emotional intelligence of uk fundraisers

Fundraisers are more emotionally intelligent than the general population in all five dimensions of emotional intelligence, and again this finding persists when controlling for the effects of education. Unlike the personality traits, there is no statistically significant difference between

Table 21: Emotional intelligence of UK fundraisers

Emotional intelligence scale	Million pound askers	All other paid fundraisers	General Population (BHPS)	General population with at least a first degree
Appraisal of own emotions • I know why my emotions change • I easily recognise my emotions as I experience them	4.35	4.28	3.83	3.86
Appraisal of others' emotions • I can tell how people are feeling by listening to the tone of their voice • By looking at their facial expressions, I recognise the emotions people are experiencing	4.44	4.37	3.86	3.83
Regulation of own emotions • I seek out activities that make me happy • I have control over my emotions	4.07	4.05	3.71	3.74
Regulation of others' emotions • I arrange events others enjoy • I help other people feel better when they are down	4.26	4.26	3.54	3.61
Utilisation of emotions • When I am in a positive mood, I am able to come up with new ideas • I use good moods to help myself keep trying in the face of obstacles	4.37	4.35	3.89	3.88

the mean scores on the emotional intelligence scale for 'million pound askers' and all other types of paid fundraiser.

Whether these findings indicate that fundraisers have different personality traits and emotional intelligence in advance of entering the profession, or gain these traits and refine this intelligence as a result of doing the job, cannot be concluded from this data. But it can be noted that many fundraisers are relatively young and inexperienced yet score highly on both tests.

Conclusions

The data presented in this chapter provides insights into the demographic, personal and social characteristics of paid fundraisers, as well as whether, and if so how, those who have raised donations of £1 million or more differ from other paid fundraisers and from the general population.

In sum, the data shows that fundraisers often have formative experiences of helping behaviour, high levels of generalised trust, a greater predilection for gift-giving to loved ones and donating blood to strangers, a willingness to facilitate social situations, a preference for community-oriented and intellectual hobbies, positive personality traits and higher levels of emotional intelligence. 'Million pound askers' are likely to be older and to have worked as a fundraiser for longer than the average fundraiser, are more likely to have benefited from being mentored and be slightly better read than their colleagues, and – in terms of personality traits – are significantly more open and less neurotic than all other paid fundraisers.

However, it is important to emphasise that just as there is no 'typical donor', there is also huge variety within the fundraising profession. Despite the patterns identified above, they are clearly not present in every fundraiser. To pick just three examples of common characteristics that are most certainly not universal: successful fundraisers can be – and are – introverted, do not give blood and do not in sing in a choir. There is no 'type' or blueprint that can be followed with the guarantee of recruiting someone who will succeed in raising any – or very large – amounts of money. But the data does suggest some interesting patterns across the fundraising profession, and among those who have raised the largest amounts, that might be usefully explored and discussed further by those interested in creating the structures most likely to increase the quantum and quality of philanthropy.

The next two chapters explore the 'science' and the 'art' of fundraising, and the chapter after that looks in close detail at what it is that fundraisers actually do in their daily work; together these three chapters shed light on how the personal qualities identified in this chapter are utilised in the everyday practices of fundraising.

Notes

1. This quote is from a personal conversation with Rachel Briggs who co-founded Hostage UK and is now CEO of Hostage US: www:hostageus.org
2. The survey was sent to a stratified random sample of 2,501 members of the Association for Healthcare Philanthropy (AHP), the Council for Advancement and Support of Education (CASE), and the National Society of Fund Raising Executives (NSFRE). To broaden the sample beyond the membership of those organisations and reach fundraisers working in less affluent non-profits who may not be able to afford membership fees, each recipient was sent two copies of the survey and encouraged to ask a non-member to complete it (Duronio and Tempel, 1997, pp xx–xxi).
3. The following attention filter was inserted in three places across the survey: 'This is an attention filter. Please select "Disagree strongly" for this statement.' Respondents who failed to pay attention, i.e. who did not select 'Disagree strongly', were removed from the sample.
4. These same three words were used in a number of the interviews conducted for this book.
5. The text describing the Introductory Certificate in Fundraising is from the Institute of Fundraising's website: www.institute-of-fundraising.org.uk/events-and-training/qualifications/introductory-certificate-to-fundraising (last accessed 25 August 2016).
6. The British Household Panel Survey ran from 1991 to 2009, and was a multi-purpose study following the same representative sample of individuals, interviewing every adult in the households included in the study. According to the study's website (www.iser.essex.ac.uk/bhps) the wave 1 panel consists of some 5,500 households and 10,300 individuals drawn from 250 areas of Great Britain. Additional samples of 1,500 households in each of Scotland and Wales were added to the main sample in 1999, and in 2001 a sample of 2,000 households was added in Northern Ireland, making the panel suitable for UK-wide research.
7. This figure appears on this NHS website: www.nhs.uk/conditions/Blood-donation/Pages/Introduction.aspx (last accessed 28 June 2016).

THREE

The science of fundraising

A 2008 *New York Times* article asked whether fundraising was due a 'Moneyball moment',[1] referring to the book (later made into a film starring the actor Brad Pitt) about an underdog baseball team that triumphed by being the first to rely entirely on sophisticated data analytics and pay no heed to conventional wisdom when buying players and selecting teams. The question arose because the author of the article, David Leonhardt, believes that charity fundraising appeals are largely based on 'common sense', 'intuition', and 'nothing more than a few rules of thumb', and quotes a series of economists who believe there is little science or empirical evidence to support the strategies employed by most fundraisers (Leonhardt, 2008, np).

The successful fundraisers interviewed for this study might well agree with Leonhardt's analysis while disagreeing with his conclusion, because they see knowledge and evidence as *necessary* but not *sufficient*, as this interviewee explains:

> I encounter quite a lot of people working in fundraising who are capable and have the technical skills but fall down because they don't get the political and contextual issues right. They don't read the weather right, they miss signals. I worry that we have sometimes encouraged people to think that if they go on enough courses then they'll become a good fundraiser. But what's most important are things you learn on the job not in the classroom: an ability to deal with complexity, to tolerate uncertainty, to see things through a donor's point of view, a kind of doggedness. And the finest fundraisers I know have a kind of boldness, have courage. I believe everyone can learn and get better at these things, but I do think there are some people who have the aptitude, have the focus at the beginning of the journey and consequently have a head-start. (Female, A, B)

All interviewees had enjoyed significant fundraising success, yet some readily admitted they had no standard practice, did not adhere to accepted techniques, had never read a book about fundraising or been on a training course. One made an analogy with other jobs that rely to some extent on innate ability: "You could deconstruct, you know, the technical ability of a premiership football player but it doesn't mean to say you could get on the pitch and play like them" (Male, A, B). Another respondent argued that certain personal qualities were of primary importance for major donor fundraisers: "Is the person likeable? Are they someone you'd want to spend time with? If not then guess what? Rich people are not going to want to spend time with them either!" (Male, A, B).

However, other interviewees take the opposite view – "I'm a firm believer that you can train people to ask for money" (Male, B) – and express concern about the lack of proof behind practice: "I've worked with some really inspirational fundraisers but, you know, you're thinking ... they're actually saying this on the hip, this is their own experience – there's nothing backing this up" (Male, A, B). Others feel that the perceived lack of rigour is deeply unhelpful: "I think it's a myth that fundraisers are 'born not made', it comes from a rather outdated view of fundraising which is, you know, 'we'll find a nice person and people will give them money'. So I think: absolutely, fundraising can be taught. Absolutely" (Female, B).

There is, therefore, a live and ongoing debate within the profession about the extent to which fundraising is a science or an art: is it based on an objective body of knowledge that can be taught, or does it rely on subjective judgements and instincts that only some people have? This chapter explores the extent to which fundraising know-how can be, and has been, codified for educational and training purposes, highlighting the key themes and difficulties that emerge in this endeavour.

This chapter begins by reviewing how fundraisers gain knowledge and their expectations regarding the combination of practical and empirical knowledge required for fundraising success, followed by the rationale and methodology for analysing the 'how to fundraise' literature. This analysis is not intended to generate a comprehensive list of all the advice on offer, but rather to describe and discuss the key themes, as well as reflections on how the overall task of fundraising is depicted in these books. There is much consistency found in the advice, alongside a number of contradictory messages on the complexity – or otherwise – of fundraising, whether fundraisers are primarily seeking instruction or inspiration, and the extent to which success can be achieved by anyone who makes the effort to master the techniques, or relies to some degree on innate qualities. These mixed messages are reflected in data from the interviews with successful fundraisers, which reveals a variety of opinions on the extent to which fundraising can be taught or not. The chapter concludes that fundraising practice is benefiting from the growth of evidence-based knowledge and a body of teachable techniques, but that success is still understood to be strongly related to the possession of personal qualities, which is the subject of the next chapter.

Fundraising training, education and occupational standards

For most of history, fundraising has been taught by the 'apprenticeship' method: learning by doing alongside an experienced colleague. As noted in Chapter 1, during the first decades of the 20th century, when the body of paid fundraisers grew rapidly, knowledge and skills were passed on informally through a process of personal tutoring (Harrah-Conforth and Borsos, 1991, p 24; Wagner, 2004, p 168). The first 'manual' on fundraising, written by Harold Seymour, did not appear until 1966 and it was almost another decade before the first courses were offered by The Fund Raising School, established in the US by Hank Rosso in 1974 (Tempel et al 2016, p xxiii).

The past few decades have seen rapid developments in the training and education of fundraisers, advancing the perceived professionalisation of this occupation and enabling it to be increasingly based on a body of verifiable and learnable knowledge and techniques. This information is codified in books, as well as taught in courses run by and for practitioners, as well as academic programmes for those wishing to study fundraising at a number of Higher Education Institutions. Professional membership bodies for fundraisers, including the UK's Institute of Fundraising, now offer training that ranges from short courses to more intensive professional development and a suite of accredited qualifications that culminates in a Masters-level diploma. Recent cooperation between the professional bodies representing fundraisers in the UK, mainland Europe, the US, and Australia has resulted in an agreed international body of knowledge for professional fundraising qualifications. In addition to these formal routes, training and support is also organised on a self-help and mutual aid basis by fundraisers working in particular parts of the UK, or focused on a cause area, or specialism within fundraising. These groups are often supported by the membership body,[2] including 12 geographically based groups (including London, Scotland and the North West), and 22 'special interest groups' (including 'corporate fundraisers', 'fundraisers working in Christian organisations' and 'sole fundraisers'). There also exist informal groups that rely on social media to organise 'fundraiser meet-ups' and social gatherings in major cities. All these self-organised groups provide a source of support, advice and opportunities for shared learning among fundraisers, while the larger and more formal groups organise events and conferences with relevant speakers and training workshops.

Despite this growing body of information, scholarship, training and educational programmes, it is not clear what proportion of fundraisers are choosing to avail themselves of these opportunities, nor the extent to which they are viewed as a sufficient pathway to success. The data in this book shows that most practitioners believe that fundraising relies on a combination of art and science, and is therefore a subject that must be 'caught' as well as 'taught', as this interviewee states: "Fundraising can be taught but you also learn by just getting on with it, ideally alongside older hands who've been there and done that. It's like public speaking, you can learn the techniques but you get better by practising" (Female, A).

More than one interviewee drew an analogy between swimming and fundraising, noting that it is not possible to learn to swim, or to fundraise, in a classroom: the student must jump in, literally and metaphorically, in order to become proficient.

Other interviewees are less convinced about the merit of any 'classroom' element:

> I'm anti all those golden rules, the '7 steps', or 'the 9 whatevers'. There's nothing wrong with being systematic and thoughtful and prepared but a lot of good fundraising is following your own instinct. The more you try to script it, the more likely it is to go wrong. (Male, A)

Many interviewees argue that success is related to innate – and often ill-defined – qualities such as 'good judgement', 'intuition' or 'the right instincts', while others resist the suggestion that it is possible to offer any template for success, saying, for example: "There is no one way or right way of doing anything in fundraising. You have to be sensitive enough to work out what is the right thing to do in any given set of circumstances" (Male, A, B). But the most common position held by the fundraisers interviewed for this study is that success derives from a combination of technical and personal skills:

> You can clearly learn all sorts of techniques and can be very effective as a result of that. There is stuff you need to take on board like how to build a campaign and all the paper techniques, as well as learning how to understand body

> language, mirroring, repeating back what the donor has said to you. But I think at the end of the day you do have to be a certain type of person. It's not going to work if you are just going through the motions. (Male, A, B)

The combination of practical and empirical knowledge required for fundraising success is reflected in the British National Occupational Standards for Fundraising. These standards, which were devised in 2008 and updated in 2013, list the skills deemed necessary for staff and volunteers responsible for raising funds (Skills Third Sector, 2013). The development of these national occupational standards is described as a necessary step towards professionalisation (a topic discussed in greater detail in Chapter 6), which succeeds in amalgamating best practice in the field with the latest academic research (Sargeant et al, 2010, p 39). As apprenticeships,[3] which are also based on nationally agreed standards, become a more widespread entry point for those starting out in fundraising, and a more popular option for those seeking career development, this concept is likely to become better known, and there will be value in exploring more closely the content of such standards, and the extent to which they reflect the reality of everyday practice as a fundraiser. But during the period of this research, the more common source of information on 'how to fundraise' was contained in books that attempt to set out what the job entails and how to master the required skills. Therefore, in order to capture and explore the science of fundraising, this chapter contains an analysis of 'how to fundraise' books, augmented by data from the survey and interviews.

Methodology

The data presented in Chapter 2 showed that a large number of fundraisers describe themselves as having 'fallen into' the job (52% of million pound askers and 42% of all other paid fundraisers) and that, once in post, the most typical method for acquiring fundraising skills and knowledge was 'learning on the job' (53% of million pound askers and 52% of all other paid fundraiser). Books also play a role as a useful source of information for acquiring skills and knowledge. Fundraisers are typically avid readers, including books related to their job, and many interviewees volunteered the name of books that they find useful and regularly recommend to fellow fundraisers. These titles were collated into a list and circulated to members of a broader group of UK fundraisers who had either completed the online survey or chosen to sign up as 'contacts' of this study, with an invitation to suggest additional books that they find particularly helpful.

The final tally of 60 books, listed in Appendix C, were written by 65 different authors, eight of whom wrote or co-wrote more than one book on the list; in alphabetical order these are: Burnett, 2002, 2006; Gurin, 1985, 1991; Mullin 1995, 1997; Panas, 1984, 1988, 2012; Ross 2002, 2008; Segal, 2002, 2008; Sargeant and Jay, 2010, 2014; Seymour, 1947, 1966. By 2010, fewer than 1,000 'how to' books had been published on fundraising (which compares poorly to the more than 300,000 books on the comparable topic of marketing [Sargeant et al, 2010, p xxiii]). As the cut-off point for the selection analysed here was four years later in 2014, the number achieving practitioner acclaim is likely just under 10% of the potential sample.

Date of publication

The earliest of the books selected for the analysis was published in 1947. *Designs for Giving* by Harold Seymour (1947) recounts the story of the US effort to raise 'national war funds' during the Second World War and is intended as a history rather than a 'how to' guide, but its provenance and enduring lessons mean it can still be found on some fundraisers' bookshelves. The same author also wrote the next oldest book on the list: *Designs for Fundraising* (1966), which was the first handbook intentionally written for fundraisers. There are only two books from the 1970s and five from the 1980s, but the numbers increase rapidly from there onwards, with 19 from the 1990s, 22 from the first decade of the 21st century, and 10 from the first third of the current decade. These dates refer to when the book was first published, as it is not possible to know which edition respondents are referring to, but a quarter (28%) of the books have been updated in later editions, some more than once, and two have reached their sixth editions (Herbst and Norton, first published in 1992; and Klein, first published 1988).

Place of publication

More than half of the books recommended by UK fundraisers were written by authors based in North America, usually with a domestic readership in mind. Not all advice travels unproblematically across the Atlantic, most obviously in relation to legal and tax issues, but also in terms of the social, economic and cultural context for philanthropy (discussed further in Chapter 5), with the latter having a particularly strong influence on how philanthropic behaviour is enacted and perceived. Some interviewees had visited North America on business, and a handful had worked in fundraising in the US, and shared examples of practices and approaches they believed would not be appropriate in the UK context. However, many interviewees also expressed the view that 'the American model' of fundraising was worth understanding and emulating because the profession is found in its most advanced form in that country (as also argued by Breeze and Scaife, 2015) and much practice from that part of the world would likely eventually become mainstream in the UK. It is therefore not surprising that so many US- and Canadian-focused 'how to fundraise' books are found on the shelves of UK-based fundraisers, even if it involves an extra effort to discern the appropriateness of the advice they contain.

Type of publication

The vast majority of books on fundraising are 'how to' guides written by practitioners drawing on their personal experiences of fundraising, and only a tiny minority are textbooks written by academics drawing on scholarly studies and evidence-based knowledge (Sargeant et al, 2010, p xxiii). Of the 60 books named by respondents in this study, just over one tenth (7) are the latter type: Rosso and Associates (1991) and later editions; Mixer (1993); Kelly (1998); Lindahl (2010); Prince and File (1994); Sargeant and Jay (2014); and Sargeant et al (2010).

The source of the advice presented in the other 53 books is largely unstated and draws on the authors' personal, and often substantial, experience of working in roles that involve fundraising, rather than empirical evidence. In other words, it is time-tested but theory-less (Kelly, 1998). In a typical example, a foreword explains that the author is sharing his 'insights, experience and wisdom' (McKinnon, 2006, p viii), and some authors even draw attention to the absence of evidence underlying their advice: 'I'm leaving it to others in other places to provide the empirical, statistical analysis that shows just how well relationship fundraising works' (Burnett, 2006, p x). In a handful of cases, the authors draw on primary research, usually interviews they have conducted themselves with fundraisers, as is the case with Flanagan (2002), Panas (1988) and Green et al (2007); but no methodological details, such as sample size or sampling strategy, are provided, which makes the robustness of the findings unknowable.

Whether the books are scholarly, anecdotal or somewhere in between, a concept that is useful for encapsulating the nature of their content is the Ancient Greek term *phronesis*, meaning 'practical wisdom'. This term was applied by Robert Payton to Hank Rosso's now-seminal handbook, *Achieving Excellence in Fundraising*, in order to highlight that its content derived from both substantive experience and study, and to underline the practical implications of the knowledge contained therein.

Advice on *doing* fundraising

As noted above, this chapter does not set out to provide a comprehensive summary of the content of 60 'how to' books. Rather, it is focused on showing on how the task of fundraising is variously – and sometimes confusingly – depicted in this literature. But it is interesting to note that there is a great deal of consensus in the advice offered on how to *do* fundraising. This is largely because the content of most books is focused on donor recruitment and donor retention, and, latterly, on the dominant paradigm of 'relationship fundraising', which involves developing and maintaining long-term relationships with donors (Sargeant and Jay, 2014, p 169).

Systematic approaches to recruiting, retaining and developing relationships with donors are commonly described as occurring within some manner of 'fundraising cycle', within which an ongoing process of research, planning, execution and evaluation occurs. The techniques, skills and processes that are used and advocated within such cycles are not a matter of great debate; however, they may be described using different terminology and packaged in innovative ways, including numbered processes, such as 'the ten steps to success' (Matheney, 1995, pp 31–9) or 'the 11 principles of stewardship' (Sprinkel Grace, 2005, pp 145–50), as well as pneumonics, such as ROPES – Research, Objectives, Programming, Evaluation and Stewardship (Kelly, 1998), or REAL – Research, Engage, Ask, Love (Pitman, 2007).

Advice on *doing* fundraising is often organised into broad topics such as planning and strategy, organisational skills and communication skills. The accord that these skillsets are necessary is reflected in comments such as: 'Strategy is the backbone of fundraising' (Herbst and Norton, 2012, p 39), or, less prosaically: 'Of course, you can fundraise without having a strategy, or planning or budgeting, in the same way as you can journey up the Amazon without consulting a map or buying provisions. But your chances of returning successfully from your venture are immeasurably increased if you think ahead' (Baguley, 2000, p 21). The importance of being organised, thorough, and good at detail have been emphasised since the first 'how to' book noted the need to 'indoctrinate' all fundraisers in the importance of 'tremendous trifles', by which was meant:

> writing a man's [sic] name the way he wants it written, answering all mail promptly and cheerfully, using good manners over the telephone, never being too busy to see visitors, always keeping the door open on every office, and above almost all, never letting it be said that 'Mr. Doakes is in conference'. (Seymour, 1947, p 21)

There is also widespread agreement that fundraisers need to have excellent communication skills, being eloquent, expressive and interesting speakers as well as patient, attentive listeners (see, for example, Woods, 1997, p 12; Burnett, 2006, p 70). Burk goes as far as to state that fundraising failure 'is actually a failure to communicate' (Burk, 2003, p 19).

The focus on what fundraisers need to *do* is, inevitably, most emphatic in the empirically based literature. For example, Kelly (1998) deals thoroughly with the organisational context and processes involved in fundraising, while Sargeant and Jay (2014) provide extensive, and extensively referenced, instructions on planning, marketing, strategy and management. Yet in the vast majority of the 'how to' books, these sort of skills are presented as necessary but not sufficient, because organising, planning, strategising and managing are said to only provide the infrastructure that enables successful fundraising to take place (Lysakowsi, 2012, p 169).

Advice on *being* a fundraiser

This literature therefore also devotes a substantial amount of space to explaining how to *be* a fundraiser. Many authors accept and advance the premise that fundraising requires a grasp of techniques but that alone is not enough, as summarised in this advice: 'The secret to rapid and astonishing success in fundraising seems to require a shift. Not a shift in what you are *doing* (although that will happen) but more of a shift in who you are *being*' (Bassoff and Chandler, 2001, p 1).

This has echoes of Gurin's suggestion that fundraising requires a distinctive point of view more than it requires a distinctive skillset (Gurin, 1985, p xii). The advice on being a fundraiser supports the assertion, developed in Chapter 5, that fundraising is a form of emotional labour. Giving is presented as an emotional act rather than a financial transaction (for example Burk, 2003, p 37; Joyaux, 2011, p 11; Prince and File, 1994, p xvi), which has implications for the emotional investment required of fundraisers (Sprinkel Grace, 2005, p 18). Therefore, as Joyaux asserts, successful fundraisers need to be more than 'effective fundraising executives who are consummate managers and proficient technicians ... more than a manager and a fundraising strategist. Lots more' (Joyaux, 2011, p 37). But the brevity of that last sentence ('Lots more') is indicative of the scant detail provided as to what exactly it is that fundraisers need to do, and how to do it, in order to be the kind of person who can successfully raise a lot of money. There is verbiage – 'Be interesting', 'Be inspiring', 'Be passionate' and so on – but what this means in practice is less clear. As Kelly notes: 'The practitioner literature [is] filled with references to "Mom and apple pie" traits desired in fundraisers, such as an appreciation for hard work and the ability to inspire people' (Kelly, 1998, p 88). Fundraisers themselves, when asked to name the characteristics and traits exhibited by colleagues they admire, are no more precise, simply suggesting that 'strong characters and warm personalities' were required (Duronio and Temple, 1997, p 159).

Content analysis of the 'how to' literature identified some key qualities for *being* a fundraiser, as opposed to *doing* fundraising, that help to flesh out expectations. According to these authors (and bearing in mind that this advice is borne of experience rather than rigorous research), successful fundraising requires traits such as:

- being passionate;
- being authentic;
- being good at interpersonal skills;
- being able to take pressure.

Being passionate

Passion is such a recurrent theme that the 'how to fundraise' literature risks being classified as romance if computers ever displace librarians. Fundraisers are told that they must be passionate about the cause, and any specific project they are raising funds for; they must inspire passion in the donors and then reciprocate that passion; and they should feel passionately about the act of asking for money. Failure to exhibit requisite genuine passion in any of these dimensions risks failure, because donors will be able to tell if the asker doesn't really care, if it's 'just a job'. So the fundraiser must ooze passion for the charity, the cause, the beneficiaries, the donors, the volunteers and the very act of asking.

Being authentic

Fundraisers must also exhibit authenticity, especially in their interactions with supporters, because: 'Donors have, out of necessity, become experts at identifying authenticity in the nonprofit staff with whom they engage. They want to know that you honestly and truly value the relationship with them because of who they are, not because of the number of zeros in their bank account' (Jones and Olsen, 2013, p 95). 'How to' authors rarely advise the aspiring fundraiser to change their personality, but rather assume they already possess the requisite qualities: 'The good news is we can be exactly who we are and still be successful fundraisers' (Pitman, 2007, p 18). This again underlines the emotional labour involved in fundraising: it is not about acting but authentically caring about the donor and the cause. For example, an interviewee described becoming emotional when a donor announced she was ready to make a big gift: "I almost cried and was hugging her, I got very tactile!" (Female, A). The fundraiser's fear that this might have been an inappropriate reaction was assuaged when the donor later said it was the moment that reassured her that she (the fundraiser) truly cared and was not simply 'doing her job'.

The implications of this are discussed further in Chapter 6, which explores whether fundraising might be better described as a vocation or a calling than as a profession. But insofar as the 'how to' literature deals with this issue, it either assumes the fundraiser's authentic instincts will be appropriate ('be exactly who you are'), or it offers more cynical and confusing advice, such as: 'Lay it on as thick as you can while still being authentic' (Axelrod, 2000, p 152).

Being good at interpersonal skills

Many of the 'how to' books discuss, explicitly or implicitly, the importance of interpersonal skills, and some devote whole chapters or sections of their books to this topic. Aspiring fundraisers are encouraged to be personable, cheerful, chatty, positive and 'immediately likeable': 'A good fundraiser should really enjoy meeting and dealing with people. A good memory for names and faces also helps' (Herbst and Norton, 2012, p 22).

This skill set is viewed as being of primary importance because, in the words of one widely read 'how to' author: 'fundraising places a high premium on people skills, [so] a superior ability to communicate and a genuine interest in people should be coveted as core talents when hiring fundraising staff. If need be, new staff can learn the technicalities of the job while on the job' (Burk, 2003, p 184).

Specific interpersonal skills required by fundraisers include an understanding of body language, because someone's true feelings might only be discernible by being alert to what is left unsaid and expressed through their physical reactions (Stroman, 2014, p 110). The fundraiser must also use his or her own body language to best effect: 'Learn how to read the prospect's body language (particularly to identify lack of real interest or failing concentration) and how to ensure yours is open and encouraging' (Wilberforce, 2010, p 130)

This ability is exemplified by an interviewee who explained that she can tell when a conversation with a prospective donor is going well by spotting signs such as their face relaxing, their body leaning forward, and unfolding of their arms: "If they sit motionless across the table from me, polite but unyielding, then I know they are only listening to the pitch because they agreed to do so when a friend asked" (Female, B). This is an example of emotional intelligence, which is widely understood as a measure of interpersonal skills. As discussed in Chapter 2, fundraisers tend to exhibit higher than average abilities in this regard.

Being able to take pressure

Fundraisers are responsible (often single-handedly, as so many charities are small) for keeping an organisation 'in business', because without the financial and other resources needed to pay the bills, the mission cannot be delivered. This creates a lot of pressure for the person carrying such a responsibility, and the 'how to' books frequently describe fundraising as hard work, demanding and complex (for example, Panas, 1988, p 24; Rosso and Associates, 1991, pp 9 and 15; Allford, 1993, p 105; Elischer, 1995; p 3), and requiring persistence, intensity, commitment and single-mindedness (for example: Panas, 1988, p 35; Norton, 2007, p 11; Herbst and Norton, 2012, p 19).

The ability to perform well under pressure is much valued in stressful situations such as fundraising offices. One interviewee (male, B) described one of the best hires he made as being the man who used to be sent out to fix the charity's photocopying machine, which frequently broke down, often at particularly inconvenient moments. The interviewee explained that he knew this man had excellent customer care skills, and was able to keep calm and provide reassurance during a 'crisis', and that this new recruit did indeed turn out to be valuable member of the fundraising team.

One characteristics that can enable someone to handle pressure is tenacity which, as discussed further in Chapter 5, is a self-identified common trait of fundraisers. To exemplify this point, one interviewee (male, A, B) described himself as being 'like a terrier' when pursuing goals he had set his mind to, such as insisting that Buckingham Palace agree a date for an event.

Preliminary discussion of 'how to' books advice

Much of the advice on doing and being a fundraiser is indistinguishable from that found in the 'how to' literature aimed at people seeking to succeed in a wide range of professions. Being passionate, authentic, having good interpersonal skills, and being tenacious in pursuit of success are clearly qualities that are valuable in many contexts. However, a distinctive feature of the 'how to' fundraising literature, when considering all 60 books *in toto* rather than any specific book, concerns some significant conflicting depictions that emerge within this body of work.

There is a great deal of consensus on the broad areas of technical knowledge and methods (what fundraisers *do*) and nothing very distinctive in relation to what fundraisers need to *be*. But alongside this broadly homogenous and commonplace advice can also be found some notable contradictions in the depiction of the nature and 'learnability' of fundraising skills and knowledge. Three particular sets of conflicting advice are:

1. 'Fundraising is easy' versus 'Fundraising requires special attributes'.
2. 'Fundraisers need instruction' versus 'Fundraisers need inspiration'.
3. 'Anyone can learn fundraising skills' versus 'Fundraiser exceptionalism'.

'Fundraising is easy' versus 'Fundraising requires special attributes'

Many of the 'how to' books promote the view that fundraising is simple, straightforward and therefore, by implication, open to anyone who wishes to try. A leading UK 'fundraising guru' Ken Burnett is a proponent of this view. Burnett writes that: 'There's no big secret to the art and science of [raising money] ... In essence, it's all pretty much common sense' (Burnett, 2006, p vii), and later in the same book he underlines his point: 'At its most simple, effective fundraising is about being nice to people' (Burnett, 2006, p 63). Burnett's view echoes that set out over three decades before by Warner (2001), in the US:

'You raise money when you ask for it, preferably face to face, from the smallest number of people, in the shortest period of time, at the least expense … *It's almost childishly simple*' (Warner, 2001, p 186, my emphasis).

As a third example, another well-regarded 'how to' author, Kim Klein, whose book is currently in its sixth edition, has a subsection entitled 'Anyone can do fundraising', within which she states that:

> fundraising is easy to learn … a course, a degree, a certification [contributes to the health and well-being of the non-profit sector but are] not required for a person to be good at fundraising, and they will never take the place of the only three things you really need to be a successful fundraiser: simple common sense, a commitment to a cause, and a basic affection for people. (Klein, 2011, p 25)

In other books, fundraising is described as 'not rocket science' (McKinnon, 2006, p vii) and 'one of the most natural things in the world. It's as simple as storytelling' (Pitman, 2007, p 11). And the oldest self-described fundraising handbook also takes this position, stating baldly that: 'Only fools and fatheads … seek to build an image of the special cult [of the fundraiser], the mystique, and the ways of an inscrutable expertise' (Seymour, 1966, p 118). Others use more moderate language, while clearly suggesting that effort and passion are what matters most:

> Being successful – there may not be any secret to it at all. If you believe in the mission of your institution and you love your work, and you do the right things at the right time, and keep persistently at it – there is every possibility you can be successful. (Panas, 1988, p 106)

Of course, people selling 'how to' books need to make the goal appear achievable and may be engaged in an effort to reassure putative fundraisers, given the widespread fear of asking for money, rather than hold a genuine belief that their trade is 'childishly simple'. But there are others who are in the same trade of selling advice and yet take a different approach, insisting that fundraising does require special skills and personal characteristics. For example, Rosso and Associates state baldly: 'Fund raising is not easy. No magic formula has ever been devised to transform a desperate wish into immediate gift funds' (Rosso and Associates, 1991, p 9).

Those who advocate that fundraising is essentially 'easy' and those who say it requires special attributes are not necessarily in total disagreement, but rather, each perspective may need contextualising. It seems that fundraisers are being encouraged to make their work *look* easy and effortless in front of donors (and to some extent colleagues), and to keep the 'secret' of the hard work involved within the community of fundraising practitioners. As Baguley states: 'Make it easy for the donor, but be aware that fundraising is not easy' (Baguley, 2000, p 226). While this approach may be useful for achieving fundraising goals, it may also contribute to misunderstanding of the fundraiser's role if colleagues and charity leaders are misled as to the true nature of the job:

> Of course we fundraisers bring some of this heat on ourselves. When we first apply for a job, we want the interviewers to believe we can solve all their problems. You want them to think you will be a miracle worker. If they hire you … that means they fell for your line and are now expecting those miracles you promised. (Perdue, 2014, p 12)

An interviewee addressed this point, noting that:

> we need to educate colleagues who don't understand what fundraising is and the complexity, you know: the stages of fundraising that we have to go through, that detail of research and analysis that we have to do, modelling that we do with our data and the segmentation of our data. There's some real science and mathematics there, but most people – including colleagues – don't understand what we do, they just think: 'oh they're rich, they've given to that institution so they're bound to give to us'. (Female, A)

Another possible resolution to the easy/special divide is to re-frame 'easy' not as effortless, but rather as simple and straightforward and nonetheless requiring significant effort and skill to pull off. This is well illustrated by an analogy with trick shots in billiards:

> On the immediate level, fundraising comes across as an incredibly simple business … [which] reminds me of those 'trick shots' that billiard masters learn how to shoot after practicing, and practicing, and practicing … When one sees the shot, it looks remarkable, almost magically easy, though

> it's not, requiring trained muscle memory and razor-sharp focus. (Israeli, 2014)

Fundraisers also have a repertoire of 'shots' that may look easy, but unlike the predictable balls and baize used in billiards, fundraisers must work with unpredictable, complicated and nuanced human beings. And, of course, the outcome of fundraising matters a lot more than success in a game of billiards.

'Fundraisers need instruction' versus 'Fundraisers need inspiration'

While many 'how to' authors no doubt strive to both instruct and inspire their readers, they tend to align more with one camp than the other. Those who lean towards instruction are more likely to describe fundraising as a systematic process and to offer an infrastructure or framework to help fundraisers organise their efforts. One of the most well known is the 'Moves Management' system developed by G. T. 'Buck' Smith, which continues to be advocated in contemporary 'how to' books (such as Joyeaux, 2011, pp 275–6; Lysakowski, 2012, pp 403 –4), while many other authors offer numbered or pneumonic lists to help readers grasp techniques, skills and processes, such as the ten steps, the 11 principles, 'ROPES, or 'REAL', as discussed above.

The 'instructors' also often provide examples to clarify advice, not just counselling fundraisers to make small talk at the start of a meeting with prospective donors, but providing specific suggestions for what to talk about. For example, Baguley suggests that 'a short period of settling in, with talk of the journey or the weather, allows people to feel comfortable with each other' (Baguley, 2000, p 143), while Pitman offers this mini-script: 'So, what do you do when you're not eating lunch at this restaurant (or whatever activity you're both doing at the time)? How long have you been doing that? Really? How did you get started?' (Pitman, 2007, p 29). Such books often also include templates for typical fundraising activities, such as a sample calendar for running a five-year campaign (Allford, 1993, p 395); checklists for fundraising essentials and sequences (Seymour, 1966, p 193); sample letters for different types of donor (Broce, 1986, pp 256–74); and step-by-step guides to running events (Axelrod, 2000, pp 183–219; Greenfield, 2002, pp 539–544).

In contrast, 'how to' books that emphasise inspiration over instruction not only omit such prescriptive elements, they can also be contemptuous of such approaches. For example, one influential UK 'fundraising guru' argues that fundraising should be creative not formulaic, and warns his readers to avoid the 'deferential me-too-ism that makes so much fundraising so banal and unsuccessful' (Smith, 1996, p 214). Perdue is particularly scathing about instructors who reduce fundraising to a formula by:

> say[ing] something like: 'Send this many letters to get this many responses to get this many appointments to get this many solicitations to get this many gifts at this average gift. Using our methods you can hire every major gift officer within 250 miles and each one will raise 15 times their annual salary forever and ever' ... Ultimately, success comes from your ability to get people to like you ... That is an art. (Perdue, 2014, pp 8–9)

Burnett affirms: 'fundraising is not, most definitely, the science of predictable responses to predictable actions based on hard-and-fast rules of experts' (Burnett, 2002, p xiii). Later in the same book he returns to this point: 'Remember that there are no rules in fundraising. Very few things work for absolutely everybody. Use your judgment to decide what is best for you, then test before you proceed' (Burnett, 2002, p 32). Likewise, one leading US expert tells fundraisers that, 'your own intuition and experience will be your most valuable guide, when deciding what, when and how to communicate' (Burk, 1993, p 113). A Canadian book offers this suggestion: 'Be smart and trust your common sense ... Speak to [the donor's] heart from yours and you will find success' (Green et al, 2007, p 183). Green et al do offer some instructional advice, but state their overall intention is to 'empower' readers and thus describe the contents of their book as 'a recipe', which should be the basis for experimentation, adapted to particular constituencies and situations (Green et al, 2007, pp 177–8). Lord's (1987) book, which is explicitly concerned with inspiring people to have a go at fundraising rather than offering detailed instruction on how to do it, uses a similar rationale for the absence of a formulaic blueprint: 'In the day-to-day practice of philanthropy, most decisions are "judgment calls" that depend on circumstance and opportunity' (Lord, 1987, p x).

One of the older 'how to' books included in this analysis insists that fundraising 'can't be written as a formula' and therefore fundraisers must avoid becoming intimidated by, or a slave to, techniques (Warner, 2001, p 21). However, others suggest that the foundation on which creativity can flourish may involve a more tried-and-tested element: 'There are no infallible "right words" to secure a major gift from every donor at every time [but] proven preparation and solicitation strategies are available to improve your levels of comfort and success' (Matheny, 1995, p iii).

Therefore, where authors sit on either side of the instructional–inspirational binary is often as much about what is possible as what is desirable. Fundraising is by necessity relentlessly innovative because efficacious approaches do not always remain so in the long term: once-successful techniques can lose their effectiveness when they become commonplace and therefore less attractive to donors (Hughes, 1996, p 184). Fundraisers need to be ready to abandon the 'old rules' once they stop working, and constantly adapt to changes in the environment and the donor population (Nichols, 1996, p 152). There are, therefore, many authors who take the middle ground, advising that both techniques and creativity are required, for example: 'Adapt the specifics, be creative' (Stroman, 2014, p 139); 'Flexibility is a virtue in any plan [because] … conditions can change (Greenfield, 2002, pp 84–5); 'Every rule is made to be broken – sometimes' (Wolf, 2011, p 48). The need to have respect for instructions but leave room for inspiration is well encapsulated by Panas, who writes: 'The great fundraisers know all of the principles, basics and mechanics. They know their trade and apply it well. But most of all, they follow their intuition' (Panas, 1988, p 12).

One interviewee explains how the instructional–inspirational routes combine in practice when supporting her junior colleagues:

> You can guide in terms of what good customer service looks like, for example you can set some parameters around 'well it would be really nice to do a letter and it would be really nice to have these paragraphs in it' or something. But the difference between a good fundraiser and a less good one is that the good one would take those tools and then they'd adapt them to their circumstance with that particular individual. They might take a key message and re-craft it and handwrite it in a Christmas card, you know. But somebody that would be following a formula would be 'right, we have to print it in this type face and we have to kind of … ' you know. The rules are there for guidance but actually, you ought to know when to bend them. (Female, A, B)

'Anyone can learn fundraising skills' versus 'fundraiser exceptionalism'

The final pair of apparently contradictory positions found in the analysis of the 'how to' literature suggests that fundraising is either a set of skills that anyone can learn if they try hard enough, or alternatively, requires some innate, or at least ingrained, qualities. This binary is a variant of the 'born or made' argument.

The academic textbooks, perhaps inevitably, are the most prominent examples of the 'learnable knowledge' camp. They do not spend any time reflecting on their audience and assume all readers are equally capable of studying and grasping the content therein. But this stance is not limited to academic authors: McKinnon baldly states: 'It's a learned skill' (McKinnon, 2006, p 15), and Elischer concurs that anyone can be a fundraiser, it 'is not an art limited to a chosen few' (Elischer, 1995, p 3).

Yet others hold the opposite view, and believe there are discernible innate or ingrained qualities that enable some people to succeed as fundraisers. Levy suggests that: 'Fundraisers see the world differently from normal folk' (Levy, 2009, p 128), while Allford insists that 'charity staff are a special breed' (Allford, 1993, p 105). One 'how to' author who also taught fundraising seminars and workshops noted that he could often spot those exceptional qualities at first glance:

> On the first day of class – before presenting any of this material – I could predict with a fair degree of accuracy who was going to be an effective fundraiser and who wasn't. It had less to do with the knowledge they carried into class and much more to do with how they interacted with me and their peers. If they looked me in the eye, offered a firm handshake, and steered the conversation away from themselves and toward the person whom they were speaking with, I knew they had [already] mastered a large part of the technique. (Wolf, 2011, p 10)

Panas agrees there is something special about those who succeed in raising funds, claiming that: 'the language of the institution or the discipline can easily be learned. The magic of fundraising cannot' (Panas 1988, p 112). Yet Broce offers a bracing riposte to this sort of sentiment: 'There is no magic in fundraising. The skills are primarily those of effective planning, organizing, management, and marketing, bolstered by good common sense' (Broce, 1986, p 5). Broce goes on to add that '[Fundraisers] are not magicians. They must be armed with the knowledge and resources to complete their tasks' (Broce, 1986, p 25). Turner (1991) analyses the dramatic language that is sometimes used to describe fundraising, and notes that even the second half of the compound word – 'raising' – suggests an act of physical accumulation that can cause fundraisers to be viewed by associates and colleagues as engaged in 'somewhat Herculean labor' (Turner, 1991, p 39). He notes that:

> Being cast in such a heroic image is helpful and flattering to fund raisers, but it has its own drawbacks. It puts pressure on fund raisers to perform at an extraordinarily high level, but it also complicates the image of fund raising by associating it with the world of high romance where heroes use magic and miracles to get their jobs done. Fund raisers would be better off with a realistic budget and some manageable time lines. (Turner, 1991, p 48)

A number of interviewees similarly rebut the suggestion that fundraisers are exceptional and in possession of singular traits that make mundane skills and practical support unnecessary: "Fundraisers are not magicians for hire, or white knights on a charger, suddenly the money will come rolling in! It's a myth that that will happen" (Female, A). "People say 'we need a fundraiser' as if it's a dark art that can be learnt. But in reality you need to be personable, organised, have basic good written skills, and someone to watch and learn from" (Female, A).

A variant on the 'exceptionalism' argument is to divide people into those who like asking for money and those who fear it (as noted, for example, by Matheny, 1995, p iii), such that the defining characteristic becomes attitude rather than ability: 'Fundraising is either something you like doing or not, recruit the former!' (Axelrod, 2000, p 235).

Another variant on the exceptionalism argument relates to the organisation's mission and the asker's intention and effort, suggesting that those lacking in these regards will find less success. In a preface addressed to fundraisers who might be feeling scared, threatened and afraid by the scale of the task facing them, Warner writes: 'Take a good, deep breath and relax … you and your worthwhile program will find the money you need … I wish you 'good luck' with the sure knowledge you won't need it because you're doing something worthy and your dedication will see you through' (Warner, 2001, p 2).

Discussion of 'how to fundraise' books

The analysis of the 'science' of fundraising, as encapsulated in the most popular 'how to' fundraising books that are read and recommended by UK fundraisers, reveals a complex and often contradictory picture of what the job entails. These different emphases – and sometimes outright inconsistencies – matter for a number of reasons: newly recruited fundraisers may struggle to comprehend expectations; colleagues – whose buy-in is known to be essential to create an internal culture of philanthropy – may lack clarity about the fundraising function; and confusion may arise between fundraisers and their managers as to the nature, purpose and execution of the role (Worth and Asp, 1994, p 27). Indeed, some of the problems associated with fundraising as discussed elsewhere in this book, notably its negative reputation, may be due to 'continuing ambiguity reflected in the literature' concerning the proper roles and responsibilities of the job (Worth and Asp, 1994, p 14).

However, the 'how to' literature is largely written by practitioners who are focused on the prosaic reality of the task at hand and rarely engage with conceptual issues that might attract attention in a more theoretically minded milieu. The resulting pragmatic tracts are aimed at fundraisers who are usually working in stressful situations with imminent deadlines, with little interest or time to pursue 'knowledge for knowledge's sake'. So despite being (on the whole) highly educated, avid readers, and keen on lifelong learning (as seen in Chapter 2), in the workplace they tend to be adherents – and consumers – of Noah's principle: 'No credit for predicting rain. Credit only for building arks' (Levy, 2009, p 7).

However, this strong pragmatic streak and desire to know 'how to do it' more than an interest in discussing 'what's it all about' runs up against the reality that fundraising (again, on the whole, and in particular in relation to major donor fundraising which is the focus of this study) resists standardisation. Donors are individuals, who respond best to approaches that are authentic and respectful of their individuality, so no two campaigns or 'asks' can be exactly alike (Prince and File, 1994, p xvii; Greenfield, 2002, p xiii; Sloggie, 2005, p 23; Johnson, 2011b, p 101; Filiz-Obay and Uler, 2016, p 1). This makes the search for consistently reliable techniques somewhat difficult. At best, the 'how to' authors can provide a 'toolbox' but cannot provide a fail-safe, step-by-step, how-to guide because 'there is no one way to do it … [it is] messy and hard to predict or even manage' (Ross and Segal, 2002, p 2).

The realisation that fundraising does not have a stable, straightforward 'blueprint for success' can be disconcerting and uncomfortable: 'Early in my career I often heard the saying "There is no one right way to raise money." I found that statement both frightening and a bit disheartening because I wanted a formula, a blueprint, or at least a game plan' (Broce, 1986, p xi). The requirement for personalisation is largely in response to the poetically put realisation that 'donors are like snowflakes' (Johnson, 2011b, p 101), and the attendant requirement for innovation to avoid being – or appearing – formulaic in approach. Fundraisers need to avoid a one-size-fits-all approach (Lloyd, 2011) and routine methods because there is a thin line between 'proven' and 'stale', and the more familiar a technique, the less effective it becomes (Lindahl and Conley, 2002, p 99). Fundraisers are therefore required to conquer the mechanics of the process, without ever appearing to have a mechanical quality to their actions (Dorsey, 1991, p xiv).

In addition, it is not just the individual qualities of donors that affect how fundraising occurs, because variation in fundraising is also a reflection of the heterogeneity among fundraisers. This relates to the findings summarised in Chapter 2 of this book; for example, the 'salesperson' type is defined as 'Loners who raise money based on their personal energy and charisma and with no need for any method or systematic approach' (Worth and Asp, 1994, p 19), while the 'leader' type pays closer attention to the moral, ethical and philosophical concerns. The latter likely see fundraising as a learnable skill and prefer instructional texts, while the former may be more likely to promote the 'magical qualities' notion and reply on inspiration.

The existence of different fundraising types is further proof that fundraisers are far more than 'mere technicians' (Lord, 1987, p 98), just as the donors they interact with are far more than walking bank accounts. Philanthropy involves meaningful and value-laden relations between living, breathing, idiosyncratic people, which is why, 'Fundraising is never neat, never predictable and a lot more fun' (Perdue, 2014, p 1).

Conclusions

This chapter has presented and discussed the findings of a content analysis of 60 widely read and recommended books on 'how to do fundraising', as nominated by UK fundraisers. While there was much consistency within the technocratic guidance, a number of contradictory positions were also identified, illustrated and discussed. Further, an overarching contradiction was identified at the heart of the 'how to' literature: that the best fundraising is intensely personal and idiosyncratic, so it defies standardisation. Donors react badly to being marketed to, so anything that belies the 'mass' nature of organised asking may have the opposite effect of what was intended. Fundraising relies on successful interactions between people who are individuals and expect to be treated as such. If 'every donor is a snowflake', and no two 'asks' can be exactly alike, then fundraisers must be continually innovative and best practice must be in perpetual motion. The creativity required to rise to this challenge, is discussed further in Chapter 6.

Such a conclusion risks lionising fundraisers, which sits oddly with their current low standing and indeed the historic problematisation of the profession. And yet:

> To be a great fundraiser you really do need to have an extraordinary array of skills and abilities. You need to be highly creative, yet extremely organised. You need to be able to speak to hundreds, yet also be stimulating company with one or two. You need to be spontaneous and flexible but also a good planner. Fundraising is a series of contradictory and paradoxical skill sets. (Farnhill, 2007, p 14)

As noted at the start of this chapter, the successful fundraisers interviewed for this study hold various views about the extent to which fundraising relies on learnt skills or innate abilities. But they do appear to support Payton's suggestion that the best guides to fundraising are examples of *phronesis* or 'practical wisdom', in the sense that the knowledge read and recommended by fundraisers is largely attained as a result of the authors' *doing* fundraising, as well as – perhaps more so than – *studying* it (Payton, 1991, p xiii).

The depiction of fundraising as an inexact art or an imprecise science that is reliant on a combination of pre-existing and learnt knowledge and personal skills, chimes with many interviewees:

> I think that a lot of fundraisers arrive in a job with the key elements in place but if they've got any sense then they keep learning from other people who are more experienced at it. You can't teach somebody the gift of the gab, you can't teach somebody the ability to be highly sociable, you certainly can't teach somebody tact, I don't think. So you either have those skills or you don't, but a smart fundraiser will learn from people. (Male, B)

Returning to where this chapter began: does fundraising need to have a 'Moneyball moment' (Leonhardt, 2008, np)? It is true that the current collective wisdom on fundraising techniques and practices is largely subjective and often based on nothing more than 'what we've always done', yet there is plenty of information identifying and describing the techniques, information, methods and knowledge that fundraisers need. However, the consensus is that there is more to successful fundraising than the possession of this skill set. The science is conceived of as necessary but not sufficient, it is the art that ensures successful implementation and results. Fundraising practice is undoubtedly benefiting from the growth of evidence-based knowledge and a body of teachable techniques, but success is still understood to be strongly related to the possession of personal qualities; notably, the ability to build authentic and meaningful relationships with a wide range of people, which is the subject of the next chapter.

Notes

1. This article is written by David Leonhardt: 'What makes people give', *New York Times*, 9 March 2008.
2. National, regional and special interest groups supported by the Institute of Fundraising are listed here: www.institute-of-fundraising.org.uk/groups (last accessed 2 January 2017).
3. For more information on apprenticeships, which are overseen by the UK government Skills Funding Agency, see www.gov.uk/topic/further-education-skills/apprenticeships (last accessed 1 January 2017).

FOUR

The art of fundraising

In contrast to the previous chapter, this chapter focuses on the non-technical aspects of fundraising. It draws on new data from interviews with successful UK fundraisers, as well as ideas in the literature, to demonstrate how social and personal skills are utilised in the 'art' of fundraising. This art involves responding creatively to the fact that every donor is unique, and that each unique donor has different intentions, attitudes and aspirations in the context of different giving scenarios. Further, the language of gift giving is, by convention, oblique, so the art involves an ability to understand what is *really* being said and desired, and to respond accordingly. As donors react badly to standardised offerings, the art of fundraising requires a tailored and highly personalised, even idiosyncratic, interaction, which is difficult to capture within the body of codified knowledge and best practice that was discussed in the previous chapter.

The birthday card dilemma

An interview with a female director of fundraising at a major UK charity began with her explaining how the morning had gone so far: she had been in a brief meeting to agree a significant budget for a new direct mail campaign, and had then had an extended discussion with a colleague debating whether or not to send a birthday card to a relatively new and potentially major donor. They had chewed over questions such as: Was it too soon to be so familiar? Or was it worse not to acknowledge the occasion? If a card was sent, should it say 'Dear Mr Smith' or 'Dear Bob'? And how warm should the greeting be? Too fulsome would come across as insincere; too measured would fail to convey the closeness desired – if not yet achieved – by the charity. These deliberations were described with a self-knowing laugh, aware that an observer would expect big budget decisions to require more introspection than the birthday card dilemma. But getting this latter sort of call right has long been key to successful fundraising. Fifty years ago, Seymour described a good fundraising campaign as 'an aggregate of the *tremendous trifles* by which any enterprise wins and holds public approval' (Seymour, 1966, p 95–6, my emphasis).

Coping with 'tremendous trifles' continues to occupy much time and energy of contemporary fundraisers, as the birthday card dilemma illustrates. Another interviewee describes "agonising" over whether or not the time was right to invite an important prospective donor to an event, while another, who had endeavoured to arrange seating plans around known and unknown animosities, reported receiving a tongue-lashing from an angry donor, saying "why the hell did you sit me next to that person? I can't stand them and haven't spoken to them for five years".

Such vignettes usefully highlight a crucial fact about fundraising that is not obvious to many observers, or even to most of their colleagues: their daily work involves juggling major strategic decisions with the minutiae of interpersonal interactions, not only with potential major donors but with all those within and outside their organisation who might potentially play some role in helping the charity to secure necessary resources. Successfully accomplishing this task, which is comprised of thousands of tiny decisions about how best to build and grow personal relationships, forms the bedrock for a secure source of voluntary income and enables those bigger strategic and budgetary decisions to be taken, not just within the fundraising department but across the charity's operations and. most importantly, its front-line work. As the funding enables the mission to be delivered, successful fundraisers know that it is worth sweating the small stuff of a greeting card.

This chapter begins by describing how data was collected from successful paid fundraisers in the UK through a series of in-depth interviews. After explaining what is meant by the 'art' as opposed to the 'science' of fundraising, there is a discussion of ideas and common metaphors offered by interviewees in their efforts to explain the art of their job. Most frequently, fundraisers describe themselves as choreographers of the various elements of donor relations and interactions with the cause, which relies on extensive, and largely hidden, organisational skills. Parallels with ideas found in the extant literature, which depict fundraisers as various types of 'middlemen', highlight the abstract and intangible nature of the job, which is likely to be a contributing factor to negative perceptions of the profession.

Methodology

In addition to the survey data discussed in Chapter 2, this book draws on data from 50 in-depth, semi-structured interviews conducted with successful paid fundraisers in the UK. There are many different types of specialisms within fundraising, including people who produce direct mail appeals, create digital fundraising campaigns and apply to institutionalised grant-makers. The focus of this study is not on those who manage such processes, but rather on those fundraisers who are themselves making – or supporting others to make – personal requests for financial donations. Fundraising in person, face-to-face, is typically found in the specialism known as 'major donor fundraising', although personal engagement also happens in other types of fundraising such as community, events and corporate fundraising.

The recruitment of a purposive sample of successful fundraisers was achieved by interviewing people who met at least one of the following criteria.

1. Hold a leadership role, typically as the director of fundraising, in a major UK charity.
2. Enjoy a high profile as an authority within the UK fundraising profession, for example, by regularly appearing as speakers at major conferences or providing comment in industry media.

In many cases, interviewees met both of the above criteria. Quotes from interviews are followed by the participant's gender, and the letters A and/or B, to indicate which of the above criteria they met. Around one fifth of interviewees had also received recognition from their peers in the form of industry awards or honorary fellowships of the Institute of Fundraising, though this latter criterion is not highlighted by quotes to avoid inadvertently identifying participants.

Two thirds (64%) of interviewees were female and their ages ranged from late twenties to mid-sixties. A wide range of cause areas were represented in the sample, including health, children, the arts, education and animal charities. While all, by definition, worked for the minority of charities that are large enough to have employees (NCVO, 2016), they ranged in size from having only one paid member of staff who fulfils all roles, including the fundraising function, to charities with thousands of paid staff.

The interviews took place between March 2013 and January 2016. Most were conducted in person at the fundraiser's place of work, a handful took place in cafes, one was held in the fundraiser's house, and one in my own house. Five interviews were conducted over the telephone in order to broaden the geographical location of interviewees in the sample, which nonetheless remained skewed towards London where the majority of major donor fundraising takes place. The length of interviews ranged from 50 minutes to over three hours, averaging around 80 minutes. The interview schedule was deliberately brief, containing just eight fairly broad questions (as listed in Appendix B), in order to avoid constraining the conversation and to maximise the opportunity for interviewees to say whatever they wanted on each topic. All interviews were captured on a digital recorder and transcribed before a process of inductive analysis and coding of the data to identify the key themes. In a handful of quotes, some details have been slightly changed to protect the confidentiality of the interviewee and/or the charitable organisation. The findings of this phase of the research form the basis of this chapter and are also woven into the other chapters.

Context for the art of fundraising

Despite the plethora of 'how to' books, designed to meet the demand for step-by-step instructions on the mechanics of fundraising, many authors readily admit that there is more to the task of asking for money than can be codified in such standardised texts. There is understood to be an art to fundraising that goes beyond the mechanical aspects (Dorsey, 1991, p xiv; Rosso and Associates, 1991), though this acknowledgement is often implicit and lacking in detailed exposition. Telling fundraisers to 'build relationships' (Burnett, 2002; Burk, 2003), to 'love' their donors (Pitman, 2007), and to treat the process 'like a romantic courtship' (Green et al, 2007, p 121) is of limited value without insights or examples of precisely how this can be achieved.

However, one explanation for such nebulous advice is that fundraising is described not as *doing* particular things but rather as *being* a particular way. As Norton explains: success derives less from *what* you know, or (contrary to widespread assumption) from *who* you know, 'but in actual fact, it is much more about *who you are*' (Norton, 2007, p 11, emphasis in original). Such injunctions suggest that the art of fundraising is reliant on inherent characteristics, but those seeking usable advice are urged to consider making existential changes: 'The secret to rapid and astonishing success in fundraising seems to require a shift. Not a shift in what you are *doing* (although that will happen) but more of a shift in who you are *being*' (Bassoff and Chandler, 2001, p 1, emphasis in original). Indeed, the 'doing' can be detrimental to the intended outcome:

> most gift officers fail [because t]hey prioritize updating spreadsheets, filling out donor reports, writing thank you notes and ranking prospects above actually getting out and meeting people. Those tasks are all important, but not one

> of them will advance a relationship toward an ask – let alone get you a gift. (Jones and Olsen, 2013, p 36)

Getting caught up in the process is problematic because it risks turning 'flesh and blood people with their own personal attitudes and preferences' into abstract cases in a database (Lord, 1987, p 12). Such an approach creates 'slick, boiler-room operations' that nonetheless lack sensitivity to the concerns and needs of those being solicited and therefore fails to forge the strong links that lead to significant and sustained support (Dorsey, 1991, pp xiv–xv).

Counterintuitively, this results in the suggestion that the goal of securing support be subordinated in order to achieve that outcome: waiting until the donor 'gives you permission' to ask (Axelrod, 2000, p 144), focusing on preserving the relationship and prioritising the prospective donor's personhood over banking a gift, because a 'depleted' donor will not give or give again (Ragsdale, 1995, pp 24, 30).

However, the art of fundraising by no means implies passivity. Building relationships with donors and prospective donors relies on the willingness of fundraisers to engage in self-disclosure to prompt reciprocal revelations and thus deepen intimacy (Ragsdale, 1995, p 21). It is accepted that donors like to talk about themselves, their families, their experiences and opinions, so in order to help donors feel comfortable and safe in revealing themselves the fundraiser must also be prepared to express personal feelings and respond to the donor's emotions. This is not unique to fundraising: for example salespeople also endeavour to 'simulate intimacy' through the trappings of personal disclosure and gift exchange in order to 'create an emotional setting for trade' (Offer, 1997, p 467). But the instrumental nature of such efforts goes unremarked in the non-profit sphere, despite expectations going far beyond what would be deemed appropriate in other professions. Fundraisers describe revealing deeply personal details in order to assist the 'spiral of mutual self-disclosure' (Offer, 1997, p 458) leading one interviewee to wonder aloud:

> Where are the boundaries? I had a meeting with someone that I really didn't know very well and they suddenly shared a horrendous personal family history. I was very aware in my mind when this story was being laid out that I had to reciprocate because it was so exposing. I thought: "If I don't offer something back then I'm not going to be able to come back to this person. I've got to find another connection to them". (Female, A)

Likewise, another interviewee explained:

> Fundraisers must be willing to open up – we can't expect donors to talk about such personal issues as their money and what's happened in their life to make them care about a topic or cause, unless we as the fundraiser reciprocate and also open up and share revealing stories about ourselves. (Female, A)

The intimacy created by this approach can result in a blurring of the professional/personal boundaries as the fundraiser becomes entangled in the lives of donors. Being invited to visit donors' holiday homes or attend family weddings might be construed as extreme versions of interactions that occur in market exchanges, such as business lunches. But when fundraisers are prominent participants in the funerals and memorial services of donors (for example, Johnson, 2011, p 55), this is arguably actual, rather than simulated, intimacy. As Matheny emphasises: 'the qualities of a good friend and a successful major donor fundraiser are one and the same' (Matheny, 1995, p 43).

How fundraisers describe their work

The successful fundraisers that I interviewed would recognise much of what is written in the literature, but as practitioners they have a distinctive perspective and used a number of different, often vivid, metaphors and analogies to encapsulate their role. In the extant literature, a number of metaphors are used to describe fundraisers: May describes them as the 'glue' that bonds donors to an organisation (May, 1997, p 19); Nagaraj (2014, np) describes fundraisers as being like Swiss army knives because they need to have a lot of tricks in one small package; and, rather poetically, Warner tells fellow fundraisers that 'You are a blend of Don Quixote and Sancho Panza: you pursue impossible dreams with both feet firmly on the ground' (Warner, 2001, p 4).

Four types of imagery that came up repeatedly in my research will be discussed here: the fundraiser as a choreographer, a swan, an honest broker and a weeble, before a brief discussion of some less frequently used metaphors.

The Choreographer metaphor

The most frequent metaphor used by interviewees when explaining the everyday reality of their work was as choreographers trying to stage-manage events in order to achieve desired outcomes. The appeal of this metaphor lies partly in the fact that a number of successful fundraisers had previously worked in the arts, including the theatre, and saw genuine parallels between directing plays and directing a fundraising department. As one interviewee explained: "You have to manage and cope with a lot of other egos, and try to get people in the right place to say the right thing" (Female, A).

This analogy was also offered as a way of emphasising that, despite assumptions about the 'prima donna' personality of some fundraisers, they are not – and should not want to be – centre-stage. Put simply: "The fundraiser sets the stage so someone else can make the ask" (Female, A, B). Therefore, fundraisers are off-stage, providing essential but unseen support to the 'true stars' – the donors, the CEO, the front-line staff, the volunteers and the beneficiaries. As one interviewee explains:

> a lot of people think a fundraiser is, you know, somebody who's going to come in, be a very big personality and is going to attract lots of donors. Now there are some of those around, sometimes that can work, but actually I think more often a fundraiser is somebody who stage-manages situations to get the right result. And that includes being *absolutely* ... somebody who's absolutely aware of what's going on everywhere. (Female, A, B, emphasis in interviewee's intonation)

Explaining how this works in practice, she gave this hypothetical explanation:

> So, for example, if the charity is approaching a major donor for £5 million. I need to make sure that when he visits the charity on Thursday he's going to be in a room with the right people, all those he has a contact point with and would enjoy meeting. I need to make sure that everybody's on-message and understands what are his particular pressure points, right down to, you know, some donors don't actually like particular words. I worked with a donor who didn't like the word 'output'. He couldn't stand it and got really

> uptight if it was used. So I had to brief everyone not to say the word 'output' because it becomes a red herring! So I think it's that, it's thinking through everything so that it all goes well, to the point where I, as the fundraiser, don't need to be in the room because it's all been organised and everyone understands what they need to do. When you think about somebody organising their wedding or just a private party, even really senior chiefs of industry will get stressed about details like choosing the wine. That's the kind of thing a fundraiser has to think about, and sort it out without anyone really noticing it's been managed, every day of the week. (Female, A, B)

On hearing this example, another fundraiser concurred and added:

> This is why it looks like an easy job, especially if the fundraiser doesn't attend the meeting because they've judged it'll go better without them being in the room. Good fundraisers are OK with not taking any credit and they'll set up a scenario and then the Chairman walks in and asks and gets the yes. So the Chairman thinks that was a five-minute job and not years of solid work leading up to that ask! And even if the fundraiser does attend, no one is aware of all the background work, so when they're, you know, on the job, it looks like they're just kind of going out for lunch for a living or sipping champagne for a living and it's quite hard to see the work behind the scenes because it's kind of in their head – the second-guessing and the choreography and so on. (Female, B)

The importance of attending to every small detail to ensure the donor has the best possible experience was emphasised by another interviewee:

> So literally if it was an event, I would make sure that everyone knew who was walking through the door so we could greet people by name – I would hold up photos of donors to my team before an event and make it a competition so they would learn them and be able to name them. And I would think about what that experience feels like from the moment the donors walked in – was there going to be a queue, was it smooth running, how do you pick up your card, is there going to be a queue for the

> cloakroom afterwards? Everything you're thinking is: what is the donor experience? So it's not just about the giving but the whole interaction with the organisation at every level. (Male, A, B)

Another interviewee described how he had choreographed (his phrase) an encounter between a potential donor and a leading figure within the cause area:

> My goal was to show a potential major donor that our charity is well connected to the biggest names in our field as I knew that would give her enough confidence in our organisation to make a transformational gift. This particular lady was attending a performance and a dinner for supporters afterwards, but she wasn't the kind of person who would want to sit at the 'top table', that's not her style, I knew she'd much prefer some informal one-on-one time with the stars. So I arranged to take her down to the side of the stage at the end to watch the curtain calls from the wings, which is an amazing experience for anyone. But I took it a step further that night, and once the auditorium was empty I walked her and her husband out onto the stage and the guys in lighting knew we were coming and they put the spotlight on us. Even the most senior person in the land is like a kid at Christmas doing that! Then when we came off stage I knew we'd 'bump into' the stars. I'd timed it so we could walk with them to the dinner, and that gave my potential donor the opportunity she really wanted for a private conversation with a performer she admired. (Male, A, B)

Such choreography only succeeds if it is done with respect for the integrity of all involved. When another fundraiser described facilitating a similar encounter, I asked whether the 'celebrity' had any inkling that she had met someone who had a lot of money that might come the way of the charity:

> No. No, no, no. No, because that would ... that would be unfair on her. She would feel used and in fact she was also sitting at dinner next to another potential major donor, who she had been briefed about. So there were two pieces of choreography going on [that evening], and the second

> was more straightforward. I think it's like directing a play, or writing a book, you know what story you want to tell and if I think about each prospect that we have, you do that analysis on that person of actually what they're interested in, who they're married to, what school did they go to, who will they know? So you actually build up a picture of that character and then you can start thinking: "how do we get them from this part of the story to that part in the story and what events need to take place to get us to that point and which other characters do we need to introduce?" (Female, A)

The job satisfaction comes from directing the right script, rather than any necessary recognition of the fundraiser's role in achieving the outcome, as another interviewee explained:

> You recognise what they [the donor] want and you give it to them. You find the right people for them to talk to, be it a scientist, be it an academic, be it a Vice-Chancellor – you recognise what they're seeking and you make it happen. That's what being a fundraiser is. You've called the play, you've made it happen – there's the satisfaction. The fact that your face isn't in the photograph at the signing of the agreement really doesn't matter in the least – you made all of that happen. (Female, A, B)

The Swan metaphor

After allusions to fundraising as choreography, the next most frequent way that interviewees described their work involved the swan metaphor, which refers to being graceful on the surface while working frantically hard behind the scenes. This chimes with fundraisers cited in the extant literature: "Most people only see advancement professionals schmoozing donors at coffees, lunches, dinners and events. They don't see the work that takes place inbetween" (quoted in Laskowski, 2016, p 16). A typical comment from my interviewees was:

> Being highly organised is key. Fundraisers are like swans, we're graceful on the surface but there's a lot of hectic activity behind the scenes.... We're charming, laid-back and fun when in public around donors and colleagues, but behind the scenes we have to be ruthlessly well-organised

> and obsessed with tiny details that others wouldn't realise matter. (Male, A, B)

Another interviewee reflects on how being swan-like can confuse colleagues, leading them to ask:

> "Don't you just hang around and chat and have nice meals for a living?" So I answer by using the swan analogy of, you know, I try to be graceful and laid-back and look like I've got all the time in the world when I'm with a potential donor or sponsor, but behind the scenes there's a huge amount of work that went into it and that needs doing still, but never kind of showing that. (Male, A)

Another interviewee made a similar point:

> Colleagues can often think all you're doing is swanning around having lunch for a living but there's so much organisation behind the scenes they don't know about. You have to almost have a split personality where you can seem like a very laid-back, kind of "I've got all the time in the world ... " But actually underneath it is a little machine clicking away. (Male, B)

Covering up the messiness of the fundraising function, and all it entails, is summarised in this final quote on the swan metaphor:

> We [fundraisers] make difficult things happen without actually telling anyone how difficult it was, or the work that's gone into doing it. And actually we can also make unpleasant people palatable, whether that's our organisation to a donor or a donor to our organisation. Our job is to smooth the edges. (Female, A, B)

The Honest Broker metaphor

Paid fundraisers have an obvious obligation to the charity paying their salary, but nonetheless many view themselves as being equally beholden to donors as they are to the organisation that is seeking funds. Some describe this scenario as being like an 'honest broker', such that "you are representing the institution to your donor and representing your donor to the institution" (Female, A). This dual allegiance is typical of a variety of professions (as discussed further in Chapter 6) and is not experienced as conflicting because it is felt that the best outcomes arise when the needs of both the charity and the donors are being met: "that's something that on a personal level governs me very strongly is that sense of fairness and that a deal has to be something that's fair for both sides and to be relatively unbiased about that" (Female, A). However, taking equal account of donor needs and concerns can confuse, or even offend, non-fundraising colleagues, as another interviewee explains: "The people that [sic] work on the programme side or the policy side are sometimes a little bit more aggressive, they want to get their point across, they're not necessarily looking for a solution for all the parties involved" (Female, A). This is arguably a result of some colleagues viewing the fundraising function as simply securing money as needed to fund projects that are decided and designed in-house, whereas successful fundraisers see their role as facilitating a respectful, two-way process. Others describe this role as a type of "intellectual arbitrage", because: "we take information between the donor and the organisation. You have to speak the language of the donor and of your institution – you're constantly translating between the two" (Male, A, B). Successful arbitration relies on the ability to communicate with both parties, and a number of interviewees jokingly described their ability to speak 'donor-ese', as one explains:

> Yes, we need to speak 'donor-ese' because there's a lot of softly stating. For example, I might say: "Would you have the time to meet?" The potential donor replies: "We are perfectly happy with our relationship with the charity and can't see it changing in the future." Translation: Might you give some money? No we're not going to! (Male, B)

Successful communication involves empathising with the donor's point of view, and explaining their perspective to charity staff and volunteers: "the fundraiser is a source, a conduit, for feeding frank feedback from the donors to the institutions" (Male, A, B). Unsurprisingly, such feedback is not always appreciated by colleagues, leading to situations where,

> We are frequently slightly detached from the organisations we represent because we have to act as an advocate for the donor, just as much as an advocate for the organisation for whom we're working. We need to be able to ask those challenging questions, either anticipated by the donor or

> asked by the donor, we need that degree of distance I think. (Female A, B)

This situation was recognised by many interviewees, with one commenting:

> Yeah, and you feel quite protective over them [the donors] sometimes. You'll put their question forward and you'll get a rolling of eyes [from colleagues] "why are they [the donor] asking me this?" It's because they are giving this level of money and they have every right. You feel yourself being quite insulted on their behalf. So there's a lot of managing you do internally, to say: "they do have the right ... ". (Male, A)

Similarly another interviewee explained:

> Unfortunately in a lot of organisations there's a sense that perhaps the cause knows best and the donor doesn't. But it's a relationship and donors have points of view and a perspective. They're often highly educated and intelligent and over-achieving people and I think one of the skills of a fundraiser is being able to balance representing the donor to the organisation in an ethical way, and sometimes that does merge into having a very friendly relationship with donors, because you might be a touch point representing that donor's interest. You might be the one person to whom they can say "actually I don't agree with that theory you're pursuing" or "I do agree with it, why aren't you doing it faster?" So it's important to be able to get some joy and pleasure from that bridging relationship and doing it in an ethical way, in a way that plays to your organisation's values and the donors' values. (Female, A, B)

Some interviewees felt their role as a go-between is coming out of the shadows and becoming recognised as a legitimate contribution by both donors and charities, as this interviewee explains:

> I think it's one of the way major donor fundraising has changed massively in the past 15 years in the UK, to become more like in the US system – we are more respected brokers now. When I first started there was more

> tit-for-tat fundraising where you give money because someone's asked you, the right person's asked you, even if you don't understand the cause. There's been a massive move, and I find it much more enjoyable now because I am talking to a donor about making sure their giving is strategic and achieving what they want it to achieve, so I get more respect because they know I'm the broker within the charity, representing their interests and giving them access to the people they want to see. They see me as the person doing that and they appreciate it. (Male, A, B)

The Weeble metaphor

When fundraisers are asked to describe the qualities needed to succeed in their job, one word recurs: tenacity. It derives from the root word 'tenacious' which is defined as: 'Holding together, cohesive; tough; not easily pulled in pieces or broken'.[1] The word is synonymous with 'chutzpah' and 'determination', as well as less positive terms like 'intransigent' and 'inflexible'. Yet most fundraisers view it as a compliment, and certainly preferable to antonyms such as 'indifference' or 'irresolution'. The word 'tenacity' appeared on a list of 'magic ingredients' named in a poll of fundraising directors (Breeze, 2013b).

Fundraisers tend to be plain talkers who eschew jargon and prefer an amusing turn of phrase. So instead of describing themselves as 'tenacious', a number of interviewees compared themselves to a weeble, which is an egg-shaped plastic toy, popular in the UK in the 1970s, weighted to keep it upright. The toy's earworm marketing jingle – 'Weebles wobble but they don't fall down' – resonates with fundraisers:

> One characteristic which I can say across a huge amount of good fundraisers I've met is the weeble factor. They get a setback and they react to a setback and go "OK, how can I ... how can I twist my way around this one?" Good fundraisers always bounce back. And the thing to watch, to stretch the weeble metaphor, is the lovely thing about weebles is they never bounce back on the same plane that you knocked them down in. So the number one characteristic I'm looking for, when I recruit a new fundraiser, is that weeble factor. (Male, B)

Bouncing back and staying positive were frequent themes in depictions of successful fundraisers: "You need to be a person who can always see an opportunity in a situation, it links to being tenacious – never say never" (Male, A). The knocks can be frequent and unpredictable, as another interviewee explains:

> you've also got to be persistent and to take being knocked back. It's tough you know, that picking up the phone. Sometimes people are really not very nice. You can get people who are really lovely but others yell "why did you call me when I'm in a meeting?" You think : "why did you pick up the phone" but you say "terribly sorry" and they yell "go away". So you've got to be robust, and feel comfortable about that when you're getting a lot of pressure. (Female, A)

One interviewee explained that being a 'tenacious weeble' also means being able to reflect on the reasons behind the knock-back, and generate a new strategy to 'get to the yes':

> You need to not give up too easily. You can't sort of stop at the first hurdle just because someone said no – it might just be "no" because it's the wrong time to ask them or you've gone to them with the wrong thing and so on. And it's being able to gauge that relationship, to work out when to, you know, when to go back if at all: is it definitely "no, that's never going to happen" or "no, just not right now"? So I think, yeah, there's something about just keeping going. Sometimes you get knocked a lot, I think, as a fundraiser and from a number of different angles and you've got to be able to just not take that personally and just keep going. (Female, A)

While choreographers, swans, honest brokers and weebles (or equivalents of these terms) were among the more common ways that fundraisers described the 'art' of their job, a number of other interesting metaphors also emerged in the interviews. Three of the more vivid – Del Boy, Chess Pawns and Chameleons – are described and briefly illustrated below.

The Del Boy metaphor

'Del Boy' is a fictional character from a UK comedy series, Only Fools and Horses, broadcast in the 1980s. He is an archetypical market trader – sharp-witted, optimistic and always dreaming up new schemes to make money. A charity chief executive who had previously worked as a fundraiser reached for this analogy to reflect on what he saw as the dominant characteristic of those charged with raising the resources so that a welfare-providing charity can fulfil its mission:

> Our fundraisers are a little bit Del Boy, a little bit risky, and sometimes that doesn't go down well with finance colleagues or even with care colleagues, but they need that ability to chance things, you want somebody who will chance things without being a chancer, if you like, who will do it in an educated way. You want to be able to excite [potential donors] with plans that aren't necessarily fully thrashed out, they haven't necessarily been fully agreed even, but you need to take donors with you, you need to inspire them about a better world. (Male, A, B)

Clearly all fundraisers want, and need, to stay on the right side of the law. So the Del Boy analogy does not refer to breaking real rules, but rather knowing the difference between what is a legal and ethical requirement and what is simply 'accepted practice' that is not necessarily applicable in all situations.

The Chess metaphor

Another interviewee, formerly an in-house fundraiser and now running a fundraising consultancy business, chose a more cerebral analogy, comparing fundraising to a game of chess in which:

> Fundraisers are the pawns on the chessboard – not the king or even a bishop. But a pawn can still win the game for you! The naïve view is to see fundraising like a game of pool, where asking is hitting the ball and it either pots or not; whereas in reality it's more like a game of chess involving context, tactics and complexity. (Male, B)

The suggestion that fundraising requires a strategic mind and a resourceful outlook is also reflected in these quotes, which offer a lay version of the 'systems thinking' described by Sargeant and Shang (2016) as crucial for 'great fundraising':

> A good fundraiser has to be able to join the dots, it's not just about the ask and the money, it's joining the dots

> internally and externally. You have to be nuancing, be flexible, thinking ahead, thinking all the time about how to nuance a situation because it's different every single time. (Male, A, B)

> You have to be resourceful and really love a challenge in the way that some people go thrill-seeking – it's a different kind of adrenaline junkie! I think fundraising is attractive to people who love to work out how to get from A to B. If you relish doing that, and then starting it all over again, then fundraising is probably a job you'd enjoy. (Female, B)

The Chameleon metaphor

The final metaphor that a number of interviewees use to describe the art of being a fundraiser is that of a chameleon: able to change, adapt and fit in as circumstances (primarily related to donor personalities) dictate. Interviewees gave many examples of this quality in practice:

> If you're talking with someone who's really soft spoken – and I'm really loud – I really have to consciously work at toning it down, meeting them where they are. I do think that takes a high emotional intelligence, to really step outside your comfort zone or to tone down whatever glaring personality traits you have. (Female, A)

> I personally think that a good fundraiser is someone who leaves their ego at the door. You're walking into a room and it's not about you, it's about the donor, so you are mirroring what they are doing and *you are going to be who they need you to be*. (Female, A, B, my emphasis)

Another comment illustrating the chameleon metaphor was: "You have to learn to dial it up or dial it down, to be willing to change your personality to suit the donor" (Female, A, B).

There are, therefore, a number of vivid ways in which successful fundraisers depict their understanding of what is meant by the 'art' of fundraising. These metaphors highlight the key qualities, attitudes and personal characteristics required to be successful at asking others for money and other resources. But however useful metaphors are as a shorthand explanation of a phenomenon, they are inevitably condensed and lack the nuance and detail of more complex representations. To describe fundraisers as 'swans' or 'weebles' is knowingly reductionist and involves emphasising one aspect at the expense of explaining the full process involved and the whole gamut of skills and qualities required for success. Collectively raising £10 billion of fundraised income each year is clearly the result of more than emulating Del Boy. More prosaic language is used in the extant literature, yet these authors also turn to metaphors and analogies in an attempt to convey how fundraisers operate.

The art of fundraising in the extant literature

The tasks involved in doing fundraising and being a fundraiser, as depicted in 'how to' books, were discussed in depth in Chapter 3. Here the focus is on how practitioner and academic texts offer a holistic perspective on the art of fundraising. As with the fundraisers themselves, these authors also often reach for metaphors, though less vivid and more technocratic terms, including the idea of fundraisers being links, connectors, matchmakers and middlemen.

Fundraisers as links

Burlingame and Hulse depict fundraisers as a 'link' in at least two respects: first, as the link between the organisations they work for and the communities served by those organisations, and second as the link between what the charity aspires to achieve and the means needed to implement that mission. Being a link in these two regards means that the fundraiser is standing 'at a critical intersection' and doing a 'complex and time-consuming' job (Burlingame and Hulse, 1991, p xxii). Echoing the 'honest broker or 'intellectual arbitrage' ideas espoused by fundraisers, being an effective link means finding ways to reconcile the often conflicting demands and expectations of people within and outside of the organisation – staff, colleagues, volunteers, trustees and donors – and to do so in a 'statesman'-like way, without compromising the quality of any of the interpersonal relationships (Burlingame and Hulse, 1991, p xxii).

Fundraisers as connectors

The idea of fundraisers as connectors is promoted by many authors. Williams states that fundraisers facilitate the philanthropic process by 'connecting[ing] values with visions, ideals with ideas, aspirations with resources and problems with solutions' (Williams, 2016, p 20).

Levy writes that fundraisers need to identify the intersection between the interests of donors and the needs of the charity and then forge the connection in order to 'easily tap' resources (Levy, 2009, p xxvi). One Australian study comes to a similar conclusion, stating that a distinguishing feature of the fundraising function, especially in relation to major gifts, is to *connect* donors to organisations (Scaife et al, 2011, p 27). Drawing on interviews with both fundraisers and donors, they describe the task as being primarily about making connections and building bonds between those seeking, and those able to give, resources. The quality of that bond is deemed crucial: 'If poorly executed it can kill a giving relationship' (Scaife et al, 2011, p 28), and they conclude that the ability of the fundraiser to make high-quality connections with supporters 'makes the difference between a long-term commitment to the cause and disengagement (Scaife et al, 2011, p 26).

Fundraisers as matchmakers

The idea of fundraising as 'matchmaking' appears relatively often in both the practice and the academic literature. Accord to Rosso and Associates: 'Fundraising is at its best when it strives to match the needs of the not-for-profit organisation with the contributor's need and desire to give (Rosso and Associates, 1991, p 7). Mutz and Murray describe fundraisers as 'matchmaker[s] of good works and good people' (Mutz and Murray, 2010, p 9), while Matheny describes fundraisers as being in the business of 'joyful matchmaking' (Matheny, 1999, p 104). The same concept goes by the name of 'co-orientation theory' in the academic literature, such that the relationship between donors and charitable organisations is founded on 'the principle of matching needs' (Kelly, 1998, p 357).

Fundraisers as 'middlemen'

Whether described as links, connectors or matchmakers, these concepts are particularly useful in explaining why fundraisers are able to do something that so many people seem to find unappealing, or even distasteful, namely, asking for money. As one interviewee explains: "The fundraiser who sees themselves primarily as a connector doesn't worry about asking for money because it's not for them!" (Female, B). This quote highlights a commonality across depictions of the art of fundraising in the literature: the focus on the fundraiser's positioning between the organisation and its supporters, and the mission and the means, in order to bring benefits to all. This perspective sees the fundraiser as essentially an intermediary or, in old-fashioned terminology, a 'middleman'.

Middlemen play a significant role across modern society, despite predictions of their demise as a result of new technology (Krakovsky, 2015). The ability for buyers and sellers of all sizes to interact directly on the internet was expected to result in 'friction free capitalism', according to Bill Gates (1995). Yet that did not come to pass, and middlemen now make up a larger part of the economy than ever before (Krakovsky, 2015, p 3). A new tranche of 'internet intermediaries' has recently arisen, which 'give access to, host, transmit and index content originated by third parties or provide Internet-based services to third parties' (OECD, 2010, p 4). As with offline middlemen, they succeed by establishing trusting relationships with, and providing value to, both buyers and sellers. Internet intermediaries help people to negotiate everything from global travel (such as TripAdvisor) to securing a local taxi (such as Uber), and from managing personal finances (such as MoneySavingExpert) to managing personal relationships (such as Facebook, Tinder).

While often experienced as direct ('friction free') connections, these technologically enabled interactions rely on overlooked – often invisible – intermediaries who try to make transactions simpler and less risky, for example, by inventing and implementing ratings systems, and by filtering content that appears in social media feeds. While the parallels between e-commerce and fundraising should not be overstretched, the evidence from both the extant literature and the new data presented in this book is that fundraisers can be understood as a type of intermediary because they exist to add value to both charities and supporters, they succeed as a result of establishing trusting relationships, and, at best, they make philanthropic interactions simpler, less risky and more enjoyable by reducing the distance between donors and recipients.

However, this is not an unproblematic depiction of what fundraisers do, because the work of middlemen is 'abstract, intangible, and often nebulous' (Krakovsky, 2015, p 10) and therefore frequently attracts contempt. Easily dismissed as parasites, incapable of productive activity, they can also be accused of reducing value as a result of the costs they incur – notably their salary and overheads, in the case of paid fundraisers. The contribution they make is not easy to discern, but to create value by facilitating transactions that would not otherwise have happened, thereby enlarging the size of the pie and making all parties better off, requires distinctive skills and practices.

The general disdain for middlemen is neatly expressed by economist Robert L. Steiner, who noted that, 'Society honors those who build better mousetraps but suspects those who market mousetraps better' (Steiner, 1976, p 2). This sentiment is probably also exacerbated by the lack of perceived professionalism involved (discussed further in Chapter 6), as there are no classes or formal education on how to be a middleman. However, their knowledge and practices are increasingly well understood by, and sometimes drawn from, social science research, such as the economics of transactions and game theory, as well as sociological studies on social networks and reputation management (Krakowsky, 2015, p 14).

Conclusions

This chapter has described and illustrated the 'art' of fundraising, which differs from the 'mechanical manipulation' typified in the scientific approach (Gurin, 1991, p 3). The literature points to a need for fundraisers to adapt a specific mindset in order to succeed at asking for money, and the new data adds detail to this exhortation by suggesting that personal qualities such as being engaging intermediaries, and avoiding getting caught up in the process are essential for significant fundraising success.

The 'art' can seem inaccessible and unteachable, as when successful fundraisers say (as one interviewee did): "Look after the donors and the rest will look after itself" (Female, B) – this is clearly of limited value to new recruits seeking direction and insight into best practice and professional expectations. This explains why the two most common methods of acquiring fundraising skills (as listed in Table 7, Chapter 2) are 'Learning on the job' and 'Learning by working alongside a more experienced fundraiser'. The next chapter draws on descriptions of both the art and the science of fundraising in order to establish what it is that fundraisers actually do.

Notes

[1] Definition from the online *Oxford English Dictionary*. Available at: www.oed.com.chain.kent.ac.uk/view/Entry/198998?redirectedFrom=tenacious#eid (last accessed 6 June 2017; log-in required).

FIVE

What do fundraisers do?

A chapter on what fundraisers do might be expected to be rather short and unrevealing. Surely the clue is in the name? But the existing literature, and the new data collected for this study, highlight the diversity and complexity of the work undertaken by fundraisers, and paint a far more nuanced picture of the everyday reality of being employed in this role than a literal interpretation of the job title suggests.

Fundraisers do far more than 'raise funds'

When I first began this research into what fundraisers do, and asked someone that very question, they responded with this joke:

> Did you hear the one about the doctor, the lawyer and the fundraiser who all die at the same time? When they reach the pearly gates of heaven, St Peter offers the doctor, who arrives first, a single wish as a reward for doing so much good on earth. The doctor asks for a million pounds and walks through the gates into eternal paradise. The lawyer, who is second in line, overhears the conversation and when his turn comes he asks for – and gets – a billion pounds. Next up comes the fundraiser. When St Peter asks what reward she'd like, she says: "I know it's a big ask, but could I have the business cards of the two people who were just in front of me?"

This joke is much loved within the fundraising world because it acknowledges and celebrates the all-consuming nature of the job, and highlights many of the qualities discussed in previous chapters, such as tenacity, opportunism and confidence in their interpersonal skills.

Contrary to public perceptions, fundraising is not solely focused on raising funds (Waters, 2016, p 423). There is one simple truth that underlies any discussion of what fundraisers do: they are *proactively* working to do whatever it takes to legally and ethically secure the resources their charity needs to fulfil its mission. As the UK's Institute of Fundraising, somewhat wearily, notes, 'This money does not appear by magic – donors need to be asked for donations' (Institute of Fundraising, 2011, p 7). It ought to be unnecessary to state this basic fact, but given the lack of awareness of the fundraising function described in my introductory chapter, it is worth emphasising that fundraisers are not sitting on the sidelines watching surprise donations come in.

As noted in the Introduction, the job of fundraising is often assumed to be exclusively focused on asking for money, but such a restricted definition is unhelpful and misleading, and even 'insultingly narrow' (Worth and Asp, 1994, p 6). The only study to quantify how paid fundraisers spend their time concludes that only just over a tenth (13%) of a typical fundraiser's working week is taken up with activities that involve directly asking for support, and the bulk of the rest of the time is spent interacting with, and building relations with, potential supporters (Duronio and Tempel, 1997, p 38). For this reason, most fundraisers do not see 'raising funds' as their central task. Indeed many, especially those who work closely with major donors and other personalised forms of fundraising, do not use the word 'fundraiser' or 'fundraising' in their job title or on their business card, preferring instead to use terms such as 'development director', 'partnerships' or 'head of philanthropy'. While this could be interpreted as typical British reticence to mentioning money, we will see in this chapter that it accurately reflects the reality of the daily tasks of the most successful fundraisers, whose work goes far beyond the isolated task of solicitation.

This chapter draws on existing literature and the new data collected for this study on both the 'art' and the 'science' of fundraising, to describe a new, comprehensive model that depicts what it is that fundraisers do. This model capture the diversity and complexity of the fundraising role, subsuming the multifarious tasks and goals under three broad types of work: fostering a philanthropic culture within the charity and in wider society; framing the needs being met by the charity, and; facilitating donations.

Each part of this triad is explained and illustrated with a range of examples, followed by a discussion of the emotional labour this entails, and introducing a new concept of 'gratitude work' as a distinctive core feature of the job of fundraising. The chapter ends with a summary and reflections on how the sociocultural context in the UK shapes and affects perceptions of what fundraisers can and must do in order to succeed.

The three 'Fs': a new framework to explain what fundraisers do

The proposed new model to explain what fundraisers do has three elements:

1. **Fostering** a philanthropic culture – both within the charity and in wider society.
2. **Framing** needs – to establish the legitimacy of the cause and educate potential donors about the existence of credible voluntary solutions.
3. **Facilitating** donations – provide a trusted and, where possible, enjoyable way for donors to respond to needs.

The Foster-Frame-Facilitate triad encompasses the multiplicity of tasks depicted in prior research and in the present study, as explained in further detail below. It is important to note that these tasks are not sequential: fundraisers must simultaneously foster, frame and facilitate, because fundraising is not a linear process (Lindahl, 2010, p 174). The description of this triad is followed by a discussion of the 'emotional labour' involved in all aspects of this work, introducing the concept of 'gratitude work' as a distinctive, though as yet overlooked, feature of the fundraising function.

Fostering a philanthropic culture

There is a known and measurable connection between fundraising success and the existence of a positive culture of philanthropy (Bell and Cornelius, 2013), such that it is difficult for fundraising to be successful in contexts where philanthropy is not understood as a legitimate, necessary and positive activity. A global comparative study finds that fundraising is more advanced in countries where there is: greater awareness of the role and contribution of philanthropy; normative expectations that prompt charitable giving; widespread social rewards, such as recognition of, and esteem for, donors; and enabling social policies, such as tax breaks for donations (Breeze and Scaife, 2015, p 588). Cumulatively, these features signal social, cultural and political encouragement for, and approval of, charitable giving, creating a more fertile environment in which fundraisers can do their work.

The benefits of fostering the right cultural context for fundraising accrue beyond the ask, as Ward explains: 'donors' post-decision concerns and emotions about the wisdom of gifts and the agents' integrity are best preempted or assuaged if their cultures accord a positive valence both to acts of charity and to the soliciting agents' (Ward, 2015, p 576). However, the reverse is also true: fundraising is more difficult in contexts that lack a generally positive culture of philanthropy. As discussed in the introductory chapter, despite most people in the UK making charitable donations (62% donated at least once in 2015 (CAF, 2016)) there remains 'an ambivalent approach to the idea and practice of charity' (Mohan and Breeze, 2015, p 2), manifested in much cynical and critical reporting of philanthropy in UK media, which deters some rich people from starting or increasing their giving (Breeze and Lloyd, 2013, pp 157–8). When philanthropic acts raise suspicions of tax-dodging, reputation-mongering and outsized egos, rather than attracting instinctive approval, this has implications for the solicitation process. For example, fundraisers are less likely to be able to leverage the 'prestige motive' to help motivate donors, as is possible in countries such as the US, where being a philanthropist remains an aspirational identity and is more likely to generate personal cachet (Harbaugh, 1997). Therefore, one consequence of a 'fundraising-unfriendly' context is that it reduces the number of tools available for the fundraiser to use. Another consequence is that it increases the fundraisers' workload because they need to fill the 'appreciation gap' and compensate for the criticism that donors may receive from other quarters, notably the media.

Given the crucial important of an enabling context, and the proactivity (as described in previous chapters) that is typical of successful fundraisers, it is unsurprising that they make efforts to shape and mould the philanthropic culture both within and without their charitable organisations. The work of fostering a philanthropic culture is essential but time-consuming, and includes at least the following four elements:

1. nurturing constituencies in which potential supporters might emerge;
2. investing in building community among potential and existing donors;
3. fostering relationships – real and imagined – between donors and beneficiaries; and
4. building a philanthropic culture within their own charitable organisation.

Nurturing constituencies in which potential supporters might emerge

Studies of charitable decision making show that donors usually give to causes with which they have had some prior personal contact

(Breeze, 2013a; Breeze and Lloyd, 2013). But given the plethora of worthy causes seeking support, a basic connection to an organisation, such as being an alumnus or attending concerts in the building, is not enough by itself to trigger philanthropic action. Rather, donors need to identify with the cause and become part of the charitable organisation's 'community of participation' (Schervish and Havens, 1997).

Interesting communications, such as alumni magazines, newsletters, emails and websites, help to build a sense of belonging to a community, especially if they include interactive elements such as sections in which readers can share their news and updates. Events that are focused on gaining and strengthening contacts rather than generating an immediate financial return, such as receptions, open days and behind-the-scenes tours are also key 'friend-raising' strategies. For potential donors capable of making significant gifts, this process involves personal and face-to-face efforts to establish and nurture relationships, with some stating that the central role of fundraiser is to offer donors meaningful participation in the charity (Prince and File, 1994, p xv). However, the shift from friend-raising to fund-raising is not clear-cut: having grown a community of participation, fundraisers cannot simply demand support from those who identify with their cause – rather, they must continue nurturing the constituencies from which donors might emerge and continue investing in, and befriending, potential supporters (Godfrey, 2016, p 89).

Investing in building community among potential and existing donors

The next stage involves investing in building community among and between potential and existing donors. In some small and local charities, it is possible that donors will know and be known to each other. But in most cases, the task of building these networks requires fundraisers to mediate a 'community of strangers' (Silber, 1998, p 139). Again, communications and events are typical methods, though more intimate and personalised activities, such as lunch with the Chair of trustees (who may themselves be one of the charity's biggest donors) or a small group meeting with an influential figure connected to the charity (for example, a renowned opera singer or a royal patron), may be suitable for subsets of potential donors judged to have a high giving capacity.

Once built, these networks can be useful in many ways, including providing 'social proof' for members who become aware of the charitable choices of peers and people they may admire, at the same time as becoming more aware of the needs of those around them (Godfrey, 2016, p 92). They can also be useful in opening up new avenues of potential support when members invite family or friends to become involved, or even to donate, as they are more likely to respond to requests from someone within their existing communities of participation. As Matheny states, 'It's true that people give to people, but it's even truer that people give to peers' (Matheny, 1999, p 12).

Fostering relationships between donors and beneficiaries

Fundraisers need large numbers of connections and relationships with people inside and outside the charity in order to perform optimally (Ferris, 2011, p xi). In addition to the obvious relationships with potential supporters, donors, colleagues and volunteers, they also need – where feasible – to be connected to the organisation's beneficiaries, because philanthropy is fundamentally about social relations between donors and recipients (Ostrander and Schervish, 1990). Both the giver and the receiver are needed for a gift transaction to take place, yet with the exception of some charitable transactions – for example, where donors provide patronage to talented artists and scholars – it is not usually possible or desirable for beneficiaries to interact directly with donors. In the past, beneficiaries were often humiliated by being made available for viewing by their benefactors 'who could not help but feel a thrill of satisfaction as they contemplated the living fruits of their benevolence' (Owen, 1965, p 61), but modern charitable transactions are more respectful of human dignity and avoid stigmatising recipients or exacerbating inequalities.

The solution to the 'missing beneficiary' puzzle has been solved in the comparable context of blood donation banks. A study shows that blood bank staff 'supplement an imagined relationship to imagined recipients with a real social relationship to real nurses at the real blood bank' (Dalsgaard, 2007, p 109). Blood bank staff accept, care for, and show appreciation to blood donors, despite not being the actual recipients of the donated blood. They offer token counter-gifts of recognition such as food and drink, as well as stickers and pin badges so the donor can signal their altruism. In this way, blood bank staff offer a 'real social relationship that provides the donor with acceptance and appreciation', which increases the likelihood they will return to donate blood again as a result of being caught up in reciprocal social interactions (Dalsgaard, 2007, pp 109, 104). This explanation is directly transferable to situations involving donations of money and other resources instead of blood. Just like blood bank staff, fundraisers take on the obligations of the absent beneficiary, giving 'the other' in the interaction a human face, accepting the gift, recognising the donor's altruism, and offering counter-gifts, such as thanks and appropriate recognition, in order to increase the likelihood of a repeat gift (although, as with any gift exchange, this is never guaranteed). The risks involved in gift-giving, and the labour of 'gratitude work', are discussed further below.

Building a philanthropic culture within charities

The final element of 'fostering' a philanthropic culture relates to activity *within* the charity. Fundraisers operate in both internal and external arenas and must dedicate substantial effort to building a culture of philanthropy within their organisation in order to support the solicitation process (Bell and Cornelius, 2013; Worth and Asp, 1994, pp 27, 37). Many fundraising handbooks emphasise that fundraising is not a solitary effort, but rather requires the support of colleagues across the organisation. For example, Holman and Sargent explain that: 'Major gift fundraising ... is the culmination of a collective effort across the organisation to create a major donor-friendly culture within your charity' (Holman and Sargent, 2006, p 138).

Many interviewees describe working in charities that lack a culture of philanthropy. The comment below also references the 'magical qualities' expected of fundraisers, discussed in Chapter 3:

> I've had bitter experiences of working in charities where they just don't care about the fundraisers: they don't back you up, they just expect you to wave a magic wand and come back nine months later with a big pot of money and no questions asked. As soon as you start asking for things like contacts, or information, they think that you're not doing your job. (Male, A, B)

Therefore, many fundraisers need to spend time convincing, educating and coaching the senior management team about fundraising (Daly, 2013, p 26) and encouraging their chief executive and trustees to embrace a donor-centred philosophy (May, 1997, p 33).

Interviewees concurred with this view, and expressed frustration at the time and effort required to explain and defend their role within the charity:

> There's still this view that fundraisers are the sales people, that we're slightly parasitic. We have to explain to non-fundraising colleagues what we do and how we do it. They think: "it's the dirty money, let's not talk about it, it's not

> the pure bit of the organization". But I think: "if we don't bring in the money, you can't do the work". (Female, A)

But interviewees also recognised their reliance on colleagues as sources of information and interesting insights to share with donors, and understood that supporters usually prefer to meet the charity's leaders and programme staff, who can share interesting stories from the front line: 'It's essential to find colleagues within the organisation who have the charisma and willingness to meet donors – their passion for the organisation is more important than their seniority. If you don't have colleagues you can present to donors then you're stuck' (Female, A, B).

This means that fundraisers are often simultaneously isolated in doing a job that is not well understood or appreciated, and yet are 'inextricably bound' to their organisation (Bloland and Bornstein, 1991, p 106) and reliant on their colleagues, because even the best fundraiser cannot have much success in an organisation that is not fulfilling its mission, is poorly run, or is not meeting the needs of clients (Dorsey, 1991, pp xvi–xvii). This codependency results in successful fundraisers accepting the task of fostering an internal culture of philanthropy as part of the job, and viewing their colleagues as part of their team: 'Good fundraisers see the finance team, you know, the support teams and the services team as all part of the same team … Poor fundraisers talk a very, kind of, 'us and them' language about the rest of the organisation and I just don't think that's effective' (Female, A, B).

A lack of collegiality can be evident when colleagues hold – and express – normative negative views about asking for money, as one interviewee related:

> I saw a colleague talking to a really important prospect [prospective donor] at a party, who could have single-handedly funded a project that I know really mattered to that colleague. So I made my way over to join them. My colleague saw me coming and I heard him turn to this man and say: "Here comes our fundraiser, watch your wallet!" (Male, A, B)

When this incident was related to other fundraisers, most groaned in recognition and said that something similar had happened – often more than once – to them. For example, another interviewee recalled this similarly excruciating incident. A trustee had agreed to set up a lunch meeting with a wealthy friend who had expressed interest in the charity's work. Once they and the fundraiser were settled at the table, the trustee stood up to walk away, saying: "Right! I'll leave you with our fundraiser to do the dirty work" (Male, A, B).

Another interviewee offered an explanation of such incidents, which helpfully illuminates a key difference between fundraisers and their colleagues. She said, of the latter: "it's because they feel uncomfortable with the situation of asking for money – they're trying to break a tension that only they are feeling!" (Female, A). The same interviewee then emphasised how crucial it is to work in a 'fundraising-friendly' environment: "Fundraisers cannot be good if they are not in a supportive environment. It's not about a huge budget, but a supportive culture" (Female, A).

Despite the difficulties, and what can be construed as unnecessary distraction, of expending energy on fostering an internal culture of philanthropy, it remains a priority for most successful fundraisers, in part because of its simple necessity but also, in the words of another interviewee: "You have to be able to inspire colleagues as well as donors, and persuade them to follow you. Its about conviction and belief. If you can't do that, you really can't do the job" (Male, A, B).

Framing needs

We turn now to the second element of what fundraisers do: framing needs to establish the legitimacy of causes and to educate potential donors about the existence of credible voluntary solutions. Gunderman explains: 'It is important for fundraisers to function in part as educators, encouraging and helping donors to understand better who they are, what they really care about, and how they can best go about making the difference they hope to make' (Gunderman, 2010, p 592).

As noted in the introductory chapter, a significant barrier to charitable action is lack of awareness of the existence and urgency of some needs (Chapman and McGuinness, 2013). This can be the result of geographical distance, living in different social worlds to those with needs, or the lack of tangibility of some needs, such as environmental issues, disaster prevention and scientific research. Therefore a key role for fundraisers is drawing attention to needs that might otherwise be neglected, and framing them in such a way as to encourage a philanthropic response. One interviewee explains: "Fundraisers are a bit like Venetian storytellers, going down to the wharf to get stories from visitors to take back to their neighbourhoods" (Male, A, B). While some people will be grateful to be alerted in this way and will respond as prompted, others will resent the intrusion of 'moralists at the feast' making demands on their private resources (MacQuillin, 2014).

Therefore this act of framing is essential and yet risks exacerbating public hostility to fundraising.

Nonetheless, the charitable sector exists to respond to demands that are not currently being met by either the state or the market (Hansmann, 1987; Salamon, 1987). Therefore, as the people charged with raising the funds to fulfil the mission, fundraisers must articulate that hitherto ineffectively expressed demand, despite knowing it will receive a hostile reaction from some quarters. Research suggests this is an effective strategy as there is empirical evidence for a 'theory of situational support', which states that information provided by fundraisers interacts with other factors, such as affinity to the cause, to prompt philanthropic behaviours (McKeever et al, 2016). This makes instinctive sense, not only because people cannot offer help when they are unaware that help is needed, but also because there is a long history of humanitarians questioning formerly unquestioned social practices, such as child labour, prison conditions and animal abuse, which has played a pivotal role in the cultural reconstruction of pain and suffering, and initiating a public, voluntary response (Halttunen, 1995). This creates an onerous responsibility for fundraisers, who are tasked with both framing needs, for example, by selecting images that represent deserving need, and proposing the appropriate response (Longmore, 2015).

The framing of needs also requires subject knowledge and patience. Major donors sometimes have a high level of expertise in the work of the organisations they support, and understandably prefer to interact with someone who can speak proficiently on the topic. In some cases, a fundraiser can call on the help of in-house experts, such as programme or policy staff. As one university-based fundraiser explained: "I have to bring in a bioscience academic to get credibility when asking for donations in that area" (Female, A). But most charities are small and becoming an 'instant expert' is another task that successful fundraisers are often obliged to take on:

> In all the charities I've worked in, the fundraisers are expected to have knowledge only second to the people actually doing the work. I enjoy that, I worked in children's charities for ten years and I understood all the policy side of things, then I moved to a medical research charity and that was a big change but I liked challenging myself. I didn't have a clue about [the disease] so the first thing I did was read everything I possibly could – I still am – that's part of

> what I love about my job, you're given the time and you're expected to get that level of knowledge. (Male, A)

Karoff confirms the view that donors want enhanced learning opportunities, and 'intellectual substance about issues and programs', and that they expect fundraisers to play a key role in this regard: 'We think fundraising that provides donors with information that goes beyond the typical case statement into a true learning experience is where the field is going. And lest this sound excessively supply side or paternalistic, donors have consistently told us that they would welcome such knowledge' (Karoff, 2005, p 52).

In some cases, donors' enthusiasm for a cause is not accompanied by any degree of specialist knowledge, so the framing needs to be done in a respectful way that allows donors to ask naïve questions "without feeling like a dinosaur" – as one interviewee put it, before going on to explain that:

> in a situation where a donor asks a really stupid question, and clearly doesn't know very much about what we do, the fundraiser has to be curious about what's led them to have that meeting in the first place. There's some bit of interest there, so can I ask the right question that is going to expand their interest? Can I get them to engage and find a way to help them think more broadly about it and become more interested? I do think that part of our role is inspiring people to be more curious, to find out, to engage more and actually to want that. (Female, A)

Facilitate donations

The third, and final, aspect of what fundraisers do is to facilitate donations by providing a trusted and, where possible, enjoyable way for donors to respond to needs. This involves at least three elements:

1. enabling people to act on altruistic intentions;
2. supporting volunteers to make the ask; and
3. providing ongoing donor care to prompt repeat gifts.

Enabling people to act on altuistic intentions

The word 'facilitate' derives from the French word *facile*, and therefore means to make an action or process easy. Crucially, it does not imply spurring or provoking an action, but rather providing assistance for something that someone already wishes to do. The prior work of fostering the philanthropic impulse and framing needs does involve trying to influence prevailing contexts such as how people think about needs and their potential response to those needs. But, despite widespread assumptions, the fundraising process does not culminate in exerting undue pressure on unwilling subjects, but rather enabling them to put their existing altruistic intentions into action.

This point was well made over 100 years ago by the African-American leader Booker T. Washington, who described in his autobiography how he raised significant sums for the Tuskegee Institute in Alabama: '*I am not a beggar* … the main rule by which I have been guided in collecting money is to do my full duty in regard to giving people who have money an opportunity to help' (Washington, 2016, p 328, my emphasis).

A more recent expression of this view states that: 'Fundraising is proclaiming what we believe in such a way that we offer other people an opportunity to participate with us in our vision and mission. *Fundraising is precisely the opposite of begging*' (Nouwen, 2010, p 16, my emphasis).

The insistence that fundraising is more about facilitation than solicitation, enabling those with resources to implement their altruistic intentions, was a common theme in the interviews, exemplified by this quote: "You're giving people the information and the evidence to enable them to do something that they want to do, you're not standing over them and saying 'You must give'!" (Male, A). Therefore – and despite widespread assumptions to the contrary – fundraising is not about talking someone into making a gift they do not wish to make. Matheny refers to this misunderstanding of what fundraisers do as the 'myth of persuasion', and notes that even many fundraisers ascribe their success in generating gifts to 'a personal power to persuade' (Matheny, 1995, pp 34–5). But however good the fundraiser's pitch, it is unlikely to change donors' views, based on decades of lived experience and social conditioning, about the nature of problems and how best to solve them. Instead of persuasion, what the fundraiser does, according to Matheny, is 'aggressive listening', which entails asking questions such as: "How do you think we should handle the problem of homelessness?" or "Welfare and unemployment have been with us forever. Any ideas on how to find solutions?" Having found out how the potential donor thinks about the problem and the solution, the fundraiser is then able to offer a funding proposal that reflects their frame of reference and is in line with the charity's philosophy and strategy.

Successful fundraisers understand that tailoring the ask to the donor's world view is the most likely route to a successful outcome, and that this is better described as a strategy of alignment, not of persuasion. Ideally, the donor will feel like a partner in achieving the charity's mission rather than a part of the fundraising process (Armson and McKenzie, 2013, p 25). While this is an ideal outcome, it also has the perverse consequence of further marginalising the fundraising function because the donor is a 'programme partner' rather than a 'product' of the fundraising department. Nonetheless, best practice among successful fundraisers reflects the axiom that: 'The idea to give must come from the donor. The facilitation of the idea is the responsibility of the [fundraiser]' (Matheny, 1995, p 43).

However, it is important to clarify that 'not persuading' is not equivalent to 'not asking'. In the introductory chapter it was clarified that direct requests are necessary to trigger the underlying motivations that lead to a wide range of altruistic behaviours (Simmons et al, 1977; Drake et al, 1982; Oliner and Oliner, 1988; Yaish and Vaese, 2001; Musick and Wilson, 2007, pp 288–91). A clear and direct request removes any ambiguity about what help is needed, and minimises the 'bystander effect', whereby a diffusion of perceived responsibility – essentially, assuming that someone else will step up – prevents otherwise well-intentioned people from offering help (Darley and Latané, 1968; Yaish and Vaese, 2001, p 4).

So the fundraiser must usually make an ask, but it may not always look like an ask to a fly on the wall, as this interviewee explains:

> You can't be very direct, it's all in the set-up, all those little nuances, the bits and pieces of how you build it and how you engage them. You want to lead somebody to a point where the conversation becomes quite mutual and quite open, It's really a conversation about helping donors to understand how they can make a difference. (Female, A)

Other interviewees note that the ask can be implicit if the preparatory work has been done well: 'I always say it's analogous to an old-fashioned courtship. People who are ready to be asked, actually ask you. I equate it to a marriage proposal – not many men get down on bended knee until they know the woman will say yes (Female, A, B). This reflects the common 'fundraising as courtship' analogy used by practitioners such that: 'by the time you are ready to ask a donor for a gift, the donor is ready to be asked' (Axelrod, 2000, p 48). However, the opacity involved in such conversations that appear to skirt around the key question can add to the confusion of colleagues about what it is fundraisers do, as this interviewee relates:

> We still have it here that, you know: "yes, you've got a team of young women, because they're all attractive, they're good at drinking champagne, you know, and they can ask rich men for money". And you think "really? You think that's what we do, we just rock up to a party, flirt and get the money?" Our donors are not stupid, they've made their money, and they're looking for an investment ... It's an equal partnership. When you're getting to ask for that significant gift, you're there as an intellectual equal. (Female, A)

Supporting volunteers to make the ask

Despite the examples above featuring paid fundraisers doing the asking, a distinctive feature of the facilitation stage is the involvement of volunteers. These are typically either members of the charity board or existing donors who are known to, or respected by, the person being asked. As one interviewee explains: "The two most powerful word in fundraising are 'join me' and that is more powerful coming from another donor or a volunteer, or from the founder or chief executive who has spent their life in the charity" (Female, A, B).

Organised philanthropy involves enabling people to act together to accomplish something worthwhile, and part of the role of fundraisers is to minimise their contribution to encourage volunteers and let them have the most credit (Payton et al, 1991, p 13). This is not simply false modesty, because it is rare that any one person is solely responsible for raising any major gift, which is usually the result of years of cultivation and good stewardship by predecessors, colleagues and volunteers (Woods, 1997, p 7). Yet etiquette demands that paid fundraisers downplay any role they have had, as it is considered 'gauche and unprofessional to claim any credit for the success of a campaign ... [instead they should] give credit to the volunteer fundraisers, and make light of [their] own role' (Gurin, 1985, p 106).

However, working through others and resisting accepting any credit for success has the consequence of heightening the invisibility of the fundraising function. As a fundraiser quoted in the extant literature remarks: 'Be sure your ego is in good shape because you will need to have a passion for anonymity' (cited in Worth and Asp, 1994, p 41). Farnhill goes so far as to compare fundraisers to windows into the charity that are absolutely transparent so that most of the time no one notices they are there (Farnhill, 2007, p 29). As discussed in Chapter 2, this willingness to forgo acknowledgement may well be related to gender dynamics, as fundraising is a female profession and therefore more likely to be an 'invisible career' (Daniels, 1988).

Providing ongoing donor care to prompt repeat gifts

Regardless of the extent to which their role is recognised and acknowledged, and whether they do it personally or through supporting volunteers, fundraisers usually do take the lead on facilitating gifts, and ideally do so in a way that is ideally pleasurable and life-enriching for donors. One study of 82 wealthy UK donors (Breeze and Lloyd, 2013) found that most (65%) believed the more professional approach of fundraisers was a significant positive factor in the recent development of philanthropy in the UK. All participants in that study reported that they gave:

> because in some way or other it enriches their life to do so. This need not mean it makes them deliriously happy (although this can be the case), but rather that giving brings a feeling of satisfaction at doing something worthwhile, or enjoyment due to the experiences it involves, or a renewed sense of meaning in life. (Breeze and Lloyd, 2013, p 100)

The facilitation process extends naturally from the ask to the post-ask experience, which involves thanking, appropriate acknowledgement, reporting back on the impact of the gift as agreed, and ongoing involvement of the donor in the life and work of the organisation. The continued involvement, cultivation, and care of those who give are a crucial and integral part of fundraising (Sprinkel Grace, 2005, p 141). This process is usually described as 'donor care' or 'donor stewardship' and is tailored, as far as possible, to the needs and preferences of each donor as these are known to be prime motivators of giving decisions (Breeze, 2013a). Gratitude is a key part of this phase, as discussed in greater detail below – however, the goal is not just to express a sincere thank you, it is about providing ongoing donor care that prompts repeat gifts by building sustainable social relationships within which the gift cycle can continue, ideally indefinitely.

Fundraising as a form of emotional labour

The level of intimacy and personal investment required to interact with potential and current donors in order to foster, frame and facilitate donations is why fundraising can rightly be described as a form of emotional labour. The term 'emotional labour' was coined by the sociologist Arlie Hochschild (1983), who wrote about 'the managed heart' of many employees in the service economy, who are required to manage their personal feelings in order to fulfil their contractual duties: for example, air stewardesses being compelled to smile while working, regardless of any personal sadness they may be experiencing or any obstreperous passengers they may be dealing with (Hochschild, 1983, pp 24-25). Hochschild's work introduced emotion into the field of organisational studies (Dutton et al, 2006, p 61), and the concept is equally applicable to understanding charitable organisations.

Expectations of how paid fundraisers must behave, and the emotions and related behaviours that are required for success in their job, are often quite explicit. These include the need to be passionate, cheerful, open (Norton, 2007, p 12); to be courageous (Holman and Sargent, 2012, p xii); to be energetic, self-confident and curious (Levy, 2009, p 41); to have patience and tact (Herbst and Norton, 2012, p 22); to have 'unbridled, unflinching, undying enthusiasm' (Panas, 2012, p 19); to be positive, funny, and humble (Hartsook, 1999, pp 21–4); to have 'a sincere interest in the donor as a person' (Stroman, 2014, p 134); and even to 'love' their donors, because they 'have to feel you care about them' (Pitman, 2007, p 49). 'How to' books for fundraisers note that giving is an emotional act rather than a financial transaction (Joyaux, 2011, p 11), and advise readers to 'harness the power of emotion … to open people's hearts and minds' (Burnett, 2006, pp 64–5).

In the present study, many fundraisers recounted situations where they felt required to use or manage their emotions in the course of their work, with a typical comment being: "when I'm having a bad day in my personal life, then I do still need to maintain a happy façade in front of the donors" (Female, A). Other interviewees confirmed that being upbeat was necessary for all types of face-to-face fundraising, not just with major donors. An interviewee who began her career as a street fundraiser explained: 'Donors read the emotions of the askers, so if I showed that I was feeling down then people would steer around me, whereas happy street fundraisers attract donors' (Female, A).

Working with major donors requires more emotional labour than other types of fundraising because it is conducted face-to-face and often involves extensive socialising outside of the office and office hours.

The demands of these social occasions exert a particular emotional pressure, as this example illustrates:

> One time I had to host a large-scale event, and there was a lot of, you know, politicians and important people like that attending. I'd broken up with my boyfriend before I arrived at the event and we'd been together for five years, so it was quite an emotional moment for me, but that was nothing that anyone in that room would know about. There's nothing that they would think was amiss in any way, shape or form and I just got on with it. Everyone had a great time and I was part of making it a great time. So, yes, you do give a lot of yourself in that way. And there have been other times when, you know, people have been barefaced rude to me and I've thought: "You know what? You've zapped the last little bit of energy that I had today and I've got another four hours before I can actually get home to bed". Sometimes this job absolutely zaps you, your emotional currency is all spent. (Female, A, B)

Another interviewee concurs:

> One does put an awful lot of one's own self into a fundraising role in a way that I think you perhaps don't have to in a more technical role. I put a huge amount of my own self into each donor. The personal investment that fundraisers need to make is very high and underrated. (Female, A, B)

Such stories of soldiering on in the face of personal and professional misery were not uncommon, but nor were the opposite scenarios where fundraisers deployed positive emotions, such as happiness, in order to demonstrate shared personal commitment to the cause, as mentioned in Chapter 3:

> I almost cried when a donor announced she was ready to make a big gift. I got very tactile and hugged her. I was worried it might be inappropriate but it seemed to reassure her that I was equally passionate about the cause and not just 'doing my job'. (Female, A)

Fundraisers also recounted how they enjoyed using their personal skills to positively influence the emotional experiences of others, as this example illustrates:

> It's amazing to be able to offer that to somebody, to facilitate that and to say, "Actually, because I'm here you've had a really great experience". I know I can make a difference to the tone of a party, and that's just a lovely thing. I quite enjoy the event organising side of the job for that reason: you can be in charge of somebody's happiness. (Female, A, B)

Other interviewees discussed the difficulty in maintaining the upbeat personality that they feel is expected of them, and which can be dented as a result of interacting with the very people who hold those expectations:

> Donors drain you, they sap your energy. Sometimes I just disappear. Sometimes I'm having a down day and I don't feel like effervescing, but you have to put your game face on. You feel so responsible – for the cause and for the donors and guests at events. So however tired I am, I put on another layer of make-up and I don't let myself yawn. (Female, A)

This is a classic illustration of emotional labour: masking and regulating one's own emotions because the job demands it and because the worker's personality is now a commodity like any other, available to 'effervesce' for the security of a salary. However, the 'commodification' argument advanced by Hochschild is not unproblematically transferable from a for-profit to a non-profit setting. Air stewardesses may 'sell their smiles' for a wage and other perks, such as free travel, but people who are paid to work in charities often also claim to be driven by higher motivations such as affinity with a particular cause or desire to make a positive difference (Handy, 1988, p 3), and see their job as a 'vocation' or a 'calling', as discussed further in Chapter 6. It may, therefore, be difficult to distinguish when a fundraiser is doing emotional labour because they have to, or because they want to. In many ways the distinction is irrelevant, as fundraisers are clearly engaged in frequent regulation of their emotions in order to succeed in their jobs: "You do have to be 'on'. You know, you have to be engaged and engaging and that takes effort. And actually if you think of fundraisers, you know, it takes a lot ... it can take a lot of *you*" (Female, A, B, emphasis in interviewee's intonation).

Fundraising has long been understood as an emotional business: 'It always was. It always will be' (Smith, 1996, p 14). The data presented in this book extends this analysis to describe fundraising as emotional labour within an emotional business, and we end this chapter by exploring a particularly crucial emotion for successful fundraising: gratitude.

Fundraising as gratitude work

While fundraising involves marshalling and managing a wide range of emotions, as described above, the emotion that recurs most frequently in my data is gratitude. This involves more than saying 'thank you' (though it is essential to do so clearly, swiftly and sincerely); it is about expressing gratitude in attitudes and actions as well as in words (Kelly, 1998, p 437; Gilchrist, 2000, p 5). Expressing gratitude also involves demonstrating that the gift was meaningful, by giving the donor information on how their money was put to work as intended (Kelly, 1998, p 440; Burk, 2003, p 10). Successful fundraisers describe being alert to, and able to create, opportunities to express thanks and give meaningful feedback, as well as devoting effort to identifying and cultivating reciprocal obligations so that their charity can benefit from the urge of others to 'repay'.

Being grateful is a quality of being thankful, as well as readiness to show appreciation for and to return kindness.[1] The sociological importance of gratitude was first noted by Simmel (1950), but was largely overlooked in the recent flourishing of studies on emotions, which tended to focus on negative emotions such as anger, grief and jealousy (for example, Stets and Turner, 2006). However, more recent studies have emphasised the significance of gratitude in building cohesive social relations, enhancing personal well-being, and encouraging helping behaviours (DeSteno et al, 2016). Given this triad of outcomes, it is unsurprising that successful fundraisers tend to be 'gratitude experts'.

As with any emotion, gratitude is manifested in both acts and attitudes. Organising thank-you letters (ideally with a thoughtful signature from someone the donor respects and admires, such as the CEO, Chair or a celebrity patron), and hosting events to thank supporters, are two of the most tangible types of 'gratitude work', but it is also manifested in the fundraiser's demeanour and willingness to use any communication or interaction as an opportunity to reinforce gratitude, as this example illustrates:

> One of our major donors is very keen on baking, so whenever I'm in a hotel (for work or pleasure) I always take the free plastic shower caps to give her when we next meet, as she says they're useful for putting over dough whilst it rises! I know she appreciates that I remembered her hobby, and handing them over is a little token of thanks as well as a good excuse to set up a meeting so I can share our latest developments and successes. (Female, A)

This exemplifies good gift-giving practice, as recommended in the 'how to' literature:

> Choosing a gift [for a donor] requires careful thought. Your decision on this point can enhance or destroy a relationship. Begin with your knowledge of the donor, his or her likes and dislikes, hobbies and activities. Instead of an expensive but impersonal gift, try to select a gift that reflects the personality of the donor. (Matheny, 1999, p 83)

Gratitude is also carefully embedded in the physical life of many charities by naming buildings and staff posts (such as 'the Smith Chair in Physics') in honour of donors, which sends a clear, public signal of recognition and gratitude that is often deeply appreciated. Reflecting on seeing his name attached to the Bramall Music Building at the University of Birmingham, Terry Bramall shares his emotional reaction: "I can't get over it; I'm still shaking when I talk about it. It's just incredible" (quoted in Breeze, 2012b, p 27).

Gratitude figures in the daily work of fundraisers in two distinct ways. First, and most obviously, fundraisers need to convey sincere gratitude on behalf of the organisation and its beneficiaries to all those who voluntarily provide resources so that the charity can fulfil its mission. This includes expressing gratitude simply for being given the time to discuss the charity (Pigeau, 2013, p 91). Second, fundraisers need to identify and generate opportunities where others feel a sense of gratitude *to* the charity, in order to build a constituency of potential donors who may decide to 'pay back' to an organisation from which they have benefited. This latter type of gratitude work is exemplified by the focus on alumni by university fundraising departments: after graduation, alumni typically receive regular updates via emails and magazines, invitations to reunions, help to stay connected with fellow alumni, and opportunities to be involved in the ongoing life of the university, for example, by providing mentoring or career advice to current students. The premise behind this effort, which absorbs 30% of total university fundraising costs (Ross-CASE, 2016, p 10), is that alumni receive significant professional and personal benefits from their association with the university, and will hopefully wish to express their gratitude by supporting their alma mater. The strategy appears to be successful, in 2014–15, over four fifths (81%) of individual gifts to universities came from their alumni (Ross-CASE, 2016, p 9).

Hospital fundraising is often explicitly focused on previous beneficiaries: in the US, this is called 'grateful patient fundraising'. In countries without privatised medicine, this may seem an unnecessary, and even objectionable, phenomenon, but – as we saw in Chapter 1 – despite the existence of the National Health Service, UK donors continue to prioritise donations to hospitals (Breeze, 2015; CAF, 2016, p 8). Furthermore, studies indicate that one function of fundraising from patients and former patients is to empower those who may be feeling disempowered by experiencing ill health (Walter et al, 2015). This is because grateful patient fundraising 'offers [patients] a way to give back, from which many gain a valid sense of meaning, contribution, and fulfillment' (Rum and Wheeler, 2016). The cycle of gratitude is clearly evident in this example: it feels uncomfortable to take (in this case, excellent medical care) without giving back, and fundraisers provide a mechanism for return gifts.

Charities without such an obvious 'constituency' of potential supporters as alumni and former patients can use other strategies to inculcate gratitude. In my first job as a fundraiser for a Catholic charity that helps young homeless people we held a 'thank you' mass for our supporters. It was a beautiful celebration with excellent music and a buffet reception afterwards, prepared by some of the people helped by the charity. I assumed we would pass around a collection plate during mass to receive donations, but my much more experienced boss said it was better to let the supporters leave the building feeling indebted to us, having enjoyed the event and the food and drink. He knew they'd be keen to pay us back and that we'd get bigger donations if we let that feeling grow for a few days. Of course, he was quite right!

Another important aspect of gratitude work is that fundraisers are willing to do 'the labour of gratitude' so that the real recipient doesn't have to. As noted above, fundraisers receive donations on behalf of the charity and the end beneficiaries, and thereby absorb any stigma, stress and humiliation of asking for help. As Offer explains: 'Giving gives rise to obligation, in other words a debt: the giver notches up an emotional and material credit, in the form of a bond on the recipient' (Offer, 1997, p 455). By inserting themselves between the donor and the recipient, fundraisers accept both the gift and its concomitant obligations, which helps to avert problems inherent in the power imbalance between those with resources and the – often powerless – end beneficiaries. Playing this role makes them 'heroes of social interaction', to use Gouldner's term (1973, p 275), because they are willing to bear the burden of unrepayable debt in a society where people prefer to avoid becoming indebted.

Fundraisers can sometimes share the burden with colleagues, and with non-vulnerable beneficiaries. For example, an orchestra may strike up 'happy birthday' for a major donor attending a concert, or a postgraduate student may meet with the donor funding his or her studies. But many fundraisers are working on behalf of beneficiaries who cannot express gratitude: not just in the case of children and vulnerable people whose privacy must be protected, but also recipients who live in distant countries; non-human end beneficiaries, such as the environment or historic buildings; charities working to prevent future harm, such as vaccination programmes and early childhood interventions; and charities working on behalf of those facing future needs but who have not yet, for example, contracted a disease or faced drowning at sea. Part of the historical development of fundraising involves the widespread raising of funds for imagined and as-yet non-existent beneficiaries, which is far removed from centuries of giving alms to visible paupers in the street. In all cases, the fundraiser has to represent and embody the end beneficiary, accept the gift and convey the gratitude that spurs further gifts.

Gratitude work can be more or less difficult as a result of the sociocultural context. For example, UK fundraisers arguably need to do more 'gratitude work' than their US counterparts, where philanthropy is more generally seen as a 'good thing' and donors can more confidently anticipate a wider positive reaction. Not all donors seek public recognition, of course; indeed a study of rich UK donors found that over two thirds (69%) had made at least one anonymous donation (Breeze and Lloyd, 2013, p 126). But when the donor is expecting or hoping for positive acknowledgement, the unpredictability of UK public opinion and media coverage of philanthropy means that fundraisers must devote more time and energy to the role of 'bearing witness' to donors' generosity. Efforts undertaken by UK fundraisers relate to filling both internal and external 'gratitude gaps'.

Internal gratitude gap

Interviewees report that non-fundraising colleagues can be unaware of the relevance of different sources of voluntary income, and the type and degree of gratitude that is subsequently required. While all donated income will appear on the same line in a charity's published accounts, a sacrificial donation from a living donor and a grant from the National Lottery[2] require different responses from charity representatives. But it is not simply a matter of more finely differentiating the sources, as different types and degrees of gratitude need to be expressed for first gifts, regular gifts, gifts after a long absence, gifts made in memory of loved ones and so on. As Sprinkel Grace advises in relation to the particular appreciation required for 'stretch gifts':

> When planning those to include in a stewardship event, do not forget the donor whose 'stretch gift' [defined as donations that are seemingly out of proportion to donor's resources] while perhaps modest by some standards, represents a major investment that is driven by the heart and value of that donor. (Sprinkel Grace, 2005, p 149)

Fundraisers therefore need to be vigilant in monitoring the meaning of the gift to the donor, responding appropriately, and filling any internal 'gratitude gap' in the organisation by, for example, prompting hand-written notes and phone calls from the CEO, or the Chair of trustees, or a particular member of staff from whom the donor would most like to receive thanks and acknowledgement.

Another common mistake made by non-fundraising colleagues is viewing the receipt of a gift as the *end*, rather than the *beginning* of a (hopefully) long-term relationship (Gilchrist, 2000, p 1). As gift theory explains, thanking is not the end of a process, but rather the necessary next step for continuing the gift-giving cycle (see, for example, Mauss, 2002; Silber, 1998). Yet, despite extensive empirical evidence that it is more efficient to invest in retention rather than recruitment activities (Sargeant, 2013), many fundraisers struggle to secure the necessary budget and time for good-quality donor stewardship.

External gratitude gap

Fundraisers working in a culture without a widespread positive appreciation of philanthropy, such as the UK, must also make extra efforts to fill the external gratitude gap, which has two dimensions.

First, as noted above, there is no guarantee that donations will receive general social approbation, indeed a critical public and media reaction is a distinct possibility, as one philanthropist explains: "You need to accept from the outset that whatever you do will be rubbished in newspapers" (quoted in Lloyd, 2004, p 234). The possibility that no one outside of the charity will notice or applaud even a very big donation means that fundraisers must work harder to reassure and thank donors, counteracting as far as they can any negative or cynical backlash, and compensating for the lack of cultural affirmation of philanthropy.

One interviewee recalled an occasion when a major charity announced its biggest-ever gift at an event attended by an 'A' list celebrity. The following day's headlines focused solely on the star's outfit, with no mention whatsoever of the philanthropic act for which she had dressed up. In such situations, unless someone makes a proactive effort to counterbalance the general apathy about a gift, and ensure the donor feels that their act was recognised and appreciated, then the gift-giving cycle risks grinding to a premature halt. Gifts need to be given, received and returned before the cycle can start again (Mauss, 2002). The 'return' phase is usually shouldered by the fundraiser, who either does or organises the gratitude work. This can be a lonely and difficult task that involves taking on a public attitude of indifference, or even contempt, especially of bigger donors. This inevitably involves some divergence of energy and resources from other fundraising tasks, and – as noted above – is one of the less obvious, but significant, differences between fundraising in the UK and the US, where fundraisers need not shoulder this burden alone.

The second aspect of the UK's gratitude gap is the lack of general awareness of philanthropically funded activity, and therefore less understanding of when 'payback' is expected. People who have lived and worked in the US often acknowledge, without prompting, what they have gained from previous generations of givers. For example, at the Carnegie medal ceremony held in Scotland in 2013, the American-born Nat Sloane talked about the gratitude his parents felt to the Carnegie Institute of Technology and how that gratitude impelled their donations in later life. At the same event, the current president of the Carnegie Corporation of New York, Vartan Gregorian, explained that his philanthropy was rooted in an awareness that "all my life I have been the beneficiary of other people's generosity" a point underlined in his autobiography (Gregorian, 2003).[3] People who perceive themselves as recipients see their donations as 'a return', which creates fertile territory for fundraisers who are then able to harness the full power of reciprocity. Kelly admonishes those who fail to see the importance of this idea: 'How foolish those fundraisers are who regard stewardship as technician tasks without any understanding of reciprocity's critical role in donor relations!' (Kelly, 1998, p 435). In the absence of this mindset – where recipients do not recognise themselves as such – fundraisers must work harder to encourage what is felt to be an initiating, rather than a reciprocating, gift.

In sum, the gratitude work undertaken by fundraisers is related to the philanthropic cultures, both within and without their organisations, and involves a more labour-intensive approach to working with supporters when the context is less conducive and when potential donors do not start from a position of feeling grateful, and therefore indebted, for what they have previously received.

Conclusions

This chapter has focused on what it is that fundraisers do in their everyday work. Drawing on the extant literature and data collected for this study, a new model was presented to capture the three key, iterative, aspects of fundraising:

1. fostering a philanthropic culture in society and within charitable organisations;
2. framing needs by establishing the legitimacy of causes and educating potential donors about the existence of credible voluntary solutions; and
3. facilitating donations by providing a trusted, life-enhancing and ongoing conduit for philanthropic giving.

This model provides further evidence that the job of fundraising involves a far wider remit than simply 'raising funds'. The level of intimacy and personal investment required to interact with potential and current donors in order to foster, frame and facilitate donations, was illustrated and formed the basis of the argument that fundraising is a form of emotional labour. While fundraising was shown to involve the marshalling and managing of a wide range of emotions, gratitude was shown to be a particularly significant, and distinctive, aspect of the work of fundraisers. The existence of a 'gratitude gap', both in typical charities and in wider UK society, such that donors rely disproportionately on fundraisers to accept, acknowledge and value their gifts, was identified as the prime reason why fundraising involves so much hard 'gratitude work'.

In sum, successful fundraisers are engaged in emotional work within an emotional business. Their time is spent on fostering, framing and facilitating philanthropy by creating conducive contexts in which philanthropy can thrive, by inspiring and educating both colleagues and donors, and by setting the stage for effective asking and giving. None of these are straightforward activities, and they require the 'art' and the 'science' described in the preceding chapters. What this amounts to in terms of the professionalisation, or otherwise, of fundraising, is the subject of the next chapter.

Notes

1. Definition from the online *Oxford English Dictionary*. Available at: www.oed.com.chain.kent.ac.uk/view/Entry/80957?redirectedFrom=gratitude#eid (last accessed 6 June 2017; log-in required).
2. The Big Lottery Fund is a quasi-governmental agency, or non-departmental public body, which distributes 40% of the money raised for good causes by the UK National Lottery. In 2014–15 this amounted to more than £1 billion in awards to projects with a social mission. For more information, see: www.biglotteryfund.org.uk/about-big (last accessed 30 December 2016).
3. This quote is from my own notes taken at the talk by Vartan Gregorian, part of the Carnegie medal ceremony held in the Scottish Parliament in Holyrood, Edinburgh on 17 October 2013.

SIX

What kind of job is fundraising?

The status of fundraising is still very much a matter of debate. Typical questions raised about the work of asking for money for a living include: Is fundraising a profession? If not, will it ever attain that status? Is it better described as a job, a career or a vocation? And is fundraising something that anyone can do, or does it require special attributes?

These questions matter because they relate directly to the shortage of talented fundraisers and subsequent recruitment crisis described in the introductory chapter. As Levy wryly notes: 'Proud and preening parents brag about their children being doctors and lawyers ... Have you ever heard a mother or father look up to the sky and say "Lord, I wish my child becomes a fundraiser!"? (Levy, 2009, p 2). Becoming a member of an established profession such as medicine or law often represents the fulfilment of a long-held dream and is a source of pride for the individual and their loved ones, yet people tend to 'fall into' fundraising (see Table 6, Chapter 2). Only a tiny percentage of current UK fundraisers (5%) say they 'always wanted to work as a fundraiser', and just under half (44%) describe it as an accidental rather than an aspirational career move.

Whether or not fundraising is a profession has attracted a disproportionate amount of attention in both the practitioner and academic literature, because for many people this label matters. In everyday usage, the word 'profession' signals a high-status occupation that commands – and deserves – respect, so it is an emotionally loaded concept (Bloland and Bornstein, 1991, pp 108–9). It impacts on practitioners' self-esteem and their perceived likelihood of being taken seriously by donors and colleagues, and consequentially their ability to raise the resources required by their organisation to achieve its charitable mission. So, for fundraising to be held in similar esteem to other, established, professions, is viewed not only as a self-serving desire by practitioners, but also as beneficial to the organisations for whom they work, as well as their clients and beneficiaries (Worth and Asp, 1994, p 50; Mixer, 1993, p 252).

This chapter begins by reviewing the debate on professionalism, exploring the different ways it is defined and why professional status matters. The claims for and against counting fundraising as a profession are then discussed, as well as alternative depictions of fundraising as a 'job', a 'calling' or a 'vocation'. In the light of the positions set out in the existing literature, and drawing on the new data collected for this study, the proposition is made that fundraising is best understood as a creative profession, which typifies the post-industrial service economy (Florida, 2012). Just as with artists, novelists, musicians and chefs, it is argued that success as a fundraiser results from a combination of creative innovation and managerial skills, and that fundraisers possess many of the traits commonly found in the creative class such as passion, openness, ability to synthesise, non-conformity and internal motivation. The chapter ends by asking whether this means that fundraising is dependent on some innate qualities, or whether anyone can learn how to be a successful fundraiser, regardless of their raw materials, if they apply themselves to the task.

The debate on professionalisation

There is a longstanding debate about what does, and what ought to, constitute a 'profession' (Tlili, 2016, p 1106). This is especially the case among sociologists for whom the topic of work has been a central concern throughout the discipline's existence (Parsons, 1968; Halford and Strangleman, 2009, p 811; Svarc, 2016, p 393). Despite its longevity, the terms of this debate have been noticeably consistent, with arguments about how to define professions fitting into one of two camps: the 'traits approach' and the 'power approach' (Tlili, 2016, p 1107).

The traits approach

Those who take the 'traits approach' argue that an occupation becomes a profession when it exhibits certain defining traits, such as an agreed body of knowledge that is taught and certified, a professional membership association, and a significant amount of autonomy in the workplace (see, for example, Macdonald, 1995). Box 1 summarises the traits that commonly feature in discussions of professionalism in relation to fundraising.

Box 1: Commonly used criteria to assess professional status

- A body of knowledge based on theory and research
- Commitment to, and identification with, the profession
- Autonomy of decision making
- A programme of formal and graduate-level education
- Professional and membership associations
- Shared standards of ethical behaviour, with accompanying sanctions
- A service orientation

Source: Based on Carbone, 1989, p 27; Kelly, 1998, pp 103–4; Scaife and Madden, 2006, p 3; Lindahl, 2010, p 82.

The power approach

Those who take the 'power approach' believe that the title of 'profession' cannot be claimed from within the ranks of the occupation but rather needs to be conferred from without, as a result of public recognition of the calibre of the expertise and the value of the service being provided. Thus, professional status relies on successful claims-making in the external environment rather than any particular progress within the occupation. Aldrich summarises this process whereby the profession 'establishes market control through convincing the public that the services it performs are vital and not readily learned by large numbers of people' (Aldrich, 2016, p 505). Power dynamics come into play in terms of the ability of any group of practitioners to make its case to a receptive audience, with inbuilt advantages for groups that enjoy pre-existing power and higher status, such as male-dominated and long-established occupations.

A combined approach

An alternative to these two camps places even higher demands on those seeking to acquire, or have bestowed, professional status. Kelly combines the 'traits' and 'power' approaches to defining a profession by listing traits that reflect those listed in Box 1, and then adding an additional criterion: that the profession is recognised by society as providing a 'unique and essential' service (Kelly, 1998, p 104).

As there is no universally agreed, definitive list of traits that are unique to occupations that are – or become – recognised as professions, the suggestion that professions are simply those that have gained the power to be known as such appears the most persuasive. The female domination of fundraising, and the relatively recent expansion of this paid workforce, also means that the 'power approach' offers a plausible explanation for difficulties encountered in achieving professional status, given normative views on gender and the lack of entrenched support.

Why does professional status matter?

Bell and Cornelius ask why fundraising is 'fighting to be recognized as a profession' (Bell and Cornelius, 2014, p 23), so it is important to note that this 'fight' exists in many occupations, including museum staff (Weill, 1990, cited in Tlili, 2016), psychiatrists (Bloch, 1997), and even chefs (Zopiatis, 2010). Professional status matters because it endows both the practice of fundraising and the fundraising practitioners with legitimacy (Bloland and Bornstein, 1991, p 69). Furthermore, the characteristics of classical professions include desirable features such as higher wages and prestige; exemption from routine, repetitive work; and lack of precariousness in the job market (Svarc, 2016); for these reasons, gaining professional status may help to attract more able recruits. Others argue that rebutting negative conceptions of fundraising is a prime driver of pursuing professional status. Drawing on Haskell's (1984) work, The Authority of Experts, Harrah-Conforth and Borsos suggest that professionalisation of fundraising is 'a demand for respect in an otherwise suspicious world, as well as an attempt to further the interests of the profession in a market economy' (Harrah-Conforth and Borsos, 1991, p 26).

However, professional status is no longer viewed as a simple binary such that an occupation is either a profession or it is not. In the current post-industrial service economy, where the position of the traditional professions has become 'uncertain and ambivalent' (Svarc, 2016, p 392), new and intermediary distinctions have been introduced. This development started with Etzioni's idea of the 'semi-professions' (1969) and now includes concepts such as 'new professionalism, extended professionalism, altered professionalism, deprofessionalization, quasi-, proto-, hybrid-, corporate-, multi-, and portfolio-professionalization' (Svarc, 2016, p 402). Others argue that professionalism is an ideal type rather than an attainable reality: 'a goal rather than a resting place' (Gurin, 1985, p 88) or 'an unreachable star' (Carbone, 1989, p 46). As Payton elaborates:

> Professionalism is an ideal: that is, it projects a vision of perfection that cannot be fully realized in reality. Professionalism is a regulative ideal: that is, it serves as a moral action-guide directing the professional toward right conduct … To be a professional [is] to make a claim to be trustworthy, not only in the sense of competence but in the moral sense as well. (Payton, 1998, p 492)

Bearing in mind the fine-grained distinctions of types of profession, and the possibility that professionalism is an aspiration rather than an achievable goal, we turn now to consider how the definitions others have offered can help us understand what kind of a job fundraising is.

Is fundraising a profession?

A handful of authors take it for granted that fundraising *is* a profession and simply describe it as such (Burnett, 2002, p 24; Greenfield, 2002; Wagner, 2002), but most choose to depict a Whiggish history of inevitable progress towards professional status, or more poetically chart the 'tide' of fundraising professionalism (Scaife and Madden, 2006, p 5). These latter depictions are exclusively reliant on the 'traits' approach, listing the generally agreed characteristics required to 'win' professional status summarised in Box 1, and measuring fundraising's success in exhibiting these traits. For example, the emergence of professional membership associations for fundraisers (Kelly, 1998, pp 116–20); professional autonomy (Carbone, 1989); the existence of codes of ethics (Sargeant and Jay, 2014, p 421); and a service orientation (Rosso and Associates, 1991; Pribbenow, 1999) have all been noted approvingly.

Most ink has been spilt discussing the growth in attention from Higher Education Institutions since the 1970s, resulting in a body of empirical and theoretical knowledge, which is cited as 'proof' that fundraising is being professionalised (Lindahl and Conley, 2002, p 98; Sargeant et al, 2010, p xxiv). Yet the 'tick' by traits is usually qualified to some degree. For example, Kelly notes discontent with the credibility of certification offered by some membership associations (Kelly, 1998, p 119); Duronio and Tempel insist that fundraisers will never enjoy the degree of autonomy enjoyed by doctors (Duronio and Tempel, 1997, p 2); and Carbone criticises the lack of uniformity in codes of ethics promoted by different parties, noting that only a third of fundraisers have satisfactory knowledge of the codes, leaving most practice to be guided by norms (Carbone, 1989, p 15).

A key problem for fundraising's claims to professionalism relates to the demand that practitioners acquire a distinct knowledge base acquired through sustained periods of training and education (Tlili, 2016, p 1108). As we saw in Tables 7 and 8 (Chapter 2), despite fundraisers having a high level of general education, most describe their expertise as 'caught not taught', with only just over a quarter (28%) possessing a relevant qualification and only a minority of those involving anything approaching sustained study. This is clearly at odds with established professions that require substantial and lengthy academic training. It is impossible to imagine a brain surgeon telling his colleague to follow the kind of advice offered in many 'how to' books: The only way to get better at this game is to take the plunge. Don't overthink it.

Furthermore, the quality of the available body of knowledge is characterised as 'a body of lore and experiences' that 'consists primarily of intuitively based, untested principles generated by practitioners' (Kelly, 1998, pp 106, 105). There have clearly been developments since 1998 when that view was published, but as recently as 2014 it was provocatively claimed that fundraising: 'remains one of the few "professions" that one doesn't need to know anything about to enter. Of course, I exaggerate to make a point but not by much' (Sargeant, 2014, p 301).

Ongoing debates over the extent to which fundraising exhibits the required traits has led many to conclude that fundraising is best described as an 'emerging' profession (as do, for example, Carbone, 1989; More Partnership/Richmond Associates, 2014b; Aldrich, 2016, p 505). An alternative to delaying professionalism until traits are satisfactorily met is proposed by Kelly, who suggests that fundraising should be incorporated into the profession of Public Relations (Kelly, 1998, p 103). However, some are satisfied that there is now sufficient evidence to call fundraising an 'established' profession (as do, for example, Tempel et al, 1997; Bloland, 2002; Bloland and Tempel, 2004; Levy, 2004).

Those who take the 'power' approach, rather than assessing the presence and absence of traits, argue that professional status must be conferred by wider society. But an Australian study highlights a very local problem in this regard: many leaders of charitable organisations are themselves unlikely to agree that fundraising is a profession (Scaife et al, 2014). Given the poor public and media image of fundraising discussed in previous chapters, which is also often shared by non-fundraising colleagues, it is unsurprising that the 'power' approach largely precludes fundraising from acceptance as a profession. However, some branches of fundraising, notably its presence in Higher Education

Institutions, where practitioners largely use the title 'development' rather than 'fundraiser', are more likely to be viewed as professionals (Worth and Asp, 1994, pp 5, 12) or at least 'new professionals' (Daly, 2013, pp 22, 28).

There is a further, less noted, barrier to fundraising's claim to be a profession. The extensive involvement of volunteers highlights the absence of a monopoly of knowledge and practice that typifies established professions such as medicine, law and accountancy. The 'fundamental' role of volunteers (Hughes, 1996, p 187) is well documented in the 'how to' literature, notably for identifying and making contact with potential donors, and for the moment of solicitation, which it is widely advised is best done by a peer rather than a paid professional. This reliance on volunteers considerably weakens, and potentially precludes, fundraising's claims to professionalism (Carbone, 1989) because the work of paid practitioners 'is shared with amateurs' (Bloland and Bornstein, 1991, p 117). Clarity over whether and when volunteers play a minor or major role in achieving success is muddied by the fundraising norm that credit should be given to volunteers and donors, rather than claimed by fundraisers. While this may sometimes be an accurate response, philanthropy professionals constantly face the difficulty of 'how to claim some sense of professional accomplishment and competence without falsely taking credit for the generosity of some or for the work of others' (Horn and Gardner, 2006, p 87).

A final distinctive factor that bears on fundraising's claim to professional status is the crucial role of emotional labour, discussed in Chapter 5. However bad-tempered or unpleasant a doctor, lawyer or accountant may be, he or she can still achieve the immediate goal of their job by implementing their learned skills and technical expertise. The experience of dealing with a disagreeable professional will undoubtedly be worse for all concerned, and a good bedside manner is known to make a 'small' difference to medical outcomes (Kelley et al, 2014), but the difference in outcome for fundraising is much starker. An obnoxious, unhappy or simply distracted fundraiser is highly unlikely to achieve their core purpose of raising the resources required by their charity.

In sum, fundraising is clearly dissimilar to traditional professions, most obviously because it does not have an agreed body of knowledge that forms the basis of examination and certification of practitioners, and also because of the reliance on volunteers, difficulties in attributing success, and the primacy of emotional labour. Fundraising therefore appears to be qualitatively different to traditional professions. However, as noted above, new types of profession are now being identified and enumerated, and the analysis presented in this book suggests that fundraisers might most accurately be described as members of the creative profession.

Fundraising as a creative profession

The second half of the 20th century saw the emergence and expansion of creative professions, replacing the technocracy that epitomised industrial societies (Galbraith, 1967) and the 'knowledge workers', such as those in the health and education sectors, who were viewed as the prime engines of growth in the post-industrial society (Bell, 1973). The 'creative class' is a source of economic value (Florida, 2012) because it harnesses human creativity to generate prosperity (Svarc, 2016, p 401). So-called 'creatocrats' now account for a large part – between a third and a half – of the workforce in North America, Europe, Asia and around the world (Florida, 2012, p viii; Svarc, 2016, p 401). Their key characteristics are captured in Box 2.

Box 2: Characteristics of creatives

- Predominantly female
- Favour openness
- Passionate*
- Confidence*
- Non-conformists
- Willing to bend and break commonly accepted rules
- Self-assured
- Risk-takers
- Possess the ability to synthesise information and perceptions
- Capable of hard work
- Patient
- Driven by internal motivations, intrinsic rewards and satisfactions**
- Reliant on colleagues and collaboration

Source: drawing primarily on *Boden, 1990, p 255; **Amabile, 1996, p 15; Florida, 2012, pp 18–22, 54, 57–8

These characteristics tally closely with the characteristics of fundraisers identified in earlier chapters of this book, and Florida's explication of how creatives work is very familiar in relation to the *modus operandi* of fundraising:

> These people engage in creative problem solving, drawing on complex bodies of knowledge to solve specific problems. Doing so typically requires a high degree of formal education and thus a high level of human capital... they are required to... think on their own, apply or combine standard approaches in unique ways to fit different situations, exercise a great deal of judgment, and perhaps even try something radically new from time to time. (Florida, 2012, p 39)

Similarly, Beeftink et al state that the work processes of 'creatocrats' can be seen as 'continuous adaptation to changing circumstances' (Beeftink et al, 2012, p 72). Their conclusions emerge from a study of architects, which contains another resonant finding: architects spend only a minor part of their working hours on design work (Beeftink et al, 2012, p 77), just as fundraisers only spend a fraction of their time on solicitation (Duronio and Tempel, 1997, p 38). Architects must simultaneously pursue design and commercial activities, as clients expect creativity but also demand organisational abilities. An architect who is highly skilled in design will lose customers if he or she forgets meetings or has poor time management (Beeftink et al, 2012, p 73), just as a fundraiser must choreograph perfectly smooth logistics, as highlighted in Chapter 4.

The same is true in other creative professions. For example, chefs need scientific mastery and artistic innovation, as their success requires both culinary and managerial skills (Zopiatis, 2010, p 459). Zopiatis's study also sheds light on how chefs have enhanced the image and reputation of their profession in recent decades as a result of positive cultural positioning, including increased media coverage of cooking, the phenomenon of the 'celebrity chef', and the expansion in tertiary training courses; whether similar strategies could assist fundraising's reputation is an interesting question.

These various studies show that success in any creative profession requires both creative and self-regulatory characteristics. The former includes a 'creative orientation to problem solving' to generate new ideas rather than adaption to the status quo (Beeftink, 2012, p 72), while the latter includes 'setting priorities, planning work activities, and monitoring time and task progress' as well as the personal management of emotional states and problem behaviours (Beeftink, 2012, pp 72,

77, 80). This combination results in an ongoing tension between creativity and organization, as the latter is necessary but potentially stifling (Whyte, 1956; Florida, 2012, pp 16–17). As Florida explains:

> Practice without process becomes unmanageable, but process without practice damps out the creativity required for innovation; the two sides exist in perpetual tension. Only the most sophisticated and aware organizations are able to balance these countervailing forces in ways that lead to sustained creativity and long-run growth. (Florida, 2012, p 27)

Creativity comes from 'communities of practice' that enable exploration and discovery (Brown and Duguid, 2000), and creatives need to be in environments that enable their creativity to flourish, with colleagues and institutional structures that are receptive to new approaches, and that will mobilise resources around their ideas (Florida, 2012, p 26). This begs the question: how many fundraisers work in such an environment? The absence of a 'culture of philanthropy' noted in Chapter 2, where only a fifth of UK fundraisers report operating in an organisation that consistently supports and promotes their efforts, may serve as a proxy for this factor.

The above descriptions and studies of creative professionals resonates strongly with the description and illustrations of the art of fundraising in Chapter 4, including the need to resist standardisation and mechanical processes, and the requirement to react in a tailored and personalised way in every interaction with each unique donor. Yet fundraisers have not – until now – been included as members of the Creative Class.

Is fundraising a job, a vocation or a calling?

There are further dimensions to the question 'What kind of a job is fundraising?', which relate to the approach fundraisers take to their work, the language they use to describe it, and any attendant consequences. Many studies have gone beyond exploring the professional status of different types of paid work, to look instead at how people think about, and approach, their occupation. This alternative focus is more in line with the findings of this study: in the interviews conducted for this book, only a handful of fundraisers raised unprompted the issue of whether or not fundraising is a profession, whereas almost all spontaneously described their feelings about being a fundraiser and how it enables them to 'make a difference' by saving and changing lives, or otherwise improving society.

Raising money may be the means by which those ends are achieved, but successful fundraisers' eyes are fixed firmly on the destination rather than the journey. In the words of a fundraiser reflecting on her profession after receiving a terminal cancer diagnosis: 'I want to know that when I die the world is a slightly better place for me having been in it. I am very lucky to work in a sector where I get paid to make this a reality' (Bardsley, 2013). This thought is echoed by one of my interviewees: "Fundraising gives you the sense that something you love is going to be better, stronger, faster because of something that you've done" (Female, A, B).

The idea of fundraising being 'more than a job' is also a dominant motif in the literature, just as the same texts emphasise that fundraising is about more than simply 'raising funds'. As noted in earlier chapters, Basil O'Connor, whose fundraising led to the elimination of polio in much of the world, described fundraising as a 'vocation' or a 'calling', and the founder of the US for-profit fundraising consultancy industry, Charles Sumner Ward, encapsulated this sentiment by saying: 'I would leave this work immediately if I thought I were merely raising money. It is raising men that appeals to me' (quoted in Cutlip, 1990, p 43). That sense of achieving something larger than proximate goals recurs throughout the extant literature. Fundraising is described as a task that 'realises dreams' (Levy, 2009, p xxvii); that is 'moral action-applied ethics' (Payton et al, 1991, p 9); 'one of the world's most powerful catalysts for change' (Burnett, 2002, p 7); and 'the activity that makes caring service possible' (Mullin, 1987). Broce argues that this approach is shared by the majority of people working as fundraisers: 'Most people enter the fund-raising profession not because it is an easy way to make a living but because it is a tangible way in which they can marshal their talents to serve others' (Broce, 1986, p 3). But this may be an idealised representation: there is minimal empirical evidence on the motivation behind choosing a career in fundraising, and what does exist – a study of why US fundraisers are in their present fundraising post rather than in this line of work – suggests that fundraisers are primarily seeking 'more challenge or responsibility' and that commitment to the cause is swiftly followed by 'additional pay or benefits' (Duronio and Tempel, 1997, p 87). It may be that fundraisers view their work as something more than a job, in part because that is how they genuinely feel, and in part because that orientation helps them to achieve greatest success. As Lord counsels: fundraisers cannot allow themselves to become 'mere technicians', but rather should be inspiring people to 'advance our civilization' (Lord, 1987, p 98).

Such grandiose sentiment is in keeping with the widespread suggestion that fundraising is a calling or a vocation, rather than 'just a job'. The type of work that is a 'calling' rather than a 'job' or a 'career' was explored in depth within a noted analysis of modern American society (Bellah et al, 1985). In this study, 'jobs' are described as focused on financial rewards, 'careers' are focused on advancement, and a 'calling' is focused on the enjoyment of undertaking fulfilling, socially useful work. These distinctions are not dependent on occupation: people in the same line of work may variously perceive it as a job, a career or a calling. Indeed, Harrah-Conforth and Borsos insist that fundraising is 'a continuum extending between philanthropic values and the mere notion of having a job. Professional fundraisers fall anywhere between these poles' (Harrah-Conforth and Borsos, 1991, p 31). However, a study of UK fundraisers found that 'outstanding' fundraising practitioners all rejected the idea of fundraising as merely a means of paying their bills: 'In every case, they were personally passionate about the profession of fundraising, the cause they were working for, and how they might personally contribute to improving the lives of their beneficiaries' (Sargeant and Shang, 2016, p 45).

Work constitutes more than a third of waking life for adults (Wrzesniewski et al, 1997, p 21), and people living in developed societies are largely concerned with meeting higher-level needs such as esteem, which involves prestige and feeling of accomplishment, and self-actualisation, which is dependent on achieving one's full potential (Maslow, 1943, 1954). People who see their work as a 'calling' report the highest levels of life and work satisfaction (Wrzesniewski et al, 1997, p 31), and fundraisers often describe their work as being immensely rewarding and satisfying (Gurin, 1985, p 93; Panas, 1988, p 71; Harrah-Conforth and Borsos, 1991, p 35; Levy, 2009, p xxvii; Shaker, 2016, p 373). That satisfaction is borne of tangible accomplishment in worthwhile causes, as Gurin explains: 'I experience that satisfaction today when I pass a museum or school that was built though a campaign I counseled, or when I read about a program or service that I had some hand in making possible' (Gurin, 1985, p 93). Likewise, Greenfield states that satisfaction comes from seeing ideas and plans come to life, of being part of an institution that carries out programmes to benefit a community (as discussed in Wagner, 2002, p 56). For these reasons, fundraising ought to be viewed as a more enticing career option than it is, but there is a widespread shortage of fundraisers and, as discussed in the introductory chapter, the dominant external view of fundraising is critical and unaware that 'fundraising breeds a form of satisfaction and reward that is unequalled nearly anywhere else' (Reinert, cited in Harrah-Conforth and Borsos, 1991, p 35).

Yet behind such lofty sentiment lies the reality that success and satisfaction in fundraising are – at least in part – the result of mundane logistical, organisational and managerial skills, as described in Chapter 3. This reality is responsible for the longstanding tension between fundraising as a calling and fundraising as a business, because it involves the idea of service and the concepts of morality and value-driven behaviour, as well as the application of commercial skills (Harrah-Conforth and Borsos, 1991, p 19). However, this tension may be experienced as fertile rather than problematic, enabling fundraisers to be 'the bridge between the mission and the marketplace', such that their success is reliant on managing conflicting values and gaining credibility in both milieu (Harrah-Conforth and Borsos, 1991, p 19).

Bridges span territories and make connections, fulfilling both mundane and imaginative functions. So too, fundraisers are situated on a continuum from those who need a job to those who aspire to change the world, though the former may transition into the latter as a result of achieving success in raising the resources to make something transformational happen. Alternatively, the work of fundraising may appeal to those with both banal and elevated concerns: those who need to pay the bills but also hope to leave their mark on the world.

Are fundraisers 'born' or 'made'?

The final question to be explored in this chapter concerns whether fundraisers are 'born' or 'made': is fundraising something that anyone can do, or learn to do, or does it require special attributes? Analysis of the 'how to' literature in Chapter 3 highlighted dissent on this point – while many authors insist that the skills and qualities are learnable, others emphasise the existence of 'fundraiser exceptionalism', such that some special and innate personal qualities are required for significant success in this field. Yet often, authors want to 'have it both ways' and therefore this question yields 'the most muddled answers in the literature' (Worth and Asp, 1994, p 42).

Having proposed in this chapter that fundraising is best viewed as a creative profession, clarity might be achieved by addressing this 'born or made' question within the context of the wider creative sector rather than in relation to the specific job of fundraising. A macro-review of research on creativity concludes that it is a capacity that is inherent in almost everyone: 'Creativity draws crucially on our ordinary abilities.

Noticing, remembering, seeing, speaking, hearing, understanding language, and recognizing analogies: all these talents of Everyman are important' (Boden, 1990, p 245, cited in Florida, 2012, p 19).

Therefore fundraising, as a creative profession, ought to be accessible to all who invest time and effort in accumulating the relevant knowledge and experience.

For those who view fundraising as more aligned with marketing, sales and communications (such as Broce, 1986; Kelly, 1998; Sargeant and Jay, 2014), the conclusion remains the same: that the requisite skills can be acquired. For example, a study of salespeople found that, despite assumptions that the highest performers would enjoy some form of innate advantage, the key success factors were found to be preparation and planning, both of which can be taught through training and coaching: thus 'average sales people can increase their performance' (Davies et al, 2009, p 27).

It therefore seems reasonable to conclude that professional fundraising skills can be learnt, despite current low levels of uptake of educational opportunities. This creates the potential for a significant shift in prowess if lengthier and more substantial study becomes the norm among fundraising practitioners. However, it also seems reasonable to conclude that not everything can be taught in the classroom, just as interviewees in this study compared fundraising to learning swimming: sometimes the student must jump in, literally and metaphorically, in order to become proficient. Once immersed in fostering, framing and facilitating philanthropy, fundraisers will gain tacit knowledge as a result of their experiences (Bloland and Bornstein, 1991, p 116), which will finesse and strengthen their understanding of the art of fundraising. Simultaneously learning via explicit instruction and by trial and error, as well as through being mentored and emulating more successful colleagues, is a lengthy process that draws on both ingrained personal qualities and newly acquired expertise. As Panas concludes: 'Learned or taught, it is quite clear that the great fundraisers are not 'made' overnight. Nor are they simply "born". It is almost certainly a happy combination of the two' (Panas, 1988, p 71).

Conclusions

This chapter has reviewed the debate on professionalism and why fundraisers strive to achieve this status. Debates about the extent of a verifiable, agreed body of knowledge, uptake of formal qualifications and reliance on volunteers were shown to undermine aspirations for fundraising to be recognised on a par with traditional professions such as medicine and the law. Even if all the required 'traits' of a profession could be demonstrated, the dominant negative feelings about paid fundraisers would likely preclude it being awarded that label as it lacks external affirmation in the external environment. This situation has consequences for the recruitment crisis in fundraising because, until it is an aspirational job that attracts the brightest and the best, it will struggle to attract sufficient talented recruits.

However, those already within the profession portray it as an immensely rewarding and satisfying career, akin to a calling or a vocation. So the barrier occurs at the point of recruitment rather than retention, as those who have experienced the 'thrill' of raising funds to make something important happen, may struggle to find similar job satisfaction elsewhere.

The status of fundraisers is affected by cultural attitudes towards wealth and associated taboos about discussing money, including 'cultural biases against those who deal with money' (Pribbenow, 1999, p 30). Because of this complex context within which UK fundraisers work, and because standardisation is anathema to fundraising success which relies instead on creative interactions and responses in any given situation, I have suggested that fundraisers most closely resemble other 'creative professionals'. Similarities in the profiles and traits of fundraisers and other members of the creative class were shown to reinforce this position.

As such, fundraisers will flourish best in a conducive environment that both nurtures and unleashes their creativity. Unfortunately, charitable organisations with a requisite 'culture of philanthropy' that consistently supports and promotes the fundraising function are currently in the minority.

The previous chapters have shown that contemporary fundraising involves a mixture of learnt and innate skills, with the balance between the two dependent on the type of fundraising task being undertaken. On the whole, impersonal fundraising (notably direct mail) relies more on proven techniques and science, whereas personal fundraising (especially major donors) is more of an art that requires planning in advance combined with creativity in the moment. This chapter has underlined the need to combine both acquired knowledge and ingrained abilities and outlooks, to achieve maximum success in fundraising. The next, concluding, chapter builds on this discussion about the kind of work involved in fundraising, as well as data and arguments presented throughout the book, to paint a picture of the 'New Fundraisers' who organise generosity in contemporary society.

Conclusion: The new fundraisers

In the introductory chapter it was noted that fundraisers are not like a light bulb 'which performs one unambiguous task ... at the flick of a switch'. Panas elaborated:

> Light bulbs are produced by the millions. All have the same components. The fundraiser is a product of background, training, heredity, a mysterious combination of skills, and almost certainly a great deal of luck ... Among the finest, most effective in the field, there is at work a magnificent alchemy of mind, spirit, and creative genius that somehow generates sums significantly greater than its parts. (Clark Kerr, quoted in Panas, 1988, p 8)

The complexity and subtlety of the fundraising role has been the subject of this book, which has sought to highlight the 'magnificent alchemy' involved in the art and science of fundraising. In this concluding chapter, I argue that we have recently witnessed the emergence of the 'New Fundraisers' who organise generosity in contemporary society. These 'New Fundraisers' exist in a necessarily complementary relationship to the already identified 'New Philanthropists' (see, for example, Handy, 2006). These two groups are shown to share many similar traits and attitudes, including shared passion for the cause and convictions about its importance; a desire for impact; and a joy in asking and giving. These similarities enable them to build mutually beneficial relationships that can achieve transformational results, despite a general lack of public affirmation in the UK for either givers or askers.

The new fundraisers

In recent years there has been extensive claims-making that a new type of donor has emerged. The 'New Philanthropist' has been the subject of many discussions and debates, newspaper articles and academic studies. One book dedicated to describing and profiling New Philanthropists, describes them as follows:

> They are individuals, still in the prime of life, who have been successful in their chosen careers … Having made enough for their own needs they now want to use their money, their skills and their abilities to get things done to create something transparently useful in society. They talk of making a difference, of giving something back ... These people want to be in the driving seat, because that's where they belong and, being by nature entrepreneurs of one sort or another, they like to fill gaps and to meet needs neglected by others. (Handy, 2006, pp 8–9)

While this argument has been critiqued for being a-historical and failing to recognise that philanthropists are always a product of their time (Breeze, 2011), and that philanthropy is always a complex and contested concept (Payton and Moody, 2008), it has nonetheless gained purchase as a useful generalisation and it is widely accepted that contemporary donors are distinctive from their forebears.

As noted in the introductory chapter, charities have also developed in reaction to changing needs, altered public expectations, and developments in the policy environment, especially in relation to public funding. As donors and charities have changed, so fundraising practice must change too (Cluff, 2009, p 377). Alongside the new context for, and expectations of, charitable provision, and the emergence of the new philanthropists, it would be surprising if fundraisers stayed irresolutely the same amid all this novelty and change.

It is therefore a key argument of this book that we are witnessing the emergence of the 'New Fundraiser' in parallel with the emergence of the 'New Philanthropists'. While the latter is far more extensively documented, having an understanding of changes in the profiles of *both* givers and askers is of similar importance for the future health of the charitable sector, because they are so closely interrelated. The skills and qualities needed to be a successful fundraiser have not changed in isolation from changes in the donor community, but rather in response to them. This makes sense given the prime importance of relationships between donors and fundraisers: successful interactions that are authentic, mutually respectful and ideally enjoyable, are the bedrock of successful fundraising outcomes and these relationships are facilitated by shared traits and outlook, such as those enumerated below.

Clearly, neither fundraisers nor philanthropists constitute homogenous groups. There is much variety among both those who ask and those who give – including gender, age, family background, education levels, personality traits, tastes, preferences and ideological outlooks.

Nonetheless, some commonalities emerge. It is also important to note that, as explored in Chapter 4, part of the art of fundraising is for askers to be chameleon-like in their willingness and ability to adapt in response to the needs and preferences of the donors. Yet the demands of authenticity mean these adaptations are generally quite superficial, related to speech patterns or dress, rather than the more profound commonalities that emerged in the data described and discussed in the preceding chapters, and summarised in Box 3, below.

Box 3: Eight similarities between 'New Philanthropists' and 'New Fundraisers'

1. Changes in demographic profiles
2. Shared passion and conviction
3. Focus on achieving transformational results
4. Commitment to cause over organisation
5. Seeking agency and power
6. Possessing contradictory characteristics
7. Lack of public affirmation
8. Finding joy in giving and asking

Eight similarities between fundraisers and philanthropists

1. Changes in demographic profiles

Most obviously, there have been significant changes in the demographic profiles of both donors and askers. The 'New Philanthropists' are characterised as being younger, more likely to be female, and more likely to have created rather than inherited their wealth (Breeze, 2011). As discussed in Chapter 2, the 'New Fundraisers' are also younger, more likely to be female, well educated, and come from a different background to their predecessors: no longer simply well connected, well-to-do ladies, or men with a military or marketing background, instead more are choosing a career in fundraising (Woods, 1997, p 10), or made their way to it gradually through related work. These demographic changes are partly the result of professionalisation, discussed in Chapter 6, and also driven by a need to abandon the 'old rules' and adapt to changes in the donor population (Nichols, 1996, p 152). As an interviewee explained: "Culturally wealth has changed hasn't it? How you earn it and what you do with it. So we, as fundraisers, need to be able to relate to how money is being made today and be able to talk to more different kinds of people" (Male, A, B).

2. Shared passion and conviction

First and foremost, both donors and fundraisers highlight that their actions are propelled by passion and a desire to use their resources – wealth, time, connections or ability to generate support – to help and promote a cause that they care about. As noted in Chapter 2, fundraisers often have a stake in the type of charitable organisation for which they work, as exemplified by the fundraiser for a hostage support charity whose uncle had been kidnapped. So too, alumni can be especially useful members of a development office, and former musicians can be successful fundraisers for arts organisations, because they all have a meaningful connection to the cause they are promoting.

Fundraisers' passion for a cause is clearly not only a result of firsthand experiences. It can also arise as a result of their beliefs and values, which can co-exist alongside – and sometimes overshadow – objectives such as career advancement (Wagner, 2004, p 170). The personal investment of fundraisers in the cause they are serving has largely been overlooked, yet the shared conviction between fundraisers and donors is of immense importance (Payton et al, 1991, p 276; Burnett, 2002, p 29). Passion for the cause is described as 'the secret of fundraising success' (McKinnon, 2006, p 11), and was widely evident as a common characteristic among the successful fundraisers that participated in this study. In the words of one interviewee: "The top motivation for fundraisers is belief in the cause, the same as it is for donors" (Female, A). This leads Scaife et al to draw the parallel between askers and donors: 'The very strong pattern from experienced fundraisers in highlighting passion and integrity as the heart of the role suggests an attitude more akin to philanthropy and philanthropists than many major givers perhaps realise' (Scaife et al, 2011, p 64).

3. Focus on achieving transformational results

The third characteristic that successful fundraisers share with major donors is a focus on achieving transformational results. Outcomes are prioritised over money targets because, in the words of one of my interviewees: "Fundraising is not about money, it's about ideas. When you have a great idea, then you cost it" (Male, A, B). This sentiment is reminiscent of O'Connor's mid-20th-century declaration that fundraising is the means not the end, and that charitable organisations 'do not exist to raise money. We do have to have money to exist. That is the whole difference' (O'Connor, 1959, p 16).

Rather than measuring success by the amount of money raised (or, in the case of donors, the amount given), the New Philanthropists and the New Fundraisers are focused on what impact is achieved with the sums that are raised or donated. The heightened focus on measurement, monitoring and evaluation, evident in the mushrooming of impact measurement conducted by UK charities (Arvidson, 2009; Ni Ogain et al, 2012; Harlock, 2013), is therefore of interest to both donors and askers.

Some commentators suggest that the reason fundraisers tend not to be unduly concerned with achieving personal recognition is because they are instead driven by results and the impact their work achieves (Wagner, 2004). This also relates to the invisibility of the fundraising role, which has been highlighted throughout this book; and the idea of fundraisers as 'backstage' directors, who set the scene for others rather than occupy the spotlight themselves, discussed in Chapter 4. Interviewees explain that the job satisfaction comes from knowing "you made all of that happen" (Female, A, B), as a fundraiser working in a medical research charity notes: "One day someone is going to get a Nobel Prize for finding the cure for this disease. Everyone will be grateful to them, but we will know we were part of that and will have to raise a glass to ourselves" (Male, A, B). This is reminiscent of philanthropists' oft-expressed hopes that their contribution will catalyse significant outcomes (see, for example, Schervish, 2003, 2005; Handy, 2006; Bishop and Green, 2008; Breeze and Lloyd, 2013, pp 90–1; Sadeh et al, 2014). Just as with philanthropy, fundraising may appear to be concerned with money, but the real goal is making change happen.

4. Commitment to cause over organisation

The focus on transformational results described in the last point leads directly to the third shared feature: a commitment to causes over particular charitable organisations. One of the defining features of new philanthropists is an impatience with the traditional institutions of charity and a preference to set up their own initiatives to pursue their chosen causes, regardless if that 'ruffles the feathers' of established charities (Handy, 2006, p 10). While paid fundraisers, by definition, need to be on the payroll of a named charity (although some operate as consultants), they are often committed to their 'field' (such as environmental causes, homelessness or animal welfare) and see fundraising as a way to deliver outcomes they believe in. This results in many paid fundraisers feeling multiple allegiances, viewing themselves as beholden to their charity and the donors, within a broader commitment to their cause area, in order to achieve successful outcomes.

5. Seeking agency and power

The search for agency and exercise of power are also motivators of both major donors and those who solicit them. Philanthropists who donate large sums of money are described as 'hyperagents', able to shape, rather than simply support, their chosen causes (Schervish, 2007, p 173). While fundraisers clearly lack the equivalent financial resources to exert such control, they make use of other resources at their disposal, including leveraging their relationships with both donors and the charity's leadership in order to achieve desired results.

Historically, as we saw in Chapter 1 and exemplified by Thomas Coram, fundraisers were people who had ideas for new charitable initiatives but, lacking sufficient economic capital to realise those ideas, deployed their social and cultural capital to approach those with financial wherewithal to acquire funding. Some fundraisers interviewed for this study depicted their ability to raise significant sums as 'the next best thing' to being a philanthropist themself, and explained how success enhanced their sense of agency. For example, a fundraiser described meeting her first campaign goal, which funded the conversion of a previously inaccessible building: "it felt powerful" (Female, A).

6. Possessing contradictory characteristics

It is often noted that philanthropists represent various contradictions. Donors such as Bill Gates, Warren Buffett and Mark Zuckerberg count among the richest people in the world, but also the most generous; they have accumulated unimaginable wealth and are now distributing enormous sums; they are winners in the free market and yet often rail against its outcomes.

So too, successful fundraisers often combine seemingly opposed characteristics. As creative professionals, they must manage the tension between creativity and organisation, as the latter is necessary but potentially stifling (Florida, 2012, pp 16–17). The swan metaphor, discussed in Chapter 4, captures how they describe appearing laid-back and relaxed when among donors and colleagues, keeping invisible the hard work and ferocious attention to detail behind the scenes. Other contradictions include being professionals who nonetheless regularly bend or break rules, and being immensely sociable, and yet often highly isolated within their organisations.

7. Lack of public affirmation

One of the most obvious commonalities between major donors and fundraisers in the UK is that neither enjoys a particularly positive public profile. Media coverage of philanthropists is often negative, even snide (Henley, 2012), and, as discussed in the introductory chapter, fundraisers in the UK have experienced an extended period of scrutiny and attack. In both cases this is, at least in part, an example of 'do-gooder derogation', such that those who are generous, or seek to inspire generosity, provoke a defensive backlash as a result of making others feel they are being morally judged and found wanting (Minson and Monin, 2011).

Similarly, MacQuillin argues that public hostility is rooted in a view that fundraisers are 'moralists at the feast', which upsets people's equilibrium: the anger directed at fundraisers and donors is said to be a proxy for the guilt that people feel at not giving (MacQuillin, 2014). So big givers and those who seek their support share an experience of public hostility, and the unintended consequence in both cases is similar: people who might otherwise have donated large sums, or helped charities to raise large sums, are deterred from doing so.

8. Finding joy in giving and asking

The final similarity between 'New Philanthropists' and 'New Fundraisers' is the extent to which they find joy in what they do, despite both acts being viewed as inherently problematic, as highlighted in the previous point. Both donors and askers frequently describe the pleasure and satisfaction to be gained from giving and getting significant sums for good causes. Philanthropy is described as life-enriching by donors who typically state that generosity brings multiple rewards and that they 'get back far more than they give' (see, for example, Breeze and Lloyd, 2013, pp 100–1; Gates, cited in Acs, 2013). Similarly, successful fundraisers are said to find 'immense' and 'genuine' joy in their work (Panas, 1988, p 32; Laskowski, 2016, p 17).

An ebullient reflection on fundraising claims: 'It's an absolutely thrilling, endorphin-releasing experience when people say yes' (McKinnon, 2006, pp 6–7). The pleasures to be gained in a fundraising career were frequent themes in the interviews conducted for this book. Successful fundraisers often used words and phrases such as "being proud", "feeling satisfied" and "getting a buzz" from doing what they see as fulfilling, socially useful work. One interviewee connected the joy he felt in his work to the joy he knew it created for the donor: 'I love fundraising. The passion I feel about what I do is because I'm giving someone with a lot of money the opportunity to do the best thing they've done all year, or all decade – or ever!' (Male, A).

This sentiment is echoed in the literature, in which fundraisers are described as 'joyful matchmakers' (Matheny, 1999, p 104) who facilitate the joy of giving (Scaife et al 2011, p 28). These quotes underline that the joy lies in the direct interaction with donors and shared pleasure in the outcomes.

The eight similarities described and discussed above point to a great deal of overlap in the experience in asking for – and giving – large sums of money. Philanthropists and fundraisers share similar motivations, drivers and pleasures, suggesting that in many ways the major donors and the major donor fundraisers are cut from the same cloth. The most obvious difference is their access to personal wealth, but even in that regard, as an interviewee commented:

> the donors are motivated by making something happen but they just happen to have the money to be able to put that into practice, and the fundraisers aren't rich but are, you know, proactive and networked and have a sort of sense of purpose in life ... I'm not saying there's a perfect overlap. but I think they're more similar than dissimilar. (Female, B)

The 'New Fundraisers' have emerged in parallel with the 'New Philanthropists'. They share much in common and need to be understand collectively, as part of broader shifts in how philanthropy is perceived and practiced at the start of the 21st century.

Conclusion

Despite the crucial importance of fundraisers in securing the resources needed to fund charitable activity on which society relies, to date we have known very little about the people who organise generosity for a living. Most research in the field of philanthropic studies has been concerned with understanding donors and uncovering the drivers of giving. While valuable findings have been produced in donor-centric studies, such research has largely overlooked the context of asking or, at best, depicted it as a binary variable such that people are either solicited, or not, with no regard for the quality of 'the ask'.

This book has sought to help rectify that imbalance by providing an extensive, empirical and theorised account of the UK's fundraising workforce. It has argued that fundraising matters because most people make charitable donations and, on the whole, their giving is prompted. Systematic generosity requires systematic solicitation, which is organised by fundraisers who have been shown to foster, frame and facilitate generosity. As the research presented in this book has shown, successful fundraisers do not just plan, manage and implement the solicitation process – there is also a large dose of creativity involved. Hence, fundraising is an art and a science, and fundraisers are best understood as a type of creative professional.

Fundraising is an inherently difficulty job in any economic climate, and that difficulty is compounded by the lack of internal support and lack of external affirmation. While both are problematic, public opinion is unlikely to shift substantially or quickly. Colleagues are more attuned to the importance of the fundraising function – therefore, making charities more fundraising-friendly is a more realistic priority. Charity leaders should re-think fundraising as an investment rather than a cost, ensure an organisation-wide culture of philanthropy, and understand that fundraising should not be focused on securing short-term survival but rather is about helping to create strong and sustainable charitable organisations.

Yet fundraisers also need to raise their sights to that further horizon. While this book has been concerned with what can be learnt from successful fundraisers, it is clearly the case that some bad practice exists. Target-driven fundraising that lacks integrity and fails to respect donors, 'neglects or even betrays its own larger purpose' (Payton et al, 1991, p 4). The words of the major donor quoted in the introductory chapter bear repetition:

> When fundraising is done by less gifted people, they keep asking for one thing after another and it's really quite eroding, but when it's done well and I really feel that I am helping to do something special that I will look back on with pride, that's a feeling of joy.[1]

Viewing fundraising as a source of joy may raise some eyebrows in the light of the widespread perception that asking for money is, at best, a 'necessary evil' rather than the 'noble profession' and 'important calling' described by Desmond Tutu (cited in Breeze and Scaife, 2015, p 570). But donors who have experienced good fundraising are the best advocates to start changing minds because they know that fundraising enables them to put their altruistic intentions into practice and ultimately enriches their lives: this is one of many reasons that givers and askers need each other.

The New Philanthropists and the New Fundraisers are united by shared traits, outlooks and goals, as well as by similar experience of criticism and condemnation. A united front would reap rewards for both.

Notes

1. This statement was made at an event on women and philanthropy held at Murray Edwards College, Cambridge, on 25 September 2015.

Appendix A: Online survey questions

Filter question 1:

This survey is only for people who currently work in the UK as paid fundraisers, either in-house, freelance or as consultants and including those on a planned career break, maternity leave or similar. Please confirm that you fit this description.

Filter question 2:

This survey is being distributed through many networks, but it is important that people only complete it once. Please confirm that this is the first time you are completing this survey.

Section 1: Experience as a paid fundraiser

1) How many years in total have you worked as a paid fundraiser?

2) What area of fundraising do you mostly work in? Please select the one option that best reflects your role.

   Major donors; Community/Individuals; Corporate; Trusts and Foundations; Legacies; Trading; Generalist (including major donors); Generalist (not including major donors); Direct marking; Digital; Other (please specify)

2a) Supplementary question only for those who select 'Generalist (including major donors)':

   Please indicate how much of your time you spend working with major donors

   Rarely; Sometimes; Around half my time; Most of my time

3) If you do not currently work with major donors, have you ever done so in the past?

4) What is the single biggest gift you have ever secured? Please note that colleagues and volunteers may have been involved in the process, for example by helping with cultivation and asking.

Section 2: Background, training and professional qualifications

5) Which statement best describes how you came to work as a paid fundraiser?

   I always wanted to work as a fundraiser; I came into this work gradually through related professional and volunteering roles; I fell into fundraising by accident; Other (please specify)

5a) Supplementary question for those who chose 'I fell into fundraising by accident':

   Before you 'fell into fundraising', what was your main occupation?

6) Please select the response that best describes your background and present situation

   Definitely disagree; Tend to disagree; Neither agree nor disagree; Tend to agree; Definitely agree

6a) I grew up in a family where it was normal to help others and to ask for help.

6b) I borrow things from, and exchange favours with, my neighbours.

6c) I always send a thank you message when I receive gifts from loved ones, friends and relatives.

6d) I enjoy gift-giving and choosing presents for loved ones, friends and relatives.

6e) I am a blood donor.

7) Do you have a professional qualification in fundraising?

7a) Supplementary question for those who answered 'Yes' to question 7:

   Which professional qualification in fundraising do you have? Please tick all that apply:

   Introductory Certificate in Fundraising; Certificate in Fundraising; Diploma in Fundraising; Advanced Diploma in Fundraising; Other (please specify)

8) Which statement best describes your experience of formal fundraising training? By 'formal fundraising training' we mean a learning experience such as a course, conference or residential which involves a commitment of time, money or both (paid either by you or your organisation).

   I have never had any formal training in fundraising, and do not believe it is necessary; I have never had any formal training in fundraising, but wish I could find the time or money to do so; I did some formal training when

I first started as a fundraiser but not any longer; I occasionally (less than once a year) do some formal training; I regularly (once or twice each year) do some formal training; I very regularly (3 times of more each year) do some formal training.

9) Please rank in order (1 = most important) what source of information has taught you most about fundraising.

Attending a course (or courses), for example run by the Institute of Fundraising or Directory of Social Change; Learning on the job; Learning by working alongside a more experienced fundraiser (excluding formal mentoring arrangements); Being mentored; Attending events (such as the Institute of Fundraising National Convention or other conferences; Reading books about fundraising; Finding information online (including via social media) about fundraising; Informal discussions with other fundraisers; Other (please specify).

10) Does the charity you currently work for (either as an employee or as your main client) have a culture of philanthropy? NB: A 'culture of philanthropy' is defined by Jeanne Belle and Maria Cornelius (2013) as: 'Most people in the organisation (across positions) act as ambassadors and engage in relationship-building. Everyone promotes philanthropy and can articulate a case for giving. Fundraising is viewed and valued as a mission-aligned programme of the organisation. Organisational systems are established to support donors. The chief executive/director is committed and personally involved in fundraising.'

Yes; Most of the time; Probably not; Definitely not

10a) Supplementary question for those who answered 'probably not' or definitely not' to question 10:

You indicated that the charity you work for either probably does not, or definitely does not have a culture of philanthropy. Does this affect your ability to fundraise?

Yes; Sometimes; No

Section 3: Attitudes and Hobbies

11) Generally speaking, would you say that most people can be trusted, or that you can't be too careful in dealing with people?

12) How often do you meet up with friends or relatives who are not living with you?

On most days; Once or twice a week; Once or twice a month; Less often than once a month

13) When you meet up with friends or relatives, which statement best describes how the gathering was organised:

I usually organise the gathering; I sometimes organise the gathering; I rarely organise the gathering

14) What are your hobbies? Please select all that apply:

Competitive sport; Non-competitive sport or exercise; Watching sport; Singing in a choir; Making music (other than singing in a choir; Visual art (e.g. painting); Performing art (e.g. amateur dramatic theatre group); Visiting art galleries; Going to the theatre; Going to the cinema; Outdoor pursuits that do not generally involve danger (e.g. walking or cycling); Outdoor pursuits that involve some degree of danger (e.g. rock climbing); Reading; Yoga, meditation or other form of relaxation; Attending night classes / part-time study of any kind; Other (please specify); I have no hobbies

15) Which statement best describes your approach to reading books (including fiction and non-fiction)?

I am an avid reader and always have at least one book on the go; I like to read and get through 3 or more books each year; I like to read but only get through 1 or 2 books a year; I don't like to read books

15a) Please indicate the kind of books you read, selecting all that apply:

Fiction (serious/literary); Fiction (lightweight/non-literary); Non-fiction; Books about fundraising or otherwise connected to my paid job; Popular social science books such as Nudge, Tipping Point, Freakonomics; Other (please specify)

Section 4: Standardised tests of Big 5 personality traits and Emotional intelligence scale

16) Personality test. Here are a number of characteristics that may or may not apply to you. Please indicate the extent to which you agree or disagree that you see yourself as someone who …

Is talkative; Tends to find fault with others; Does a thorough job; Is depressed, blue; Is original, comes up with new ideas; Is reserved; Is helpful and unselfish with others; Can be somewhat careless; Is relaxed, handles stress well; Is curious about many different things; Is full of energy; Starts quarrels with others; Is a reliable worker; Can be tense; Is ingenious, a deep thinker; Generates a lot of enthusiasm; Has a forgiving nature; Tends to be disorganised; Worries a lot; Has an active imagination; Tends to be quiet; Is generally trusting; Tends to be lazy; Is emotionally stable, not easily upset; Is inventive; Has an assertive personality; Can be cold and aloof; Perseveres until the task is finished; Can be moody; Values artistic, aesthetic experiences; Is sometimes shy, inhibited; Is considerate and kind to almost everyone; Does things efficiently; Remains calm in tense situations; Prefers work that is routine; Is outgoing, sociable; Is sometimes rude to others; Makes plans and follows through with them; Gets nervous easily; Likes to reflect, play with ideas; Has few artistic interests; Likes to cooperate with others; Is easily distracted; Is sophisticated in art, music or literature

17) Emotional Intelligence scale.

Please indicate the extent to which you agree with the following statements:

I know why my emotions change; I easily recognise my emotions as I experience them; I can tell how people are feeling by listening to the tone of their voice; By looking at their facial expressions, I recognise the emotions people are experiencing; I seek out activities that make me happy; I have control over my emotions; I arrange events others enjoy; I help other people feel better when they are down; When I am in a positive mood, I am able to come up with new ideas; I use good moods to help myself keep trying in the face of obstacles

Concluding section: Socio-demographic questions

i) Are you male or female?

ii) What age band do you fall in?

Under 30; 30–39; 40–49; 50–59; 60+

iii) In which region of the UK do you live?

Scotland, Wales; Northern Ireland; London; East Midlands; East of England; North East; North West; South East; South West; West Midlands; Yorkshire and the Humber

iv) What is the highest level of academic qualification you have achieved?

GCSEs/'O' levels or equivalent; 'A' levels/Highers/Baccalaureate or equivalent; First degree (e.g. BA, BSc); Masters degree; PhD; None

iva) Supplementary question for those who indicated that they have got at least a first degree:

Was the subject of your university-level studies relevant to a career in fundraising?

Yes; Maybe; No

Appendix B: Interview questions

1) How did you get into fundraising?

2) Do you believe that fundraisers are born or made?

3) How can you tell that someone is a good fundraiser?

4) How can you tell that someone hasn't 'got it'?

5) What distinctive qualities do good fundraisers *tend* to have?

6) Are there any essential qualities that fundraisers *must* have?

7) Who is the best fundraiser you know? Why?

8) Is there anything else you would like to add?

Appendix C: List of 'How to fundraise' books in Chapter 3 analysis

Ahern, T. (2009) *Seeing Through a Donor's Eyes: How to make a persuasive case for everything from your annual drive to your planned giving programme to your capital campaign*, Medfield, MA: Emerson & Church.

Allford, M. (1993) *Charity Appeals: The complete guide to success*, London: J. M. Dent & Sons.

Axelrod, T. (2000) *Raising More Money: A step-by-step guide to building lifelong donors*, Seattle, WA: Raising More Money Publications.

Baguley, J. (2000 [1996]) *Successful Fundraising*, 2nd edn, Stafford, UK: Bibliotek Books.

Bassoff, M. and Chandler, S. (2001) *RelationShift: Revolutionary fundraising*, San Francisco, CA: Robert D. Reed Publishers.

Broce, T. F. (1986) *Fund Raising: The guide to raising money from private sources*, 2nd edn, Norman, OK: University of Oklahoma Press.

Burk, P. (2003) *Donor-Centred Fundraising*, Chicago: Burk and Associates Ltd.

Burnett, K. (2002 [1992]) *Relationship Fundraising*, 2nd edn, San Francisco: Jossey-Bass.

Burnett, K. (2006) *The Zen of Fundraising*, San Francisco: Wiley.

Carnie, C. (2000) *Find the Funds: A new approach to fundraising research*, London: Directory of Social Change/CAF.

Eastwood, M. and Norton, M. (2010 [1992]) *Writing Better Fundraising Applications*, London: Directory of Social Change.

Elischer, T. (1995) *Teach Yourself Fundraising*, London: Hodder & Stoughton.

Farnhill, J. (2007) *The Porcupine Principle and Other Fundraising Secrets*, London: Directory of Social Change.

Flanagan, J. (1999 [1991]) *Successful Fundraising: A complete handbook for volunteers and professionals*, 2nd edn, New York: McGraw-Hill.

Gilchrist, K. (2000) *Looking After Your Donors*, London: Directory of Social Change.

Green, F., McDonald, B. and van Herpt, J. (2007) *Iceberg Philanthropy: Unlocking extraordinary gifts from ordinary donors*, Ottawa, ON: The FLA Group.

Greenfield, J.M. (2002) *Fundraising Fundamentals: A guide to annual giving for professionals and volunteers*, New York: John Wiley & Sons.

Gurin, M.G. (1985) *Confessions of a Fundraiser: Lessons of an instructive career*, Washington DC: The Taft Group.

Gurin, M.G. (1991) *Advancing Beyond the Techniques in Fund Raising, Rockville*, MA: Fundraising Institute.

Hartsook, R. (1999) *Closing that Gift! How to be successful 99% of the time*, 2nd edn, Wichita, KS: ASR Philanthropic Publishing

Herbst, N.B. and Norton, M. (2012 [1992]) *The Complete Fundraising Handbook*, 6th edn, London: Directory of Social Change.

Holman, M. and Sargent, L. (2012 [2006]) *Major Donor Fundraising*, 2nd edn, London: Directory of Social Change.

Johnson, T. J. (2011) *10 Critical Factors in Fundraising: The little green book for chief executive officers*, Oklahoma City: JTJ Publishing.

Jones, R. C., and Olsen, A. (2013) *Rainmaking: The fundraiser's guide to landing big gifts*, Createspace Independent Publishing platform.

Joyaux, S. P. (2011) *Strategic Fund Development: Building profitable relationships that last*, 3rd edn), Hoboken, NJ: Wiley.

Kelly, K. S. (1998) *Effective Fundraising Management*, New York and London: Routledge.

Klein, K. (2011 [1988]) *Fundraising for Social Change*, 6th edn, San Francisco, CA: Jossey-Bass.

Levy, R. (2009) *Yours for the Asking: An indispensable guide to fundraising and management*, Hoboken, NJ: John Wiley & Sons.

Lindahl, W. (2010) *Principles of Fundraising: Theory and practice*, Sudbury, MA: Jones and Bartlett.

Lord, J. G. (1987) *The Raising of Money: Thirty-five essentials every trustee should know*, Cleveland, OH: Third Sector Press.

Lysakowski, L. (2012) *Fundraising for the Genius*, Rancho Santa Margarita, CA: CharityChannel Press.

Matheny, R. E. (1999 [1994]) *Major Gift Solicitation Strategies*, Washington, DC: CASE.

McKinnon, H. (2006) *Tiny Essentials of Monthly Committed Giving*, Melrand, France: White Lion Press.

Mixer, J.R. (1993) *Principles of Professional Fundraising: Useful Foundations for Successful Practice*, San Francisco: Jossey-Bass.

Mullin, R. (1995) *Foundations for Fund-Raising*, Hemel Hempstead, Herts: ICSA Publishing Limited.

Mullin, R. (1997) *Fundraising Strategy*, London: CAF/ICFM.

Mutz, J. and Murray, K. (2010 [2000]) *Fundraising for Dummies*, 3rd edn, Hoboken, NJ: Wiley Publishing, Inc.

Norton, M. (2007) *Need to Know? Fundraising*, London: HarperCollins.

Nouwen, H. (2010) *A Spirituality of Fundraising*, Nashville, TN: Henri Nouwen Society.

Panas, Jerold (1984) *Mega Gifts: Who gives them, who gets them?* Chicago: Bonus Books.

Panas, J. (1988) *Born to Raise: What makes a great fundraiser, what makes a fundraiser great?*, Chicago: Bonus Books Inc.

Panas, J. (2012 [2009]) *Asking: A 59-Minute Guide to Everything Board Members, Volunteers, and Staff Must Know to Secure the Gift*, Medfield, MA: Emerson & Church.

Pitman, M. (2007) *Ask Without Fear: A simple guide to connecting donors with what matters to them most*, Greenville, SC: Standish and Wade Publishing.

Prince, R. A. and File, K. M. (1994) *The Seven Faces of Philanthropy: A new approach to cultivating major donors*, San Francisco: Jossey-Bass.

Ross, B. and Segal, C. (2002) *Breakthrough Thinking for Nonprofit Organizations*, San Francisco: Jossey-Bass.

Ross, B. and Segal, C. (2008) *The Influential Fundraiser: using the psychology of persuasion to achieve outstanding results*, San Francisco: Jossey-Bass.

Rosso, H. and Associates (1991) *Achieving Excellence in Fund Raising*, San Francisco: Jossey-Bass.

Sargeant A and Jay, E. (2014 [2004]) *Fundraising Management: Analysis, planning and practice*, 3rd edn, London: Routledge.

Sargeant, A., Shang, J. and Associates (2010) *Fundraising Principles and Practice*, New York: John Wiley & Sons.

Seymour, H. (1947) *Designs for Giving: the story of the National War Fund, Inc. 1943–1947*, New York and London: Harper & Brothers.

Seymour, H. (1966) *Designs for Fund-Raising: Principles, Patterns, Techniques*, New York: McGraw Hill.

Sloggie, N. (2005) *Tiny Essentials of Major Gift Fundraising*, Melrand, France: White Lion Press.

Smith, G. (1996) *Asking Properly: The art of creative fundraising*, London: White Lion Press.

Sprinkel Grace, K. (2005) *Beyond Fundraising: New strategies for nonprofit innovation and investment*, Hoboken, NJ: Wiley.

Stanois, G. (ed.) *The Vigilant Fundraiser: 12 steps to fundraising success*, Toronto: Civil Sector Press.

Stroman, M. K. (2014) *Asking about Asking: Mastering the art of conversational fundraising*, Rancho Santa Margarita, CA: CharityChannel Press.

Warner, I. (2001 [1975]) *The Art of Fundraising*, Lincoln, NE: iUniverse.com.

Warwick, M. (2009) *Fundraising When Money is Tight: A strategic and practical guide to surviving tough times and thriving in the future*, San Francisco: Jossey-Bass.

Wilberforce, S. (2010 [1998]) *Legacy Fundraising*, 3rd edn, London: Directory of Social Change.

Wolf, T. (2011) *How to Connect with Donors and Double the Money You Raise*, Medfield, MA: Emerson & Church.

References

Acs, Z. (2013) *Why Philanthropy Matters: How the wealthy give and what it means for our economic well-being*, Princeton, NJ: Princeton University Press.

Aldrich, E. E. (2016) 'Fundraising as a profession', in E. Tempel, T. L. Seiler and D. F. Burlingame (eds), *Achieving Excellence in Fundraising*, 4th edn, Hoboken, NJ: Wiley.

Allford, M. (1993) *Charity Appeals: The complete guide to success*, London: J. M. Dent & Sons.

Amabile, T. (1996) *Creativity in Context*, Boulder, CO: Westview Press.

Andreoni, J. (1990) 'Impure altruism and donations to public goods: a theory of warm-glow giving', *The Economic Journal*, 100(401): 464–477.

Andreoni, J. (1998) 'Towards a theory of charitable fundraising', *Journal of Political Economy*, 106: 1186–1213.

Andreoni, J. (2006) 'Philanthropy', in S. Kolm and J. M. Ythier (eds), *Handbook of the Economics of Giving, Altruism and Reciprocity*, North-Holland: Elsevier.

Andreoni, J. and Payne, A. A. (2011) 'Is crowding out due entirely to fundraising? Evidence from a panel of charities', *Journal of Public Economics*, 95(6): 334–343.

Armson, M. and McKenzie, A. (2013) 'Launching a new middle donor programme and making it work,' *International Journal of Nonprofit and Voluntary Sector Marketing*, 18: 24–39.

Arvidson, M. (2009) *Impact and Evaluation in the UK Third Sector: reviewing literature and exploring ideas*, TSRC working paper 27, University of Birmingham: Third Sector Research Centre.

Axelrod, T. (2000) *Raising More Money: A step-by-step guide to building lifelong donors*, Seattle, Washington: Raising More Money Publications.

Baguley, J. (2000 [1996]) Successful fundraising, 2nd edn, Stafford, UK:

Balgarnie, R. (2003 [1877]) *Sir Titus Salt, Baronet: His Life and its Lessons*, Cleckheaton, West Yorkshire: Hart and Clough Ltd.

Bardsley, J. (2013) 'Being diagnosed with cancer has given me a new perspective on fundraising', *Third Sector*, 19 August 2013.

Barman, E. (2007) 'An institutional approach to donor control: from dyadic ties to a field-level analysis', *American Journal of Sociology*, 112(5): 1416–1457.

Barrick, M. R. and Mount, M. K. (1991) 'The Big Five personality dimensions and job performance: a meta-analysis', *Personnel Psychology*, 44(1): 1–26.

Barrick, M. R., Mount, M. K. and Judge, T.A. (2001) 'Personality and performance at the beginning of the new millennium: what do we know and where do we go next?' *International Journal of Selection and Assessment*, 9(1–2): 9–30.

Barry, J. and Brooks, C. (eds) (1994) *The Middling Sort of People: Culture, Society and Politics, 1500–1800*, Basingstoke: Palgrave Macmillan.

Bassoff, M. and Chandler, S. (2001) *RelationShift: Revolutionary Fundraising*, San Francisco, CA: Robert D. Reed Publishers.

Beeftink, F., van Eerde, W., Rutte, C. G., and Bertrand, J. W. M. (2012) 'Being successful in a creative profession: the role of innovative cognitive style, self-regulation, and self-efficacy', *Journal of Business Psychology*, 27(1):71–81.

Behlmer, G. K. (1982) *Child Abuse and Moral Reform in England, 1870–1908*, Stanford, CA: Stanford University Press.

Bekkers, R. (2005) *It's Not All in the Ask: Effects and Effectiveness of Recruitment Strategies Used by Nonprofits in the Netherlands*, paper presented at the 34th annual ARNOVA conference, Washington, DC.

Bekkers, R. and Wiepking, P. (2011) 'A literature review of empirical studies of philanthropy: eight mechanisms that drive charitable giving', *Nonprofit and Voluntary Sector Quarterly*, 40(5): 924–973.

Bell, D. (1973) *The coming of post-industrial society*, New York, NY: Basic Books.

Bell, J. and Cornelius, M. (2013) *Underdeveloped: A National Study of Challenges Facing Nonprofit Fundraising*, San Francisco, CA: CompassPoint Nonprofit Services and the Evelyn and Walter Haas, Jr. Fund.

Bellah, R., Madsen, R., Sullivan, W., Swidler, A. and Tipton, S. (1985) *Habits of the Heart: Individualism and commitment in American life*, Berkeley, CA: University of California Press.

Bennett, R. and Savani, S. (2011) 'Sources of new ideas for charity fundraising: an empirical study', *Creativity and Innovation Management*, 20(2): 121–139.

Bernholz, L., Skloot, E., and Varela, B. (2010) *Disrupting Philanthropy: Technology and the future of the social sector*, Durham, NC: Duke University: Center for Strategic Philanthropy and Civil Society.

Bishop, M. and Green, M. (2008) *Philanthrocapitalism: How the rich can save the world*, New York: Bloomsburg Press.

Black, M. (ed) (1992) *A cause for our times: Oxfam - the first 50 years*, Oxford: Oxfam and Oxford University Press.

Black, M. (2009) 'Obituary: Guy Stringer', *The Guardian*, 27 July 2009.

Bloch, S. (1997) 'Psychiatry: An impossible profession?', *Australian and New Zealand Journal of Psychiatry*, 31(2): 172–183.

Bloland, H. G. (2002) 'No longer emerging, fundraising is a profession', *The CASE International Journal of Education Advancement*, 3(1): 7–21.

Bloland, H. G. and Bornstein, R. (1991) 'Fund raising in transition: strategies for professionalisation', in D. F. Burlingame and L. J. Hulse (eds), *Taking Fund Raising Seriously: Advancing the Profession and Practice of Raising Money*, San Francisco: Jossey-Bass.

Bloland, H. G. and Tempel, E. R. (2004) 'Measuring professionalism', *New Directions for Philanthropic Fundraising*, 43: 5–20.

Blumenstyk, G. (2014) 'Building a better major-gifts officer', *Chronicle of Higher Education*, 23 September 2014.

Boden, M. (1990) *The Creative Mind: Myths and mechanisms*, New York: Basic Books.

Bourdieu, P. (1984) *Distinction: A Social Critique of the Judgement of Taste*, London: Routledge.

Bourdieu, P. (1986) 'The forms of capital', in J. E. Richardson (ed) *Handbook of Theory of Research for the Sociology of Education*, Westport, CT: Greenwood Press.

Bowles, S. (2016) *The Moral Economy: Why Good Incentives Are No Substitute For Good Citizens*, New Haven, CT: Yale University Press.

Breeze, B. (2006) *UK Philanthropy's Greatest Achievements*, London: Institute for Philanthropy.

Breeze, B. (2011) 'Is there a "New Philanthropy"?', in C. Rochester, G. Campbell Gosling, A. Penn, M. Zimmeck (eds) *Understanding Roots of Voluntary Action; Historical Perspectives on Current Social Policy*, Brighton: Sussex Academic Press.

Breeze, B. (2012a) 'Donor and Governmental Perceptions of Philanthropy', in CGAP (ed.) *Philanthropy and a Better Society*, London: Alliance Publishing Trust.

Breeze, B. (2012b) *Coutts Million Pound Donor Report 2012*, London: Coutts & Co.

Breeze, B. (2013a) 'How Donors Choose Charities', *Voluntary Sector Review*, 4(2): 165–183.

Breeze, B. (2013b) 'Agent Provocateur: Can British fundraisers afford to up their tenaciousness?', *Fundraising Magazine*, January 2013.

Breeze, B. (2015) *Coutts Million Pound Donor Report 2015*, London: Coutts & Co.

Breeze, B. and Lloyd, T. (2013) *Richer Lives: Why rich people give*, London: Directory of Social Change.

Breeze, B. and Scaife, W. (2015) 'Encouraging generosity: the practice and organization of fund-raising across nations', in P. Wiepking and F. Handy (eds), *The Palgrave Handbook of Global Philanthropy*, Basingstoke: Palgrave Macmillan.

Breeze, B., Halfpenny, P. and Wilding, K. (2015) 'Giving in the United Kingdom: philanthropy embedded in a welfare state society', in P. Wiepking and F. Handy (eds), *The Palgrave Handbook of Global Philanthropy*, Basingstoke: Palgrave Macmillan.

Bremner, R. H. (1988) *American Philanthropy*, Chicago: University of Chicago Press.

Bristow, W. (2011) 'Enlightenment', in *The Stanford Encyclopedia of Philosophy* (summer 2011 edn). Available at: http://plato.stanford.edu/archives/sum2011/entries/enlightenment

Broce, T. F. (1986) *Fund Raising: The guide to raising money from private sources*, 2nd edn, Norman, OK: University of Oklahoma Press.

Brookes, A. C. (2014) 'Why fund-raising is fun', New York Times, 29 March 2014. Available at: www.nytimes.com/2014/03/30/opinion/sunday/why-fund-raising-is-fun.html

Brown, L. (ed.) (1993) *The New Shorter Oxford English Dictionary on Historical Principles*, Oxford: Oxford University Press.

Brown, J. S. and Duguid, P. (2000) *The Social Life of Information*, Boston, MA: Harvard Business School Press.

Bryant, W.K., Slaughter, H.J., Kang, H. and Tax, A. (2003) 'Participating in philanthropic activities: donating money and time', *Journal of Consumer Policy,* 26: 43–73.

Bureau of Labor Statistics, *Current Population Survey: Labor Force Statistics 2016–17*, Washington, DC: US Department of Labor.

Burk, P. (2003) *Donor-Centred Fundraising*, Chicago: Burk and Associates Ltd.

Burlingame, D. F. and Hodge, J. M. (1997) 'Editors' notes', *New Directions for Philanthropic Fundraising*, 16 (summer), pp 1-3.

Burlingame, D. F. and Hulse, L. J. (1991) *Taking Fund Raising Seriously: Advancing the profession and practice of raising money*, San Francisco: Jossey-Bass.

Burnett, K. (2002 [1992]) *Relationship Fundraising*, 2nd edn, San Francisco: Jossey-Bass.

Burnett, K. (2006) *The Zen of Fundraising*, San Francisco: Wiley.

Burnett, K. (2010) 'In praise of the transformational fundraising entrepreneur'. Available at: www.kenburnett.com/BlogEntrepreneur.html

Cabinet Office (2011) *Giving White Paper*, London: HM Government.

Cabinet Office (2016) 'Community life survey 2015–16. Statistical bulletin'. Available at: www.gov.uk/government/uploads/system/uploads/attachment_data/file/539102/2015_16_community_life_survey_bulletin_final.pdf (last accessed 4 January 2017).

CAF (2016) *UK Giving 2015: An overview of charitable giving in the UK during 2015*, West Malling, Kent: Charities Aid Foundation.

Caldicott, L. (2013) 'How to recruit a great fundraiser,' *Civil Society*, 16 April. Available at: www.civilsociety.co.uk/fundraising/how-to-recruit-a-great-fundraiser.html

Cannadine, D. (2013) *Fred Freeman Annual Lecture on Philanthropy*, University of Liverpool, 12 November 2013. Available at: www.wolfson.org.uk/media/2352/fred-freeman-annual-lecture-on-philanthropy.pdf

Carbone, R. F. (1987) *Fundraisers of Academe*, College Park, MD: University of Maryland, Clearing House for Research on Fundraising.

Carbone, R. F. (1989) *Fund Raising as a Profession*, Monograph No. 3, College Park. MD: University of Maryland, Clearinghouse for Research on Fundraising.

Carlyle, T. (1841) *On Heroes, Hero-Worship, and the Heroic in History*, London: Chapman and Hall.

Chapman, T. and McGuinness, B. (2013) 'Consuming values in a social market: making choices about volunteering and non-volunteering', *Social and Public Policy Review*, 7(1): 1–17.

Charities Act (2006) Available at: www.legislation.gov.uk/ukpga/2006/50/pdfs/ukpga_20060050_en.pdf (last accessed 4 January, 2017).

Charity Commission (2016) *Charity Fundraising: A guide to trustee duties (CC20)*, London: Charity Commission.

Clifford, D., Geyne-Rajme, F., Smith, G., Edwards, R. Buchs, M. and Saunders, C. (2013) 'Mapping the environmental third sector in England: a distinctive field of activity?', *Voluntary Sector Review*, 4(2): 241–264.

Clohesy, W. W. (2003) 'Fundraising and the articulation of common goods', *Nonprofit and Voluntary Sector Quarterly*, 32(1): 128–140.

Clotfelter, C.T. (1992) (ed.) *Who Benefits from the Nonprofit Sector?* Chicago, Chicago University Press.

Cluff, A. (2009) 'Dispelling the myths about major donor fundraising', *International Journal of Nonprofit and Voluntary Sector Marketing*, 14(4): 371–377.

Conry, J. C. (1991) 'The feminization of fund raising', in D. F. Burlingame and L. J. Hulse (eds), *Taking Fundraising Seriously: Advancing the profession and practice of raising money*, San Francisco: Jossey-Bass.

Conte, J.M. (2005) 'A review and critique of emotional intelligence measures', *Journal of Organizational Behaviours*, 26(4): 433–440.

Croteau, J.D. and Smith, D.A. (2012) *Making the Case for Leadership: Profiles of chief advancement officers in higher education*, Lanham, MD: Rowman and Littlefield.

Cunningham, H. (2007) *Grace Darling: Victorian heroine*, London: Continuum Books.

Cunningham, H. (2015) 'The multi-layered history of western philanthropy', in T. Jung, S. Philips and J. Harrow (eds), *The Routledge Companion to Philanthropy*, London: Routledge.

Cunningham, H. and Innes, J. (eds) (1998) *Charity, Philanthropy and Reform: From the 1690s to 1850*, Basingstoke: Macmillan.

Cutlip, S. (1990) *Fundraising in the United States: Its role in America's philanthropy*, 2nd edn, New Brunswick, NJ: Transaction Publishers.

Cutlip, S (1998) 'Foreword', in K. S. Kelly, *Effective Fundraising Management*, New York and London: Routledge.

Dale, E. (2014) 'The story behind the gift: an exploratory study of gender, discourse, and million-dollar donations', *International Society for Third Sector research (ISTR) conference*, Muenster, Germany (22–24 July 2014).

Dalsgaard, S. (2007) '"I do it for the chocolate": An anthropological study of blood donation in Denmark', *Distinktion: Journal of Social Theory*, 14: 101–117.

Daly, S. (2013) 'Philanthropy, the new professionals and higher education: the advent of Directors of Development and Alumni Relations', *Journal of Higher Education Policy and Management*, 35(1): 21–33.

Daniels, A. K. (1988) *Invisible Careers: Women civic leaders from the volunteer world*, Chicago: University of Chicago Press.

Darley, J. M. and Latané, B. (1968) 'Bystander intervention in emergencies: diffusion of responsibility', *Journal of Personality and Social Psychology*, 8(4, pt 1): 377–383.

Davies, I., Le Meunier-FitzHugh, K., Ryals, L. J. and Ward, R. (2009) *Improving the Sales Force: Linking sales meeting behaviour to sales success*, Cranfield: Silent Edge/Cranfield School of Management.

Davies, K.A., Lane, A.M., Devonport, T.J. and Scott, J.A. (2010) 'Validity and reliability of a Brief Emotional Intelligence Scale (BEIS-10)', *Journal of Individual Differences*, 31(4): 198–208.

Davis, H. L. (2010) 'Feeding the World a Line? Celebrity Activism and Ethical Consumer Practices from Live Aid to Product Red', *Nordic Journal of English Studies*, 9(3): 89–117.

de Las Casas, L., von Poortvliet, M., Abercrombie, R. and Bagwell, S. (2013) *Money for Good UK: Understanding donor motivation and behaviour*, London: New Philanthropy Capital.

Derrida, J. (1992) *Given Time: 1. Counterfeit Money*, Chicago and London: University of Chicago Press.

DeSteno, D., Condon, P. and Dickens, L. (2016) 'Gratitude and compassion', in L. Barrett, M. Lewis and J. Haviland (eds), *Handbook of Emotions*, New York: Guilford Press.

Dibdin, J. C. (2010 [1894]) *The Book of the Lifeboat: With a complete history of the Saturday Lifeboat movement*, Charleston, SC: Nabu Press.

Dorsey, E. (1991) 'Foreword', in D. F. Burlingame and L. J. Hulse (eds), *Taking Fund Raising Seriously: Advancing the Profession and Practice of Raising Money*, San Francisco: Jossey-Bass.

Drake, A.W., Finkelstein, S.N. and Sapolsky, H.M. (1982) *The American Blood Supply*, Cambridge, MA: MIT Press.

Duronio, M. A. and Tempel, E.R. (1997) *Fund Raisers: Their careers, stories, concerns and accomplishments*, San Francisco: Jossey-Bass.

Dutton, J. E., Worline, M. C., Frost, P. J. and Lilius, J. (2006) 'Explaining compassion organizing', *Administrative Science Quarterly*, 51(1): 51–96.

EAB (2014) *Inside the Mind of a Curious Chameleon*. Education Advancement Board. Available at: www.eab.com/-/media/EAB/Research-and-Insights/AF/Infographics/29205-EAB-AF-Curious-Chameleon.pdf

Einstein, M. (2012) 'Charities shouldn't let corporate marketers set the agenda', *Chronicle of Philanthropy*, 29 April. Available at: www.philanthropy.com/article/Don-t-Let-Corporate/156653

Elischer, T. (1995) *Teach Yourself Fundraising*, London: Hodder & Stoughton.

Emerson Andrews, F. (1950) *Philanthropic Giving*, New York: Russell Sage Foundation.

Etzioni, A. (1969) *The Semi-Professions and Their Organisation: Teachers, nurses, social workers*, New York: Free Press.

European Fundraising Association (2014) *Fundraising in Europe*, Amsterdam: EFA. Available at: www.efa-net.eu/images/pdf/efa_survey_mar_2014.pdf

Farnhill, J. (2007) *The Porcupine Principle and Other Fundraising Secrets*, London: Directory of Social Change.

Ferris, P. (2011) 'Foreword', in M. Hancks, *Getting Started in Prospect Research: What you need to know to find who you need to find*, Rancho Santa Margarita, CA: CharityChannel Press.

Filiz-Ozbay, E. and Uler, N. (2016) *Demand for Giving to Multiple Charities: Theory and experiment*, College Park, MD: Department of Economics, University of Maryland.

Flanagan, J. (2002) *Successful Fundraising: A complete handbook for volunteers and professionals*, New York: McGraw-Hill.
Flannery, J. A. and Smith, K. M. (2011) *Sir Henry Wellcome: Backwood to Knighthood*, Leeds: Boston Spa Media.
Florida, R. (2012) *The Rise of the Creative Class, Revisited*, New York: Basic Books.
Franks, S. (2013) *Reporting Disasters: Famine, aid, politics and the media*, London: C. Hurst & Co.
Frumkin, P. (2006). *Strategic Giving: The art and science of philanthropy*, Chicago and London, University of Chicago Press.
Fry, H. (1917) *Royal Guide to the London Charities*, London: Chatto & Windus.
Fukuyama, F. (1995) *Trust: The Social virtues and the creation of prosperity*, New York: The Free Press.
Fund Raising Standards Board (2014) *FRSB Complaints Report 2014: An overview of charity fundraising complaints from 2013*, London: FRSB. Available at: www.fundraisingregulator.org.uk/wp-content/uploads/2016/10/FRSB_Complaints-Report_2014-1.pdf
Galbraith, J.K. (1967) *The New Industrial State*, Boston, MA: Houghton Mifflin.
Garcia, C. (2016) 'So you think you can fundraise?' *CASE Currents*, November. Council for Advancement and Support of Education.
Gates, B. (1995) *The Road Ahead*, New York: Viking Press.
Gilchrist, K. (2000) *Looking After Your Donors*, London: Directory of Social Change.
Gladwell, M. (2009) *Outliers: The story of success*, London and New York: Penguin.
Glennie, A. and Whillans-Welldrake, A. G. (2014) *Charity Street: The value of charity to British households*, London: IPPR.
Godfrey, J. (2016) 'Engaging HNWI Indians', *Journal of Development Policy and Practice*, 1(1): 89–113.
Gouldner, A. W. (1973) *For Sociology: Renewal and critique in sociology today*, London: Allen Lane.
Grant, P. (2014) Philanthropy and Voluntary Action in the First World War: Mobilizing charity, Abingdon, Oxon and New York: Routledge.
Gray, B. K. (1905) *A History of Philanthropy: From the dissolution of the monasteries to the taking of the first census*, London, Frank Cass & Co.
Green, F., McDonald, B. and van Herpt, J. (2007) *Iceberg Philanthropy: Unlocking Extraordinary Gifts from Ordinary Donors*, Ottawa, ON: The FLA Group.
Greenfield, J. M. (2002) *Fundraising Fundamentals: A guide to annual giving for professionals and volunteers*, New York: John Wiley & Sons.

Gregorian, V. (2003) *The road to home: My life and times*, New York, NY: Simon & Schuster.

Gunderman, R. (2010) 'The Social Role of Fundraising', in A. Sargeant and J. Shang (eds), *Fundraising Principles and Practice*, New York: John Wiley & Sons.

Gunstone, B. and Ellison. G. (2017) *Insights into Charity Fundraising: Why people give and their experience of donating*, London: Institute of Fundraising.

Gurin, M. G. (1985) *Confessions of a Fundraiser: Lessons of an instructive career*, Washington, DC: The Taft Group.

Gurin, M. G. (1991) *Advancing Beyond the Techniques in Fund Raising*, Rockville, MA: Fundraising Institute.

Guyatt, M. (2000) 'The Wedgwood slave medallion: values in eighteenth-century design', *Journal of Design History*, 13(2): 93–105.

Gurin, M.G. and Van Til, J. (1990) 'Philanthropy in its historical context', in J. Van Til and associates, *Critical Issues in American Philanthropy*, San Francisco, CA: Jossey-Bass.

Habermas, J. (1989 [1962]) *The Structural Transformation of the Public Sphere: An inquiry into a category of bourgeois society*, Cambridge, MA: MIT Press.

Halford, S. and Strangleman, T. (2009) 'In search of the sociology of work: past, present and future', *Sociology*, 43(5): 811–828.

Halttunen, K. (1995) 'Humanitarianism and the pornography of pain in Anglo-American culture', *American Historical Review*, 100: 303–334.

Handy, C. (1988) *Understanding Voluntary Organizations*, London: Penguin.

Handy, C. (2006) *The New Philanthropists*, London: William Heinemann.

Hansmann, H. B. (1987) 'Economic theories of nonprofit organizations', in W. W. Powell (ed.), *The Nonprofit Sector: A research handbook*, New Haven, CT: Yale University Press.

Harbaugh, W. (1997) 'What do donations buy? A model of philanthropy based on prestige and warm glow', *Journal of Public Economics*, 67: 269–284.

Harlock, J. (2013) 'Impact measurement practice in the UK third sector: a review of emerging evidence', *TSRC working paper* 106, Birmingham: University of Birmingham: Third Sector Research Centre.

Harrah-Conforth, J. and Borsos, J. (1991) 'The evolution of professional fund raising 1890–1990', in D. F. Burlingame and L. J. Hulse (eds), *Taking Fund Raising Seriously: Advancing the profession and practice of raising money*, San Francisco: Jossey-Bass.

Hartsook, R. (1999) *Closing that Gift! How to be successful 99% of the time*, Wichita, KS: ASR Philanthropic Publishing.
Haskell, T. (1984) *The Authority of Experts: Historical and theoretical essays*, Bloomington, IN: Indiana University Press.
Healy, K. (2000) 'Embedded altruism: blood collection regimes and the european union's donor population, *American Journal of Sociology*, 105(6): 1633–1657.
Healy, K. (2004) 'Altruism as an organizational problem: the case of organ procurement', *American Sociological Review*, 69(3): 387–404.
HEFCE (2012) *Matched Funding Scheme for Voluntary Giving: 2008–2011 outcomes*. Available at: www.hefce.ac.uk/pubs/year/2012/cl,142012
Henley, J. (2012) 'The new philanthropists', *The Guardian*, 7 March 2012. Available at: www.theguardian.com/society/2012/mar/07/new-philanthropists-wealthy-people
Herbst, N. B. and Norton, M. (2012 [1992]) *The Complete Fundraising Handbook*, London: Directory of Social Change.
Hibbert, S. and Horne, S. (1997) 'Donation dilemmas: a consumer behaviour perspective', *Journal of Nonprofit and Voluntary Sector Marketing*, 2(3): 261–274.
Hochschild, A. (1983) *The Managed Heart: Commercialization of human feeling*, Berkeley and Los Angeles, CA: University of California Press.
Holman, M. and Sargent, L. (2012 [2006]) *Major Donor Fundraising*, 2nd edn, London: Directory of Social Change.
Home Office (2005) *A Generous Society: Next steps on charitable giving in England*, London: Home Office.
Horn, L. and Gardner, H. (2006) 'The lonely profession', in W. Damon and S. Verducci (eds), *Taking Philanthropy Seriously: Beyond noble intentions to responsible giving*, Bloomington and Indianapolis, IN: Indiana University Press.
House of Lords (2017) *Stronger Charities for a Stronger Society*, London: The Stationery Office.
Hufton, O. (1998) 'The widow's mite and other strategies: funding the Catholic Reformation. The Prothero Lecture', *Transactions of the Royal Historical Society*, (8): 117–137.
Hufton, D. O. (2008) 'Faith, hope and money: the Jesuits and the genesis of fundraising for education, 1550–1650', *Historical Research*, 81: 585–609.
Hughes, J. (1996) 'Beyond the rattling tin: funding and fundraising', in C. Hanvey and T. Philpot (eds), *Sweet Charity: The role and workings of voluntary organisations*, London: Routledge.
Ilchman, W. F., Katz, S. N. and Queen II, E. L. (1998) (eds) *Philanthropy in the World's Traditions*, Bloomington, IN: Indiana University Press.

Institute of Fundraising (2009) *The State of UK Fundraising 2009: Mapping fundraising and income generation in the UK*, London: Institute of Fundraising.

Institute of Fundraising (2011) *The Good Fundraising Guide*, London: Institute of Fundraising.

Institute of Fundraising (2013) *Who's Doing the Asking? Diversity in the fundraising profession*, London: Institute of Fundraising.

Institute of Fundraising (2015) *Introductory Certificate in Fundraising, Unpublished training materials*, London: Institute of Fundraising Academy.

Israeli, G. (2014) *Why 'how matters' to fundraisers*. Available at: https://fundraisingcompass.com/2014/10/08/why-how-matters-to-fundraising/

James, E. (1990) 'Economic theories of the nonprofit sector', in H.K. Anheier and W. Seibel (eds), *The Third Sector: Comparative studies of nonprofit organizations*, Berlin and New York: De Gruyter.

Jasper, C. R. and Samek, A. K. (2014) 'Increasing charitable giving in the developed world', *Oxford Review of Economic Policy*, 30(4), pp 680-696.

Jeavons, T. (1991) 'A historical and moral analysis of religious fund raising', in D. F. Burlingame and L. J. Hulse (eds), *Taking Fund Raising Seriously: Advancing the profession and practice of raising money*, San Francisco: Jossey-Bass.

Jencks, C. (1987) 'Who gives to what?', in W. Powell (ed.), *The NonProfit Sector: A research handbook*, New Haven, CT: Yale University Press.

John, O. and Srivastava (1999) *The Big-Five Trait Taxonomy: History, measurement and theoretical perspectives*, University of California at Berkeley. Available at http://moityca.com.br/pdfs/bigfive_John.pdf (last accessed 3 June 2017).

Johnson, J. (2011a) 'The major donor dilemma', *Charity Insight*, 6.

Johnson, T. J. (2011b) *10 Critical Factors in Fundraising: The little green book for chief executive officers*, Oklahoma City: JTJ Publishing.

John of Salisbury (W. J. Millor, H. E. Butler and C. N. L. Brooke, eds) (1955) *The Letters of John of Salisbury Volume 1: The Early Letters (1153–1161)*, London, Nelson.

Jones, M. G. (2013 [1938]) *The Charity School Movement: A Study of Eighteenth Century Puritanism in Action*, Cambridge: Cambridge University Press.

Jones, R. C., and Olsen, A. (2013) *Rainmaking: The fundraiser's guide to landing big gifts*, Createspace.

Jordan, W. K. (1959) *Philanthropy in England 1480–1660: A study of the changing pattern of English social aspirations*, London: George Allen & Unwin.

Joslyn, H. (2016) 'Half of fundraisers start careers by age 27, according to new data', *Chronicle of Philanthropy*, 21 March. Available at: www.philanthropy.com/article/Half-of-Fundraisers-Start/235780

Joyaux, S. P. (2011) *Strategic Fund Development: Building profitable relationships that last*, 3rd edn, Hoboken, NJ: Wiley.

Kanazawa, S. (2016) '"To vote or not to vote": charity voting and the other side of subscriber democracy in Victorian England', *The English Historical Review*, 131(549): 353–383.

Karoff, H.P. (2005) 'The public and private persona of philanthropy:tThe donor challenge', *New Directions for Philanthropic Fundraising*, 47 (Spring), pp 43-58.

Kaye, M. (2005) 1807–2007: *Over 200 years of campaigning against slavery*, London: Anti-Slavery International.

Kelley, J., Kraft-Todd, G., Schapira, L., Kossowsky, J. and Riess, H. (2014) 'The influence of the patient–clinician relationship on healthcare outcomes: a systematic review and meta-analysis of randomized control trials', *PLoS ONE* 9(6): e101191. DOI: 10.1371/journal.pone.0101191.

Kelly, K. S. (1997) 'From motivation to mutual understanding: shifting the domain of donor research', in D. F. Burlingame (ed.), *Major Issues Facing Fundraising*, New York: John Wiley & Sons.

Kelly, K. S. (1998) *Effective Fundraising Management*, New York and London: Routledge.

King, S. (2006) *Pink Ribbons, Inc*, Minneapolis, MN: University of Minnesota Press.

Klein, K. (2011 [1988]) *Fundraising for Social Change*, 6th edn, San Francisco: Jossey-Bass.

Knott, R. A. (1992) *The Making of a Philanthropic Fundraiser: Instructive example of Milton Murray*, San Francisco: Jossey-Bass.

Komter, A. (2005) *Social Solidarity and the Gift*, Cambridge: Cambridge University Press.

Konrath, S. (2016) 'The joy of giving', in E. R. Tempel, T. L. Seiler and D. F. Burlingame (eds), *Achieving Excellence in Fundraising*, Hoboken, NJ: Wiley.

Krakovsky, M. (2015) *The Middleman Economy: How brokers, agents, dealers, and everyday matchmakers create value and profit*, Basingstoke: Palgrave Macmillan.

Krass, P. (2002) *Carnegie*, Hoboken, NJ: John Wiley & Sons.

Laskowski, T. (2016) '5 ways to nurture new talent', *CASE Currents*, November 2016. Council for Advancement and Support of Education. Available at: www.case.org/Publications_and_Products/2016/November_2016/5_Ways_to_Nurture_New_Talent.html

Lee, S. (1998) 'The moral maze of raising cash', *The Guardian*, 28 June 1998, www.sumption.org/oldsite/obit.html (last accessed 24 July 2017).

Lee, S. and Mullin, S. (2006) 'Prospect research policy, privacy, and ethics', in T. Hart, J. M. Greenfield, P. M. Gignac and C. Carnie (eds), *Major Donors: Finding big gifts in your database and online*, San Francisco: Wiley.

Leonhardt, D. (2008) 'What makes people give?', *The New York Times*, 9 March. Available at: www.nytimes.com/2008/03/09/magazine/09Psychology-t.html

Levy, J. D. (2004) 'The growth of fundraising: framing the impact of research and literature on education and training', *New Directions for Philanthropic Fundraising*, 43, special issue, pp.21–30.

Levy, R. (2009) *Yours for the Asking: An indispensable guide to fundraising and management*, Hoboken, NJ: John Wiley & Sons.

Lindahl, W. (2010) *Principles of Fundraising: Theory and practice*, Sudbury, MA: Jones and Bartlett.

Lindahl, W. E. and Conley, A. T. (2002) 'Literature review: philanthropic fundraising', *Nonprofit Management and Leadership*, 13(1): 91–112.

Lloyd, S. (2002) 'Pleasing spectacles and elegant dinners: conviviality, benevolence, and charity anniversaries in eighteenth-century London', *The Journal of British Studies*, 41(1): 23–57.

Lloyd, T. (2004) *Why Rich People Give*, London: Association of Charitable Foundations.

Lloyd, T. (2011) 'The major donor dilemma', *Charity Insight*, 6.

Longmore, P. (2015) *Telethons: Spectacles, disability and the business of charity*, Oxford: Oxford University Press.

Looney, C.A. and Looney, J.K. (2005) 'Attracting top talent and retaining stars', *New Directions for Philanthropic Fundraising*, 49: 99–108.

Lord, J. G. (1987) *The Raising of Money: Thirty-five essentials every trustee should know*, Cleveland, OH: Third Sector Press.

Lowe, J. (2001) *Bill Gates Speaks: Insights from the world's greatest entrepreneur*, New York: John Wiley & Sons.

Lysakowski, L. (2012) *Fundraising for the Genius*, Rancho Santa Margarita, CA: CharityChannel Press.

Macdonald, K.M. (1995) *Sociology of the Professions*, London: Sage.

Macfarquhar, L. (2015) *Strangers Drowning: Grappling with impossible idealism, drastic choices, and the overpowering urge to help*, New York: Penguin.

Macqueen, A. (2004) *The King of Sunlight: How William Lever cleaned up the world*, London: Transworld.

MacQuillin, I. (2014) 'Moralists at the feast: what really drives public hostility to fundraising?' Blogpost. Available at: http://blogs.plymouth.ac.uk/criticalfundraising/2014/09/30/opinion-moralists-at-the-feast-what-really-drives-public-hostility-to-fundraising

Marts, A. (1961) *Man's Concern for His Fellow Man*, New York: W. F. Humphrey Press.

Maslow, A. H. (1943) 'A theory of human motivation', *Psychological Review*, 50(4): 370–96.

Maslow, A. H. (1954) *Motivation and Personality*, New York: Harper and Row.

Matheny, R. E. (1995) 'Communication in cultivation and solicitation of major gift donors', *New Directions for Philanthropic Fundraising*, 10: 33–44.

Matheny, R. E. (1999) *Major Gift Solicitation Strategies*, 2nd edn, Washington, DC: CASE.

Mauss, M. (2002 [1950]) *The Gift*, London: Routledge Classic.

May, J. A. (1997) 'Meshing development efforts with major gift fundraising', *New Directions for Philanthropic Fundraising*, 16: 17–30.

May, M. and Broomhead, P. (2014) *UK Small Charity Sector Skills Survey 2014/15*, London: The Foundation for Social Improvement.

McKeever, B. W., Pressgrove, G., McKeever, R. and Zheng, Y. (2016) 'Towards a theory of situational support: A model for exploring fundraising, advocacy and organizational support', *Public Relations Review*, 42: 219–222.

McKinnon, H. (2006) *Tiny Essentials of Monthly Committed Giving*, Melrand, France: White Lion Press.

McLoughlin, J. (2014) 'Major gift fundraisers and philanthropists: reframing a crucial interaction', paper presented at Voluntary Sector and Volunteering Research Conference 2014, London, UK.

Meer, J. (2016) *Does Fundraising Create New Giving?*, Working Paper 22033, National Bureau of Economic Research, Cambridge, MA: NBER.

Micklewright, J. and Schnepf, S. (2009) 'Who gives charitable donations for overseas development?', *Journal of Social Policy*, 38(2): 317–341.

Minson, J. A. and Monin, B. (2011) 'Do-gooder derogation: putting down morally motivated others to defuse implicit moral reproach', *Social Psychological and Personality Science*, 3(2): 200–207.

Mixer, J. R. (1993) *Principles of Professional Fundraising: Useful Foundations for Successful Practice*, San Francisco: Jossey-Bass.

Mohan, J. and Breeze, B. (2015) *The Logic of Charity: Great expectations in hard times*, Basingstoke: Palgrave Macmillan.

Mohan, J. and Breeze, B. (2016) *Evidence submitted to the House of Lords Select Committee on Charity*. Available at http://data.parliament.uk/writtenevidence/committeeevidence.svc/evidencedocument/select-committee-on-charities/charities/written/37072.html

Mohan, J. and Gorsky, M. (2001) *Don't Look Back?: Voluntary and charitable finance of hospitals*, London: Office of Health Economics.

Moody, M. and Breeze, B. (2016) *The Philanthropy Reader*, London: Routledge.

Moore, S. (2010) *Ribbon Culture: Charity, compassion and public awareness*, Basingstoke: Palgrave Macmillan.

More Partnership (2012) *Review of Philanthropy in UK Higher Education: 2012 status report and challenges for the next decade*, a report to the Higher Education Funding Council for England, London: More Partnership.

More Partnership/Richmond Associates (2014a) *An Emerging Profession: The Higher Education Philanthropy Workforce*, a report to the Higher Education Funding Council for England, London: More Partnership and Richmond Associates.

More Partnership/Richmond Associates (2014b) *Higher Education Fundraising Toolkit: A guide to recruiting and retaining the best people for an emerging profession*. Available at: www.morepartnership.com/library/HE_Fundraising_Toolkit.pdf (last accessed 17 July 2016).

Morgan, K. (1993) *Bristol and the Atlantic Trade in the Eighteenth Century*, Cambridge: Cambridge University Press.

Morison, S. E. (1998 [1935]) *The Founding of Harvard College*, Cambridge, MA: Harvard University Press.

Mullin, R. (1987) *The Fundraising Cycle: The shortest book on fundraising, ever*. Available at: www.sofii.org/node/442 (last accessed 17 June 2017).

Mullin, R. (1995) *Foundations for fund-raising*, Hemel Hempstead: ICSA Publishing Limited.

Mullin, R. (1997) *Fundraising strategy*, London: CAF/ICFM.

Mullin, R. (2007) 'Two thousand years of disreputable history', in J. Mordaunt and R. Paton (eds), *Thoughtful Fundraising: Concepts, Issues and Perspectives*, Abingdon, Oxon: Routledge.

Musick, M. and Wilson, J. (2007) *Volunteers: A social profile*, Bloomington, IN: Indiana University Press.

Mutz, J. and Murray, K. (2010) *Fundraising for dummies*, 3rd edn, Hoboken, NJ: Wiley Publishing, Inc.

Nagaraj, A. J. (2014) *Gifted and Talented: What makes a top fundraiser in the age of venture philanthropy?* Presentation at Fundraising Insights – New Research Findings conference, held at the University of Westminster, London on 28 March 2014.

Nasaw, D. (2006) *Andrew Carnegie*, London: Penguin.

NCVO (2010) *Funding the Future: A 10 year framework for civil society*, London: NCVO.

NCVO (2014) *UK Civil Society Almanac 2014*, London: NCVO.

NCVO (2015) *UK Civil Society Almanac 2015*, London: NCVO.

NCVO (2016) *UK Civil Society Almanac 2016*, London: NCVO.

Neilson, L., Brouard, F. and Armenakyan, A. (2012) *Fundraising Methods: Past, Present and Future*, Ottawa, Canada: Sprott Center for Social Enterprises, Carleton University.

New Englands first fruits (1643) *New Englands first fruits: in respect, first of the counversion of some, conviction of divers, preparation of sundry of the Indians 2. Of the progresse of learning, in the colledge at Cambridge in Massachusetts bay. With divers other speciall matters concerning that countrey*, London: Printed by R. O. and G. D. for Henry Overton. Available at: https://archive.org/details/NewEnglandsFirstFruitsInRespectFirstOfTheCounversionOfSome (last accessed 8 August 2016).

Nichols, J. (1996) 'Fundraising in the USA and the United Kingdom: Comparing today with directions for tomorrow', *Journal of Nonprofit and Voluntary Sector Marketing*, 2(2): 148–153.

Ni Ogain, E., Lumley, T. and Pritchard, D. (2012) *Making an Impact: Impact measurement among charities and social enterprises in the UK*, London: New Philanthropy Capital.

Norton, M. (2007) *Need to Know? Fundraising*, London: HarperCollins.

Nouwen, H. (2010) *A spirituality of fundraising*, Nashville, TN: Henri Nouwen Society.

O'Connor, B. (1959) *The Place of the National Voluntary Health Organisation in American Life*, Address to Midwest conference of United Community Funds and Councils of America, Hotel LaSalle, Chicago, Inc. 5 March 1959.

OECD (2010) *The Economic and Social Role of Internet Intermediaries*, Organisation for Economic Cooperation and Development. Available at: www.oecd.org/internet/ieconomy/44949023.pdf

Offer, A. (1997) 'Between the gift and the market: the economy of regard', *Economic History Review*, 50(3): 450–476.

Okasha, S. (2013) 'Biological Altruism', in *Stanford Encyclopedia of Philosophy*. Available at: http://plato.stanford.edu/entries/altruism-biological

Okten, C. and Weisbrod, B. (2000) 'Determinants of donations in private nonprofit markets', *Journal of Public Economics*, 75(2): 255–272.

Oliner, S. P. and Oliner, P. M. (1988) *The Altruistic Personality: Rescuers of Jews in Nazi Europe*, New York: The Free Press.

ONS (2013) *Full Report – Graduates in the UK Labour Market 2013*. Office for National Statistics. Available at: http://webarchive.nationalarchives.gov.uk/20160105160709/http://www.ons.gov.uk/ons/dcp171776_337841.pdf (last accessed 3 June 2017).

Oppenheimer, D. M. and Olivola, C. Y. (2011) *The Science of Giving: Experimental approaches to the study of charity*, New York: Psychology Press.

Osteen, M. (ed.) (2002) *The Question of the Gift: Essays across disciplines*, London and New York: Routledge.

Ostrander, S. and Schervish, P. (1990) 'Giving and getting: philanthropy as a social relation', in J. Van Til (ed.), *Critical Issues in American Philanthropy: Strengthening theory and practice*, San Francisco: Jossey-Bass.

Owen, D. (1965) *English Philanthropy 1660–1960*, London: Oxford University Press.

Packard, V. (1957) *The Hidden Persuaders*, Brooklyn, NY: Ig Publishing.

Panas, Jerold (1984) *Mega Gifts: Who gives them, who gets them?* Chicago: Bonus Books.

Panas, J. (1988) *Born to Raise: What makes a great fundraiser, what makes a fundraiser great?*, Chicago: Bonus Books Inc.

Panas, J. (2012) *Asking: A 59-Minute Guide to Everything Board Members, Volunteers, and Staff Must Know to Secure the Gift*, Medfield, MA: Emerson & Church.

Parsons, T. (1968) 'Professions', in D. Sills (ed.), *International Encyclopedia of the Social Sciences*, 2nd edn, New York: Macmillan.

Payne, D. (2006) 'London's charity school children: the 'scum of the parish'', *Journal for Eighteenth-Century Studies*, 29(3): 383–397.

Payton, R.L. (1991) 'Foreword', in H. Rosso (ed.), *Achieving Excellence in Fund Raising: A comprehensive guide to principles, strategies and methods*, San Francisco: Jossey-Bass.

Payton, R.L. (1998) 'A tradition in jeopardy', in C. T. Clotfelter and T. Ehrlich (eds), *Philanthropy and the Nonprofit Sector in a Changing America*, Bloomington, IN: Indiana University Press.

Payton, R.L. and Moody, M. P. (2008) *Understanding Philanthropy: Its meaning and mission*, Bloomington and Indianapolis, IN: Indiana University Press.

Payton, R.L., Rosso, H. and Tempel, E.R. (1991) 'Taking fundraising seriously: an agenda', in D. F. Burlingame and L. J. Hulse (eds), *Taking Fundraising Seriously: Advancing the profession and practice of raising money*, San Francisco: Jossey-Bass.

Perdue, P. E. (2014) *May I Cultivate You? Careers in fundraising*, Norfolk, VA: Petar Publishing.

Philanthropy Review (2011) *A Call to Action to Encourage More People to Give and People to Give More. Recommendations from the Philanthropy Review*, London: The Philanthropy Review.

Pigeau, L. (2013) 'Train volunteers on "making the ask"', in G. Stanois (ed.), *The Vigilant Fundraiser: 12 steps to fundraising success*, Toronto: Civil Sector Press.

Piliavin, J. A. and Charng, H.-W. (1990) 'Altruism: a review of recent theory and research', *Annual Review of Sociology*, 16: 27–65.

Pink, D. H. (2012) To Sell is Human, Edinburgh: Canongate.

Pinker, S. (2011) *The Better Angels of our Nature: A history of violence and humanity*, London: Penguin.

Pitman, M. (2007) *Ask Without Fear: A simple guide to connecting donors with what matters to them most*, Greenville, SC: Standish and Wade Publishing.

Pribbenow, P. P. (1999) 'Love and work: rethinking our modes of professions', *New Directions for Philanthropic Fundraising*, 26: 29–50.

Prince, R. A. and File, K. M. (1994) *The Seven Faces of Philanthropy: A new approach to cultivating major donors*, San Francisco: Jossey-Bass.

Prochaska, F. (1988) *The Voluntary Impulse: Philanthropy in modern Britain*, London and Boston, MA: Faber and Faber.

Prochaska, F. (1990a) 'Philanthropy', in F. M. L. Thompson (ed.), *The Cambridge Social History of Britain 1750–1950*, Cambridge: Cambridge University Press.

Prochaska, F. (1990b) *Women and Philanthropy in Nineteenth-century England*, Oxford: Clarendon Press.

Prochaska, F. (1992) *Philanthropy and the Hospitals of London: The Kings Fund 1897–1990*, Oxford: Clarendon Press.

Prochaska, F. (1995) *Royal Bounty: The making of a welfare monarchy*, New Haven, CT: Yale University Press.

Pudelek, J. (2014a) 'Change makers: RNLI', *Third Sector*, 17 March. Available at: www.thirdsector.co.uk/change-makers-rnli/communications/article/1285184

Pudelek, J. (2014b) 'Fundraising leadership is "pale, stale and male"', *Civil Society*, 16 October. Available at: www.civilsociety.co.uk/news/fundraising-leadership-is--pale--stale-and-male-.html

Putnam, R. D. (1993) *Making Democracy Work: Civic traditions in modern Italy*, Princeton NJ: Princeton University Press.

Radley, A. and Kennedy, M. (1995) 'Charitable giving by individuals: a study of attitude and practice', *Human Relations*, 48(6): 685–709.

Ragsdale, J.D. (1995) 'Quality communication in achieving fundraising excellence', *New Directions for Philanthropic Fundraising*, 10: 17–32.

Red Cross (n.d.) 'The founding of the British Red Cross'. Available at: www.redcross.org.uk/About-us/Who-we-are/Museum-and-archives/Historical-factsheets/The-founding-of-the-British-Red-Cross

RNLI (n.d.) Origin of the The Lifeboat Saturday Movement (photocopy from archives, no publication details available).

Rooney, P. and Frederick, H. (2007) 'Bank of America Study of High Net Worth Philanthropy'. Available at: http://newsroom.bankofamerica.com/files/press_kit/additional/BAC_Portraits_of_Donors_Report_12-07-07.pdf (last accessed 6 June 2017).

Rose-Ackerman, S. (1982) 'Charitable giving and "excessive fundraising"', *The Quarterly Journal of Economics*, 97(2): 193–212.

Ross, B. and Segal, C. (2002) *Breakthrough Thinking for Nonprofit Organizations*, San Francisco: Jossey-Bass.

Ross, B. and Segal, C. (2008) *The Influential Fundraiser: Using the psychology of persuasion to achieve outstanding results*, San Francisco: Jossey-Bass.

Ross-CASE (2016) *Giving to Excellence: Generating philanthropic support for UK higher education.* The Ross-CASE report 2016, London: Council for Advancement and Support of Education.

Rosso, H. (2015) 'A philosophy of fundraising', in E.R. Tempel, T.L. Seiler and D.F. Burlingame (eds), *Achieving Excellence in Fundraising*, Hoboken, NJ: Wiley.

Rum, S. and Wheeler, J. (2016) 'Instituting and teaching ethical standards for grateful patient fundraising', *Journal of Clinical Oncology*, 34(12): 1423–4.

Sadeh, J., Tonin, M. and Vlassopoulos, M. (2014) 'Why Give Away Your Wealth: An Analysis of the Billionaire's View', Discussion Papers in Economics and Econometrics, paper 1417, University of Southampton. Available at www.personal.soton.ac.uk/mv1u06/Pledge_Sep_2014.pdf

Saint, D. (2011) 'The major donor dilemma', *Charity Insight*, 6.

Salamon, L. (1987) 'Partners in public service: toward a theory of government-nonprofit relations', in W. W. Powell (ed.), *The Nonprofit Sector: A Research Handbook*, New Haven, CT: Yale University Press.

Sargeant, A. (2013) 'Donor retention: what do we know and what can we do about it?' *The Nonprofit Quarterly*, Summer: 12–23.

Sargeant, A. (2014) 'A retrospective – charitable giving: towards a model of donor behaviour, *Social Business*, 4(4): 293–323.

Sargeant, A. and Jay, E. (2014) *Fundraising Management: Analysis, planning and practice*, 3rd edn, London: Routledge.

Sargeant, A. and Shang, J. (2011) *Growing Philanthropy in the United Kingdom*, London: Institute of Fundraising.

Sargeant, A. and Shang, J. (2016) 'Outstanding fundraising practice: how do nonprofits substantively increase their income?', *International Journal of Nonprofit and Voluntary Sector Marketing*, 21(1): 43–56.

Sargeant, A., Shang, J. and Associates (2010) *Fundraising Principles and Practice*, New York: John Wiley & Sons.

Saxton, J. and Madden, M. (2010) 'How Can the New Government Increase the Size of the Funding Cake?', paper commissioned by the NCVO Funding Commission.

Scaife, W. and Madden, K. (2006) 'Change Agents or Counting the Change: Insights to the role of fundraisers in Australian society and issues facing their professionalization', paper presented to the Social Change in the 21st Century Conference Centre for Social Change Research at Queensland University of Technology, 27 October 2006.

Scaife, W., McDonald, K. and Smyllie, S. (2011) *A Transformational Role: Donor and charity perspectives on major giving in Australia*, Brisbane, Australia: The Australian Centre for Philanthropy and Nonprofit Studies, Queensland University of Technology.

Scaife, W., Williamson, A. and McDonald, K. (2014) 'Mind the Gap! Fundraisers and their nonprofit organizational leaders do think differently and this difference matters'. Paper presented at the ANZTSR 14th Biennial Conference, November 18–20, 2014, Otautahi/Christchurch, Aotearoa, New Zealand.

Schervish, P. (2003) *Hyperagency and High Tech Donors: A new theory of the new philanthropists*, Boston, MA: Boston College Social Welfare Research Institute.

Schervish, P. (2005) 'Major donors, major motives: the people and purposes behind major gifts', *New Directions for Philanthropic Fundraising*, 47: 59–87.

Schervish, P. (2007) 'Why the wealthy give: factors which mobilize philanthropy among high net worth individuals', in A. Sargeant and W. Wymer Jr (eds), *The Routledge Companion to Nonprofit Marketing*, London: Routledge.

Schervish, P. and Havens, J. G. (1997) 'Social participation and charitable giving', *Voluntas*, 8(3): 235–260.

Schuman, M.A. (2007) *Bill Gates: Computer mogul and philanthropist*, New York: Enslow publishers.

Schwittay, A. (2015) *New Media and International Development: Representation and effect in microfinance*, London: Routledge.

Seymour, H. (1947) *Designs for Giving: The story of the National War Fund, Inc. 1943–1947*, New York and London: Harper & Brothers.

Seymour, H. (1966) *Designs for Fund-Raising: Principles, Patterns, Techniques*, New York: McGraw-Hill.

Shaker, G. G. (2016) 'Personal solicitation', in E. R. Tempel, T. L. Seiler D. F. Burlingame (eds), *Achieving Excellence in Fundraising*, 4th edn, Hoboken, NJ: Wiley.

Shapely, P. (2000) *Charity and Power in Victorian Manchester*, Manchester: The Chetham Society.

Sherrington, M. (2015) 'Yesterday's trail-blazing and pointers for tomorrow. Listen up'. Blogpost. Available at http://101fundraising.org/2015/08/yesterdays-trail-blazing-and-pointers-for-tomorrow-listen-up

Silber, I. (1998) 'Modern philanthropy: reassessing the viability of a Maussian perspective', in N. J. Allen (ed.), *Marcell Mauss Today*, Oxford and New York: Berghahn.

Silber, I. (2012) 'The angry gift: a neglected facet of philanthropy', *Current Sociology*, 60(3): 320–337.

Simmel, G. (1950) 'Faithfulness and gratitude', in K. H. Wolff (ed.), *The Sociology of Georg Simmel*, Glencoe, IL: The Free Press.

Simmons, R. G., Klein, S. D. and Simmons, R. L. (1977) *Gift of Life: The social and psychological impact of organ transplantation*, London: Wiley.

Singer, P. (2010) *The Life You Can Save: How to play your part in ending world poverty*, New York: Random House.

Singer, P. (2011 [1981]) *The Expanding Circle: Ethics and sociobiology*, Princeton, NJ: Princeton University Press.

Singer, P. (2015) *The Most Good You Can Do: How effective altruism is changing ideas about living ethically*, New Haven, CT: Yale University Press.

Skills Third Sector (2013) 'Fundraising: National Occupational Standards'. Available at: www.institute-of-fundraising.org.uk/library/fundraising-national-occupational-standards

Sloggie, N. (2005) *Tiny Essentials of Major Gift Fundraising*, Melrand, France: White Lion Press.

Smith, C. (2014) 'What makes us generous?' Big Questions online, Science of Generosity project. Available at: www.bigquestionsonline.com/2014/05/27/what-makes-generous

Smith, C. and Davidson, H. (2014) *The Paradox of Generosity: Giving we receive, grasping we lose*, New York: Oxford University Press.

Smith, G. (1996) *Asking Properly: The art of creative fundraising*, London: White Lion Press.

Smith, G. (2009) 'A profile of Britain's founding fathers of modern fundraising'. Available at: http://sofii.org/article/harold-sumption-guy-stringer-cbe-and-sir-leslie-kirkley-cbe

Sokolowski, W. (1996) 'Show me the way to the next worthy deed: towards a microstructural theory of volunteering and giving', *Voluntas*, 7(3): 259–78.

Spencer, H. (1896) *The Study of Sociology*, New York: D. Appleton and Company.

Sprinkel Grace, K. (2005) *Beyond Fundraising: New strategies for nonprofit innovation and investment*, Hoboken, NJ: Wiley.

Squire, W. (2014) *University Fundraising in Britain: A transatlantic partnership*, Leicester: Troubador Publishing Ltd.

Steiner, R. L. (1976) 'The prejudice against marketing', *Journal of Marketing*, 40(3): 2–9.

Stets, J. and Turner, J. (eds) (2006) *Handbook of the Sociology of Emotions*, New York: Springer.

Stroman, M. K. (2014) *Asking about Asking: Mastering the art of conversational fundraising*, Rancho Santa Margarita, CA: CharityChannel Press.

Sumption, H. (1995) *Yesterday's Trail-blazing and Pointers for Tomorrow: Harold Sumption Remembers …* , Hertford: Brainstorm Publishing.

Svarc, J. (2016) 'The knowledge worker is dead: what about professions?', *Current Sociology*, 64(3): 392–410.

Swindoll, C. (2015) 'The future of fundraising', *Stanford Social Innovation Review*, 2 January.

Tempel, E. R., Cobb, S. and Ilchman, W. F. (eds) (1997) 'The professionalisation of fundraising: implications for education, practice, and accountability', *New Directions for Philanthropic Fundraising*, 15: 111–126.

Tempel, E. R., Seiler, T. L. and Burlingame, D. F. (eds) (2016) *Achieving Excellence in Fundraising*, 4th edn, Hoboken, NJ: Wiley.

Titmuss, R. M. (1970) *The Gift Relationship: From human blood to social policy*, London: George Allen & Unwin.

Tlili, A. (2016) 'In search of museum professional knowledge base: mapping the professional knowledge debate onto museum work', *Educational Philosophy and Theory*, 48(11): 1100–1122.

Turner, R. C. (1991) 'Metaphors fund raisers live by: language and reality in fundraising', in D. Burlingame and L. Hulse (eds), *Taking Fund Raising Seriously: Advancing the profession and practice of raising money*, San Francisco: Jossey-Bass.

Waddington, K. (2000) *Charity and the London Hospitals: 1850–1898*, Martlesham, Suffolk: Boydell and Brewer.

Waddington, K. (2003) 'Subscribing to a democracy? Management and the voluntary ideology of the London hospitals, 1850–1900', *English Historical Review*, 118(476): 357–379.

Wagner, G. (2004) *Thomas Coram, Gent*, Woodbridge, Suffolk: The Boydell Press.

Wagner, L. (2002) *Careers in Fundraising*, New York: John Wiley & Sons.

Wagner, L. (2004) 'Fundraising', in D. F. Burlingame (ed.), *Philanthropy in America: A comprehensive historical encyclopedia*, Santa Barbara, CA: ABC-CLIO Inc.

Walker, C., Pharoah, C., Marmolejo, M. and Lillya, D. (2012) UK *Corporate Citizenship in the 21st Century*, London: CGAP/Directory of Social Change.

Walker, R. L. (2015) *Footprints in Aggieland: Remembrances of a Veteran Fundraiser*, College Station, TX: Texas A&M University Press.

Walter, J. K., Griffith, K. A. and Jagsi, R. (2015) 'Oncologists' experiences and attitudes about their role in philanthropy and soliciting donations from grateful patients,' *Journal of Clinical Oncology*, 33(32): 3796–801.

Ward, M. (2015) 'Cognition, culture and charity: sociolinguistics and "donor dissonance" in a Baptist denomination', *Voluntas*, 26: 574–603.

Warner, I. (2001 [1975]) *The Art of Fundraising*, Lincoln, NE: iUniverse.com.

Washington, B. T. (2016 [1907]) 'I am not a beggar', in M. Moody and B. Breeze (eds). *The Philanthropy Reader*, London: Routledge.

Waters, R. D. (2016) 'The current landscape of fundraising practice', in T. Jung, S. Philips and J. Harrow (eds), *The Routledge Companion to Philanthropy*, London: Routledge.

Waterson, M. (2011) *A Noble Thing: The National Trust and Its benefactors*, London: Scala Publishers Ltd.

Weil, S. (1990) *Rethinking the Museum and Other Meditations*, Washington, DC: Smithsonian Institution Press.

White, D. (2007) *Charity on Trial: What you need to know before you give*, Fort Lee, NJ: Barricade Books.

Whitman, A. (1972) 'Basil O'Connor, polio crusader, dies', *New York Times*, 10 March 1972.

Whyte, W. (1956) *The Organization Man*, New York: Simon and Schuster.

Wilberforce, S. (2010 [1998]) *Legacy Fundraising*, 3rd edn, London: Directory of Social Change.

Williams, K. (2016) 'Leadership: A position or proposition?', *Advancing Philanthropy*, winter. Available at www.afpnet.org/files/ContentDocuments/16-23 Leadership Winter 2016.pdf

Wolf, T. (2011) *How to Connect with Donors and Double the Money You Raise*, Medfield, MA: Emerson & Church.

Woods, E. W. (1997) 'Profiling major gift fundraisers: what qualifies them for success', *New Directions for Philanthropic Fundraising*, 16: 5–16

Wooster, M. M. (2000) *The Birth of Big Time Fundraising*, Philanthropy Roundtable. Available at: www.philanthropyroundtable.org/topic/excellence_in_philanthropy/the_birth_of_big_time_fundraising

Worth, M. J. and Asp II, J. W. (1994) *The Development Office in Higher Education: Toward an understanding of the role*, ASHE-ERIC Higher Education Report, no. 4, Washington, DC: Graduate School of Education and Human Development, George Washington University.

Wrzesniewski, A., McCauley, C., Rozin, P. and Schwartz, B. (1997) 'Jobs, careers, and callings: people's relations to their work', *Journal of Research in Personality*, 31: 21–33.

Wuthnow, R. (1991) *Acts of Compassion: Caring for others and helping ourselves*, Princeton, NJ: Princeton University Press.

Yaish, M. and Vaese, F. (2001) 'Alchemies of altruism: motivations and opportunities in the rescue of Jews in Nazi Europe', Working Paper, Nuffield College, Oxford and Yale University. Available at: http://soc.haifa.ac.il/~yaish/workinprogress/AlchemiesofAltruism.pdf

Young, D. R. (1986) 'Entrepreneurship and the behavior of nonprofit organizations: elements of a theory', in S. Rose-Ackerman (ed.) *The economics of nonprofit institutions: studies in structure and policy*, New York: Oxford University Press.

Yörük, B. (2009) 'How responsive are charitable donors to requests to give?', *Journal of Public Economics*, 93(9): 1111–1117.

Yörük, B. (2012) 'Do fundraisers select charitable donors based on gender and race? Evidence from survey data', *Journal of Population Economics*, 25: 219–243.

Zopiatis, A. (2010) 'Is it art or science? Chef's competencies for success', *International Journal of Hospitality Management*, 29: 459–467.

Zunz, O. (2011) *Philanthropy in America: A History*, Princeton, NJ: Princeton University Press.

Index

Note: Page numbers in *italics* indicate figures and boxes. Page numbers followed by an n refer to end-of-chapter notes.

A

B

C

W

Y